Cooking Up a Storm

Cooking Up a Storm

RECIPES LOST AND FOUND FROM
THE TIMES-PICAYUNE OF NEW ORLEANS

EDITED BY MARCELLE BIENVENU & JUDY WALKER

CHRONICLE BOOKS
SAN FRANCISCO

Library of Congress Cataloging-in-Publication Data available.

ISBN: 978-0-8118-6577-7

Manufactured in the United States of America

Designed by Marc English Design
Typesetting by Rebecka Marie D'Angleterre

10 9 8 7 6 5 4

CHRONICLE BOOKS LLC
680 SECOND STREET
SAN FRANCISCO, CALIFORNIA 94107
WWW.CHRONICLEBOOKS.COM

This book is dedicated to the citizens of the Gulf Coast, whose lives were changed forever by the events of August 29, 2005, and whose determination to keep on cooking the foods of their culture inspired this project.

CONTENTS

Acknowledgments

OVER THE YEARS, thousands of readers have contributed their recipes to the Food pages of *The Times-Picayune*. This cookbook would not have been possible without their desire to share, even after many suffered their own catastrophic losses. We must thank dozens of people whose recipes are in this book, many of whom we know only by their initials, as well as the inspirational Maureen Detweiler, Phyllis Marquart, and Brian Reid.

The chefs of New Orleans are key ingredients in the area's international reputation for food, and they are just the nicest people you ever want to meet. It is our honor to include many of their recipes here. Thanks to them so much for sharing.

A daily newspaper is the work of many hands and clever brains. The importance of the enduring work of former *Times-Picayune* food writers to this book cannot be overstated, including that of retired food editor Dale Curry and freelance columnists Constance Snow, Paulette Rittenberg, Elizabeth Pearce, and the late Myriam Guidroz and Leon Soniat.

Many others at the newspaper have contributed in significant ways. For years, copy editor Louann Dorrough tracked down countless recipe corrections, an art in itself. Invaluable help on this project came from the newspaper's head librarian Nancy Burris, book editor Susan Larson, and restaurant writer Brett Anderson, as well as Ann Maloney, Mary Lou Atkinson, Mark Lorando, George Berke, Maria Montoya, Jerry McLeod, Kenny Harrison, Elizabeth Mullener, and the rest of the features and news art departments. Thank you, copy desk chief Paula Devlin, for a meticulous edit of the manuscript, and to computer genius Tom Couvillion, for technical help in our time of dire need. The team of talented *Times-Picayune* photographers and photo editors are a critical part of the newspaper Food pages, and we would like to give a special shout-out to the photo staff, whose work illustrates parts of this book. And special thanks to features editor James O'Byrne, who stayed with the book through hell and metaphorical high water, and to editor Jim Amoss and publisher Ashton Phelps, for believing in the project and seeing it to completion.

Our heartfelt thanks to Doe Coover, for her passion and her endless patience. And to Chronicle project editor Amy Treadwell, Sarah Billingsley, Michael Morris, Ben Kasman, Molly Jones, Doug Ogan, and the rest of the crew at Chronicle Books, who have not simply supported and believed in this book from the moment they learned about it, but have believed in our city, traveling here since Katrina, to gut houses and pound nails and hang drywall. We will be forever grateful.

To our families, Dave and Mack Walker and Rock Lasserre (Marcelle's husband) who are always supportive in our endeavors: big hugs and sincere thanks!

—Marcelle Bienvenu
—Judy Walker

Introduction

In the early morning hours of Monday, August 29, 2005, Hurricane Katrina smashed through New Orleans. By Tuesday morning, levees and seawalls had collapsed, triggering a flood that washed away virtually an entire American city.

Beginning in the hours leading up to the storm and continuing through its devastating effects and the many months of difficult struggles that followed, *The Times-Picayune* of New Orleans has served as a strong voice for its city and a beacon of recovery. On October 27, eight weeks after the storm and just two weeks after the staff members of *The Times-Picayune* were able to return to their building in downtown New Orleans from their exile in Baton Rouge, the Food section resumed publication. The city still lay in ruins. The death toll still mounted every day. More than 250,000 people were still living in exile. And every day, the people who did return took a grim inventory of the homes, businesses, jobs, and irreplaceable objects collected over a lifetime that now lay in ruins.

The editors at the newspaper had long known about New Orleans' deep and abiding relationship with its food. But in the aftermath of Hurricane Katrina, they were about to get a lesson in just how profound that connection was, and remains, today. In New Orleans, food is culture. Food is family. Food is comfort. Food is life.

In the immediate aftermath of the storm, a diaspora spread across America. Displaced citizens from New Orleans began to cook their comfort foods, bringing their indigenous dishes to places like Salt Lake City, Minneapolis, and Pittsburgh—places where people didn't know étouffée from café au lait.

Back home, people were anxious for their favorite restaurant, corner grocery store, sandwich shop, or neighborhood cafe to reopen. They wanted a roast beef po-boy dripping with gravy, a bowl of rich gumbo, or maybe just a cup of café au lait and a hot beignet to give them both physical and spiritual sustenance as they tried to rebuild their shattered homes and lives. Each time one of the city's world-class restaurants reopened its doors, it would immediately become packed with patrons desperate for some sense of normalcy, and longing to celebrate their traditions amid the ruins.

At the newspaper, a frenetic dialogue immediately commenced with readers, as they sought to replace their treasured recipe collections, most of them gathered over a lifetime and destroyed after lying underwater for three weeks. A faithful reader named Phyllis Marquart suggested to food editor Judy Walker a new theme for the recipe exchange column. On October 27, 2005, Walker invited readers to participate in "Rebuilding New Orleans, Recipe by Recipe." "Exchange Alley" (the column is named after a street in the French Quarter) became the avenue to reclaim recipes. Walker paired readers searching for recipes with those who still had theirs. She would print letters from those seeking recipes and ask for responses, which she included in the column a week or two later. Sometimes Walker was able to find the recipes in the paper's archives. At other times, readers filled the request from their own recipe clippings. A week after a reader's request for Baked Stuffed Oysters (page 119) was printed in "Exchange Alley," another reader sent a copy of the recipe she had clipped from the newspaper twenty years before.

A letter from one resident of a storm-devastated community who lost all her recipes was typical: "Thank you so much for this project! The one recipe I really need is the mirliton casserole. It tasted like my Grandma's. I had tried to duplicate her recipe over the years but never quite could. I made the recipe for Thanksgiving after it was in the paper and my mother wondered where I got the old

family recipe!" Beneath the letter, Walker reprinted the lost recipe.

"Exchange Alley" quickly became a weekly swap-fest on the pages of the newspaper, with readers requesting not just recipes they had originally read in *The Times-Picayune*, but all manner of local favorites, many of them developed by the city's famous chefs, or served for decades in one of its legendary restaurants. Readers wrote in asking for the tasso shrimp dish from Commander's Palace (page 122), the signature oyster recipe from Mosca's (page 130), the stuffed crabs from LeRuth's (page 142), and the shrimp remoulade from the old Roosevelt Hotel (page 45), where Governor Earl K. Long conducted his famous trysts with stripper Blaze Starr.

Then, Judy Laine wrote from her temporary digs in tiny Talisheek, Louisiana, "The bad news is I lost everything in New Orleans, my home (water up to the roof), our business and rental, and broke both my legs the night of the storm and couldn't get to the hospital for two days because of all the trees down on highways. My husband set the legs as best he could."

After this harrowing account of her Katrina experience, what was foremost in Laine's mind? Food. "I know I am not the only one who lost all their recipes and recipe books," Laine continued. "I was thinking maybe you could all come up with a cookbook of all the recipes you printed over the years."

As dozens of these letters arrived, a portrait began to emerge of a community trying to rebuild its rich culinary history, one lost recipe and one comfort meal at a time. The newspaper's editors decided Laine was onto something. This was the genesis of *Cooking Up a Storm: Recipes Lost and Found from The Times-Picayune of New Orleans,* a collection of classic New Orleans dishes.

The newspaper's editors asked veteran cookbook writer Marcelle Bienvenu—author of *Who's Your Mama, Are You Catholic,* and *Can You Make a Roux?,* and co-author of four cookbooks with Chef Emeril Lagasse—to take on the task of building a cookbook from these many requests. The result is a collection that includes internationally known New Orleans dishes such as Barbecued Shrimp (page 120) and Red Beans and Rice (page 205), along with quirkier local dishes, such as Schwegmann's Spaghetti Sauce with Meatballs (page 208) and Bananas Foster Pie (page 254).

Bienvenu, who writes "Cooking Creole", an immensely popular weekly column in *The Times-Picayune,* understands that in New Orleans, it's not just about the food, but also about the stories that go with the recipes, which explain how they came to be and who created them. *Cooking Up a Storm* does not just teach you how to make Corinne Dunbar's Oyster and Artichoke Appetizer (page 36), but it also tells the tale of Corinne's decision, in 1935, to open a restaurant on the ground floor of her stately St. Charles Avenue mansion. She equipped it with her household furnishings, silver, and crystal, and as the streetcars rattled by, she served delightful food made with fresh local ingredients for more than fifty years.

Along with a classic recipe for red beans and rice, you'll discover the amusing way that Louis Armstrong honored this signature dish, traditionally eaten on Monday in New Orleans. You'll also learn about the Schwegmann brothers' decision, in 1946, to open Schwegmann Brothers Giant Super Market, a one-stop local institution where you could buy a goldfish, get your eyeglasses, shop for a window air-conditioner, eat a fresh po-boy and, oh yeah, "make your groceries." John Schwegmann's spaghetti sauce recipe, which he advertised in the paper, became legendary, and was much requested after the storm.

You'll meet Dorothea Scaglione, a Brooklyn native who came to New Orleans and spread her recipe for New York–Style Cheesecake (page 276) throughout the city. And you'll visit St. Martinville and Catahoula, small Cajun fishing villages where the women make delicious old-fashioned pies called Tartes à la Bouillie (page 284), which are made with a blackberry, coconut, or custard filling.

You'll make the acquaintance of "Mr. Al" Pierce, founder of the famous Bon Ton Cafe, regarded as the first authentic Cajun restaurant in the city. More than fifty years ago, Al's wife developed a memorable recipe for bread pudding (page 322), which was requested so often that the restaurant printed it up and handed it out to patrons on request. You'll even pick up a little etiquette from Marcelle's Cajun mother, who always taught her children, "Don't eat boiled crawfish in front of people you don't know." And you will hear some storm stories about loss and triumph, about courage and perseverance, and about a culinary community dedicated to comfort food and healing.

Cooking Up a Storm is a compendium of the very best of New Orleans cuisine, from seafood and meat to cocktails and desserts. But it also tells the story, recipe by recipe, of one of the great food cities in the world, and the determination of its citizens, in the face of adversity, to preserve and safeguard their culinary legacy.

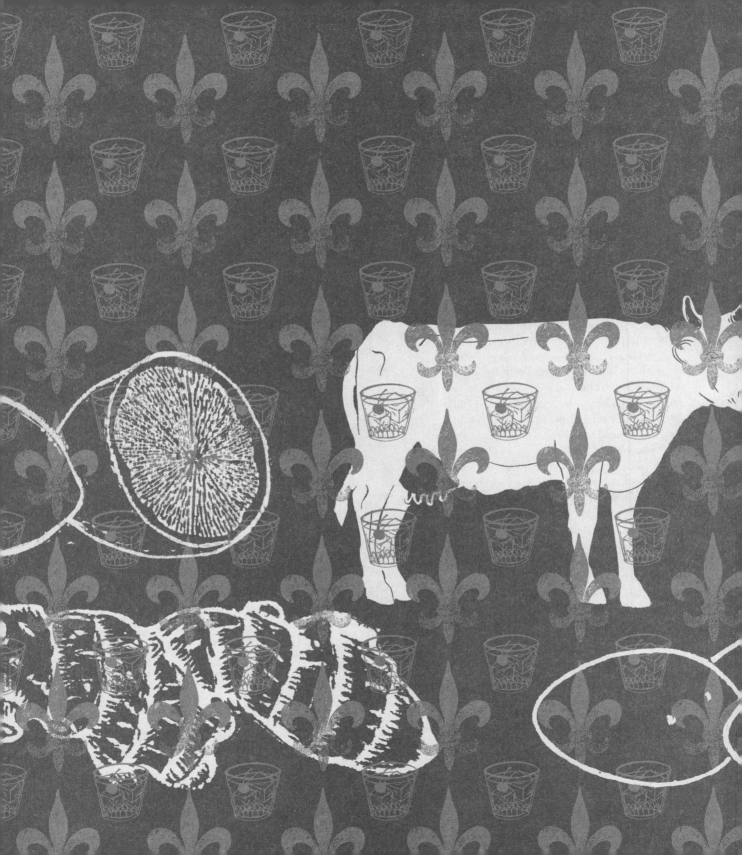

COCKTAILS

According to Stanley Clisby Arthur, in his 1944 book Famous New Orleans Drinks and How to Mix 'Em, *the cocktail originated in New Orleans. He tells us that a gentleman named Antoine Amédée Peychaud fled Saint-Domingue (which is now Haiti) in 1793 after a slave uprising and found refuge in New Orleans.*

Peychaud, an apothecary, brought with him a secret family recipe for a liquid tonic that was to become known as bitters. He set up shop in a building that still stands in the 400 block of Royal Street in the French Quarter, where he combined his bitters with Cognac and dispensed the drink to remedy stomach ailments. Arthur tells us: "He poured portions into what we now know as an egg-cup, the old-fashioned double-end egg-cup. This particular piece of crockery, known to the French-speaking population as a coquetier (pronounced ko-k-tay) was, in all probability, forerunner of the present jigger—-the name given the double-end metal contraption holding a jigger (1½ ounces) in the big end, and a pony (1 ounce) in the little end, which we now use to measure portions for mixed drinks."

It is Arthur's belief that the pronunciation of the coquetier *may have sounded like* cocktail *because of the "thickened tongues of the imbibers."*

And now you know!

In New Orleans, any time is a good time for a cocktail. A spicy Bloody Mary (page 18), a cool Milk Punch (page 23), or a smooth Ramos Gin Fizz (page 24)—called an eye-opener by the locals—are the poisons of choice to enjoy before brunch. A Sazerac (page 25) is often enjoyed before lunch or dinner.

Of course there are some who opt to wander through the French Quarter sloshing their hurricanes from Pat O'Brien's. Then there are those who like to sip on a Pimm's Cup at the Napoleon House, at the corner of Chartres and St. Louis, for a refreshing afternoon delight. It really doesn't matter what and where you imbibe, as long as you sip slowly and enjoy.

COCKTAILS

Bloody Mary

EVERYBODY IN NEW ORLEANS and south Louisiana has a favorite recipe for this popular eye-opener. It's ideal for serving at brunch. Better make a couple of batches if you're expecting company! Some people like to add a dash of prepared horseradish; others prefer to rim the glass with their favorite seasoning mix.

{MAKES 4 SERVINGS}

4 cups thick tomato juice
1 teaspoon salt
1 teaspoon black pepper
½ teaspoon celery salt
1 tablespoon Worcestershire sauce
8 to 10 drops Tabasco sauce, or to taste
2 teaspoons fresh lime juice
6 to 7½ ounces vodka
Chipped ice for serving
Lime wedges for garnish

Combine all the ingredients except the ice and lime wedges in a large pitcher and chill for at least 1 hour. Stir before serving. Pour into tall glasses filled with chipped ice, and garnish with lime wedges. ✄

Bushwacker

IF YOU HAVEN'T enjoyed a Bushwacker on a hot summer day on the beach at Pensacola, Florida, then you are missing out. Some versions, including this one, are made with ice cream, two kinds of rum, crème de cacao, and Kahlúa. Others include Coco Lopez and cream rather than ice cream.

This is the recipe most people requested, which was given to Marcelle Bienvenu by Stephen Bartlett, a New Orleanian who now lives in Gulf Breeze, Florida. Be careful, they go down easy!

{MAKES 2 SERVINGS}

3 to 4 scoops vanilla ice cream
3 ounces dark rum
1½ ounces light rum
¾ ounce crème de cacao
¾ ounce Kahlúa
Ice
Dash of 151 rum (optional)

Put the ice cream, rums, crème de cacao, and Kahlúa in a blender and pulse to blend. Add enough ice to come within 1 or 2 inches of the top of the blender container, and blend until smooth. If the mixture freezes, add a few drops of water.

Pour into two old-fashioned glasses and top each drink with a dash of the 151 rum, if desired. 🍀

Creamy Brandy Alexander

IF YOU WANT to indulge just a bit, this is a delightful after-dinner drink to offer to guests. It can be whipped up ahead of time and stored in the freezer until ready to serve

{MAKES 6 TO 8 SERVINGS}

½ gallon vanilla ice cream, slightly thawed
15 ounces brandy
10½ ounces dark crème de cacao
½ cup heavy cream
Fresh mint for garnish
Toasted Coconut Cookies (page 311)
　　or another crispy cookie for serving

Combine all the ingredients except the mint and cookies in a blender, and process until smooth. Serve immediately or store in the freezer.

Garnish with fresh mint and serve with cookies. ❧

Galatoire's Eggnog

THE HOLIDAYS JUST wouldn't be the same without a thick, rich, and creamy eggnog, which most people in south Louisiana adore. This one seems to have all the right ingredients.

{MAKES 10 SMALL SERVINGS}

5 large eggs
1 cup plus 2 tablespoons sugar
1 cup half-and-half
1 cup heavy cream
⅛ teaspoon grated nutmeg, plus more for garnish
½ teaspoon vanilla extract
3 ounces bourbon
3 ounces brandy
3 large egg whites

In a large heavy-bottomed saucepan, whisk together the eggs and sugar. Stir in the half-and-half. Cook over medium-low heat, stirring constantly, until the mixture is thick enough to coat a metal spoon with a thin film and reaches at least 160 degrees F. Remove from the heat.

Stir in the cream, nutmeg, vanilla, bourbon and brandy. Cool, then cover and refrigerate until ready to serve.

Just before serving, beat the egg whites in a large bowl with an electric mixer on high speed until stiff peaks form. Use a rubber spatula to gently fold them into the eggnog. Serve cold in punch cups and sprinkle each serving with nutmeg. ❧

Milk Punch

In January 2004, Constance Snow, who wrote the recipe exchange column for several years, offered this milk punch recipe in anticipation of the Carnival season. Rich milk punch is the traditional eye-opener for a leisurely brunch down South, even as far south as Cuba, where it is made with dark rum instead of brandy or bourbon, and is known as *ponche de leche*. No matter which poison you choose, the drink also makes a soothing fireside nightcap.

{MAKES 8 SERVINGS}

12 ounces brandy or bourbon (or dark rum for the Cuban version)

4 cups half-and-half

¼ cup confectioners' sugar

2 teaspoons vanilla extract

½ cup heavy cream, whipped

Nutmeg for sprinkling

In a large pitcher, stir together the liquor, half-and-half, confectioners' sugar, and vanilla until the sugar is completely dissolved. Refrigerate for 3 hours or overnight.

Serve in small crystal cups or stemmed glasses, topped with a dollop of whipped cream and a sprinkle of nutmeg. Alternatively, pour into a small punch bowl, float whipped cream on top, and sprinkle with nutmeg. ❧

NOTE: *To make one drink, pour 1½ ounces of brandy, bourbon, or dark rum into a cocktail shaker and add ½ cup of half-and-half, 1½ teaspoons of confectioners' sugar, and ¼ teaspoon of vanilla. Add 5 or 6 ice cubes and shake until well blended and frothy. Strain into a small crystal cup or stemmed glass. Top with a dollop of whipped cream (if desired) and sprinkle with nutmeg.*

Ramos Gin Fizz

THIS DRINK IS believed to have been invented in the 1880s by Henry C. Ramos at his bar in New Orleans. The drink was made famous, however, by the Roosevelt Hotel (which later became the Fairmont), where Huey P. Long, the Louisiana governor, and later senator, was a regular customer. Huey loved a Ramos Gin Fizz so much that he once took the bartender from the Roosevelt with him on a trip to New York to show the big city bartenders how to make the drink properly.

{MAKES 1 SERVING}

1 tablespoon confectioners' sugar
1 tablespoon fresh lemon juice
1½ teaspoons fresh lime juice
1 small egg white
1 tablespoon orange-flower water
3 ounces milk
1¼ ounces gin
Ice

Combine all the ingredients in a cocktail shaker and shake until well blended. Strain into a 7-ounce old-fashioned glass.

Sazerac

ACCORDING TO THOSE well versed in the history of the cocktail, the Sazerac was probably first mixed in a French Quarter bar on Exchange Alley in 1859. (The name originated from a particular brand of imported Cognac, Sazerac-de-Forge et Fils, favored by the locals.) Almost a century later, in 1949, the Roosevelt Hotel obtained the rights to use the Sazerac trademark when they opened the Sazerac Bar next to the hotel on Baronne Street.

With the change came a new era: ladies were finally served. The old Sazerac Bar allowed women to enter only on Mardi Gras. Hurricane Katrina shuttered the hotel, which had later been renamed the Fairmont. As of this writing in 2008, the Fairmont is slated for renovation as a Waldorf-Astoria hotel, when the name will return to The Roosevelt. This is the Fairmont's recipe.

{MAKES 1 SERVING}

3 dashes of Herbsaint
1 lump sugar
1 tablespoon water
2 dashes of Peychaud bitters
Dash of Angostura bitters
Chipped ice
1¼ ounces rye whiskey
Squeeze of fresh lemon juice
Lemon twist for garnish

Coat a chilled old-fashioned glass with the Herbsaint and then pour out the excess. In a 10-ounce glass, dissolve the sugar in the water and add the bitters, chipped ice, and rye whiskey. Stir well and strain into the glass. Add the lemon juice and garnish with the lemon twist to serve. ❧

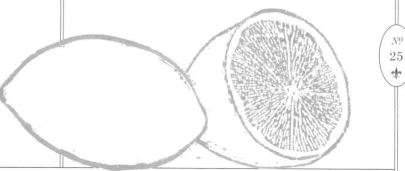

APPETIZERS

When Marcelle was a youngster growing up in the small but historic town of St. Martinville in Acadiana (south Louisiana), the word "appetizer" was not in her vocabulary. However, her mother and her mother's friends did know about hors d'oeuvres and took great pride and time making dainty finger food for tea parties and cocktail affairs.

But, oh, when Marcelle visited New Orleans with her parents, she quickly came to know such delights as shrimp remoulade (page 45), which literally brought tears to her eyes and made her nose run; luscious oysters Bienville (page 42); and rich crabmeat Remick (page 37). In fact, she was happy dining on just a few appetizers.

It's practically a given that any kind of gathering, be it a casual lunch, an elegant dinner party, or an impromptu supper, is prefaced by "a little something" to whet one's appetite before having the actual meal. New Orleanians pride themselves on delicacies as simple as Lady Helen's Cheese Straws (page 33) to nibble on while sipping on a glass of white wine or a cocktail. Then again, if the occasion warrants, there might be something more sophisticated, such as Chef Frank Brigsten's Marinated Crab Claws with Green Onion Sauce (page 34). But no matter what the appetizer is—stuffed artichokes (page 46), warm-from-the oven oyster patties (page 40), or Drago's Famous Char-Broiled Oysters (page 38)—you are sure to enjoy these warm-ups to a meal.

Appetizers

Better Than Better Cheddar

Better Cheddar is a New Orleans party staple, one of many scrumptious prepared foods sold at Langenstein's, an Uptown New Orleans grocery institution (with another location in Metairie). After a reader asked for a recipe for this favorite cheese spread, P.D. of New Orleans replied, "I hope someone from Langenstein's will respond with the real recipe, but in case they don't, below is a guess at a recipe that my friends pulled together years ago. It is very similar, and actually tastes even a little better than the real thing. It uses the homemade Creole Mayonnaise recipe from the Junior League of New Orleans' 1994 *Jambalaya* recipe book, altered slightly. We have all enjoyed this recipe for many years."

{MAKES ABOUT 2 POUNDS}

1 pound smoked Gouda cheese, shredded
1 pound sharp white cheddar cheese, shredded
3 green onions, chopped (white and green parts)
1 cup walnuts, chopped
Homemade Creole Mayonnaise (recipe follows)

In a large bowl, mix together the first 4 ingredients with enough Creole mayonnaise to get the consistency of a cheese spread. ❦

Homemade Creole Mayonnaise

{MAKES ABOUT 1½ CUPS}

1½ cups vegetable oil
1 large egg
1 tablespoon Creole mustard, homemade (page 341), or store-bought, or any coarse, grainy brown mustard
1½ tablespoons white vinegar
1½ tablespoons fresh lemon juice
¼ teaspoon paprika
1 teaspoon prepared yellow mustard
1 teaspoon salt
Dash of Tabasco sauce

Pour ¼ cup of the oil into a blender. Add the egg, Creole mustard, vinegar, lemon juice, paprika, yellow mustard, salt, and Tabasco, and blend. Add the remaining 1¼ cups of oil in a steady stream with the blender running. ❧

Blue Cheese Puffs

NEW ORLEANIANS LOVE their blue cheese, and a frequent contributor to the Food pages shared this recipe one year in time for Super Bowl parties. "Don't blink after setting these out—you will miss seeing them disappear!" he wrote. They are a variation of *gougères*, the savory French cousin of cream puffs. The recipe makes two dozen, not nearly enough if you're having guests, so consider doubling it.

{MAKES ABOUT 2 DOZEN}

Butter for greasing, plus 4 tablespoons
¾ cup water
¾ cup all-purpose flour
3 large eggs, at room temperature
¼ pound blue cheese, crumbled

Preheat the oven to 400 degrees F and butter two baking sheets.

In a heavy saucepan, bring the 4 tablespoons of butter and water to a boil over high heat. Remove the pan from the heat. Add the flour to the butter and water, and beat with a wooden spoon until the mixture leaves the sides of the pan and forms a smooth ball. Add the eggs, one at a time, beating until smooth after each addition. Stir in the blue cheese. Let the batter sit for 15 minutes.

Drop the batter by rounded tablespoons, 2 inches apart, onto the prepared baking sheets. Bake until golden, 20 to 30 minutes. Serve warm or at room temperature. 🌸

Caponata

CAPONATA—A SICILIAN dish that can be served as a salad, side dish, or appetizer—is ideal to make when summer vegetables are plentiful. Toss it with pasta to serve for a casual summer supper. It's a versatile, delicious combination of eggplant, onions, tomatoes, olives, capers, and sometimes anchovies and pine nuts. Because of the large Sicilian population in New Orleans, this dish is a favorite. You can leave the skins on the eggplant, or peel them if you wish. If you serve the caponata as an appetizer, accompany it with toasted pita chips or toasted croutons.

{MAKES ABOUT 7 CUPS}

2 large eggplants, peeled and cut into ½-inch cubes

1 tablespoon salt

½ cup olive oil

2 cloves garlic, mashed

2 cups chopped onions

2½ cups coarsely chopped Italian plum tomatoes (canned or fresh)

1½ cups chopped celery

1 cup chopped kalamata olives

1 cup Italian olive salad, drained (page 344)

¼ cup capers, drained

½ cup pine nuts, toasted (optional)

¼ cup red wine vinegar

2 tablespoons sugar

Black pepper

Cayenne pepper

Sprinkle the eggplant with the salt and let stand in a colander for 20 to 30 minutes. Rinse with cool water and pat dry.

Heat the olive oil over medium heat in a large heavy pot. Add the eggplant and cook, stirring often, until it is soft and tender, about 20 minutes. Remove the eggplant from the pot with a slotted spoon and set aside.

Add the garlic and onions to the pot and cook, stirring often, just until they are soft, 3 to 4 minutes. Add the tomatoes, celery, olives, and olive salad. Cook until the celery is tender, 8 to 10 minutes. Return the eggplant to the pot and add the capers and pine nuts (if using).

In a small saucepan over medium heat, combine the vinegar and sugar and stir until the sugar dissolves. Pour over the eggplant mixture. Season to taste with more salt and black and cayenne peppers. Continue cooking over medium heat, stirring occasionally, until the mixture thickens, about 20 minutes. Serve at room temperature or slightly chilled. The mixture can be stored in an airtight container in the refrigerator for up to 1 week. 🌾

Lady Helen's Cheese Straws

THIS RECIPE, SENT in by Marianne Hayden-Whitmore, belonged to the late Lady Helen Hardy, an Uptown resident known widely for her cheese straws. At one time, Lady Helen's Cheese Straws was one of the most requested recipes in the newspaper files.

Cheese straws are popular all year, but especially during the Christmas holidays. Once they are baked and cooled, they can be stored in an airtight container for up to 1 week. They also freeze well.

{MAKES ABOUT 120 CHEESE STRAWS}

2 cups all-purpose flour

1¼ teaspoons baking powder

½ teaspoon salt

¾ cup (1½ sticks) margarine or butter, at room temperature

15 ounces extra-sharp cheddar cheese, grated, at room temperature

5 or 6 good dashes of Tabasco sauce

1 teaspoon cayenne pepper

Preheat the oven to 300 degrees F. Lightly coat a cookie sheet with nonstick cooking spray.

Sift the flour once. Add the baking powder and salt, sift again, and set aside.

With your hands, mix the margarine and cheese well in a large bowl. Add the Tabasco, cayenne, and flour and mix well.

Place the dough in a cookie press and squeeze out rows the entire length of the cookie sheet, spacing them at least ½ inch apart. Bake for 10 minutes. Lower the oven temperature to 225 degrees F and bake the cheese straws until they are straw-colored, but not browned, about 15 minutes. If you think the straws are browning too fast, leave the oven door open.

About 2 to 3 minutes before the end of the baking time, use a small sharp knife to cut the straws crosswise into strips. ❧

Frank Brigsten's Marinated Crab Claws with Green Onion Sauce

In August 2006, the Great American Seafood Cook-off was held in New Orleans. It was a showcase not just for the chefs but also for each state's fish and seafood bounty. Maryland's Timothy Recher gilded the lily by stuffing jumbo lump crabmeat into a crispy soft-shell crab. California's John Nye made cioppino, the seafood soup invented in San Francisco. Naomi Everett came all the way from Alaska to make a colorful roulade of halibut, salmon, and crab. And Frank Brigsten's "rebuilt Louisiana seafood platter" touched all the bases, with separate preparations of baked oysters, crabmeat Thermidor, marinated crab claws, grilled drum fish with shrimp and pistachio-lime sauce, and a jalapeño and shrimp coleslaw. The seafood platter is one of the signature dishes at Brigsten's, his restaurant in the Riverbend neighborhood of New Orleans.

Here is the recipe for the marinated crab claws.

{MAKES 8 SERVINGS}

GREEN ONION SAUCE

1 large egg yolk

1 cup thinly sliced green onions (white and green parts)

1 teaspoon salt

½ teaspoon black pepper

2 tablespoons white vinegar

1 cup vegetable oil

MARINADE

½ cup red wine vinegar

1 tablespoon Creole mustard, homemade (page 341) or store-bought, or any coarse, grainy brown mustard

1 tablespoon paprika

1 teaspoon minced garlic

½ teaspoon salt

½ teaspoon dried oregano leaves

1 teaspoon sugar

1 cup olive oil

3 large, wide cucumbers

24 Louisiana blue crab claws, cracked

For the green onion sauce: In a food processor, combine the egg yolk, green onions, salt, black pepper, and white vinegar. With the processor running, slowly add the vegetable oil in a thin stream until fully incorporated. Refrigerate until ready to serve.

For the marinade: In a mixing bowl, combine the red wine vinegar, Creole mustard, paprika, garlic, salt, oregano, and sugar. Slowly add the olive oil, whisking constantly until fully incorporated.

Trim the ends off the cucumbers and cut them so you have a total of 8 slices, each 2 inches thick. From one end of each slice, hollow out the seeds to form a cup.

Marinate the crab claws for 15 minutes. Remove from the marinade and drain. To serve, spoon 2 tablespoons of Green Onion Sauce into each cucumber cup. Place 3 crab claws into each cup.

Chiqui's Creole Cream Cheese Dip

AFTER A READER wrote to "Exchange Alley" asking for a recipe, the request was filled immediately, by the creator of the recipe, no less. Chiqui (pronounced CHICK-ee) Collier is an experienced caterer, cookbook author, and instructor at the New Orleans Cooking Experience.

"This recipe was the result of a last-minute announcement by one of our cooking class students that she was allergic to the oyster appetizer we had taught in class and were about to serve in the dining room," Collier wrote in an e-mail. Although the student said she didn't need an appetizer, Collier would have none of that. "I checked in our fridge and our kitchen and garden and just started to put things together," she said. The result was a hit. "I'm always asked for the recipe so I finally wrote it down."

{MAKES ABOUT 2 CUPS}

1 (8-ounce) package Philadelphia cream cheese, at room temperature

1 (8-ounce) container Creole cream cheese, homemade (page 339) or store-bought, or 4 ounces ricotta cheese and 4 ounces crème fraîche, at room temperature

2 to 3 tablespoons chopped, oil-packed sun-dried tomatoes

2 tablespoons thinly sliced green onions (white and green parts)

2 tablespoons Worcestershire sauce

1 to 2 teaspoons of a combination of chopped fresh rosemary, thyme, chives, and parsley

Kosher salt

Cayenne pepper, red pepper flakes, or hot sauce

¼ teaspoon granulated garlic, or to taste

Assorted crackers for serving

Blend all the ingredients in a large mixing bowl. Transfer to a serving bowl and serve with assorted crackers. ❧

Corinne Dunbar's Oyster and Artichoke Appetizer

CORINNE LOEBER DUNBAR was born in 1879 in New Orleans and was one of ten children. In 1935, while her husband was suffering from an extended illness during the Great Depression, she decided to open a restaurant in the downstairs portion of their home at 1716 St. Charles Avenue. In order to make the atmosphere similar to a gracious home rather than a typical restaurant, she used family furniture, silver, and crystal.

Following the table d'hôte tradition of several other restaurants in the city, she served a set meal made from seasonal ingredients from the nearby markets. She supervised everything from shopping to service, but she looked to her longtime household cook, Leonie Victor, to turn out the cuisine for which the restaurant became famous. After Dunbar's death, the restaurant was sold and later moved to 1617 St. Charles Avenue. It closed in 1988. Her signature dish was this oyster and artichoke appetizer. The recipe for this famous dish was a long-held secret. In the 1950s, Victor wrote the recipe on a napkin for Maureen Detweiler's mother, who was a frequent diner there. Detweiler shared the recipe with *The Times-Picayune*.

{MAKES 6 TO 8 SERVINGS}

Juice of 1 lemon (about 3 tablespoons)

4 large artichokes, trimmed

10 tablespoons butter

1½ tablespoons all-purpose flour

3 tablespoons minced green onions (green parts only)

18 oysters with their liquor

1 (7-ounce) can mushrooms, chopped, with their liquid

Salt

Black pepper

½ cup fine dry bread crumbs

Bring a large pot of salted water to a boil, add the lemon juice, and boil the artichokes until the leaves pull out easily. Drain when the artichokes are cool enough to handle. Scrape the flesh off each leaf into a bowl and discard the leaves. Cut the hearts into large pieces, add to the bowl, and set aside.

Preheat the oven to 350 degrees F.

Heat a large saucepan. Melt 8 tablespoons of the butter over medium heat; add the flour and stir slowly until lightly browned. Add the green onions, oysters and liquor, mushrooms and liquid, and salt and pepper to taste, and simmer for 10 minutes.

Place the artichoke flesh and hearts in a medium casserole dish. Add the oyster mixture and top with bread crumbs. Dot with the remaining 2 tablespoons of butter, cut into bits. Bake until lightly browned and bubbly, 15 to 20 minutes. Serve immediately. ❧

Crabmeat Remick

WHEN THE PONTCHARTRAIN HOTEL opened in the 1920s, sweet fresh lump crabmeat topped with a mayonnaise-based sauce became a popular dish at the hotel's Caribbean Room. We understand this dish was also served at the Stork Club in New York City in the 1950s, so it may or may not have originated here. Although the identity of Remick eludes us, the recipe continues to be a local favorite.

The ingredients are simple and the recipe is easy to prepare. A rich dish, it is usually served in small portions as an appetizer, but you can certainly offer it as an entrée, accompanied by nothing more than a green salad tossed with a vinaigrette dressing and hot, crusty French bread.

{MAKES 6 ENTRÉE OR 12 APPETIZER SERVINGS}

1½ cups mayonnaise

1 teaspoon tarragon vinegar

½ cup chili sauce

1 teaspoon dry mustard

2 tablespoons fresh lemon juice

1 teaspoon paprika

1 teaspoon Tabasco sauce

Dash of celery salt

1 pound lump crabmeat, picked over for shells and cartilage

6 to 12 slices bacon (depending on size of ramekins used), fried until crisp

Preheat the oven to 400 degrees F.

In a small mixing bowl, combine the mayonnaise, vinegar, chili sauce, dry mustard, lemon juice, paprika, Tabasco, and celery salt. Mix well.

Divide the crabmeat evenly among six large ramekins or twelve small ones. Spoon the sauce generously over the crabmeat and top each with a bacon slice.

Bake for 15 minutes, or until the sauce bubbles. If you want to brown the tops, put them under the broiler for 1 to 2 minutes. ❧

Drago's Famous Char-Broiled Oysters

SINCE THIS RECIPE was published in the newspaper in January 1998, readers have asked for it many times. It is a signature dish of Drago's Seafood Restaurant in Metairie. As the butter drips onto the grill, the resulting flare-ups create the characteristic smoky taste of the dish. If you wish to serve the oysters on oyster plates, simply place them on the plates when they come off the grill.

{MAKES 4 TO 6 APPETIZER OR 2 ENTRÉE SERVINGS}

1 pound (4 sticks) butter or margarine
½ teaspoon black pepper
2 tablespoons chopped garlic
24 large raw oysters on the half shell
¼ cup grated Parmesan cheese
¼ cup grated Romano cheese
¼ cup chopped fresh parsley

Combine the butter with the pepper and garlic in a small saucepan. Heat until the butter is melted.

Prepare a hot fire in a charcoal grill or preheat a gas grill. Put the oysters on the grill and spoon the butter mixture over the oysters. Then sprinkle a pinch of each cheese and a pinch of parsley onto each oyster. Broil until the oysters puff up, about 3 to 5 minutes. Serve at once. 🌺

Eggplant Fritters

EGGPLANT IS A popular vegetable in south Louisiana's summer gardens, and it is used in many local dishes: eggplant and rice dressing, fried eggplant, eggplant casseroles, eggplant stuffed with shrimp and crabmeat, and eggplant fritters. These fritters make a great appetizer when dabbed with a bit of remoulade sauce (page 45; minus the shrimp) or tartar sauce (page 345).

{MAKES ABOUT 6 SERVINGS}

1 pound eggplant, peeled and cubed

1 teaspoon baking powder

⅓ cup all-purpose flour

½ teaspoon sugar

⅛ teaspoon ground nutmeg

1 teaspoon salt

Pinch of cayenne pepper

Vegetable oil for deep-frying

Cook the eggplant cubes in a large heavy skillet over medium heat, adding just enough water to keep the eggplant from sticking to the bottom. Stir often. When the eggplant is tender, remove from the heat, mash well with a fork, and cool slightly.

In a large mixing bowl, combine the eggplant, baking powder, flour, sugar, nutmeg, salt, and cayenne. Mix well.

Heat about 4 inches of oil in a deep, heavy pot or electric fryer to about 360 degrees F. Drop the eggplant mixture by tablespoonfuls into the oil and fry until golden brown, about 2 to 3 minutes per batch. Drain on paper towels. You can season the fritters with more salt if you wish. ❧

McKenzie's Oyster Patties

McKENZIE'S PASTRY SHOPPES, which at one time numbered over twenty, were a popular spot on New Orleans's culinary landscape for sixty-five years. When they closed their doors in 2001, locals lamented the loss of such favorites as buttermilk drops, wine cakes, turtles (chocolate-pecan delicacies), and a plethora of other baked goods.

During Carnival season, McKenzie's could barely keep up with the demand for their brioche-style king cakes. Ladies in the Garden District clamored for their dainty ladyfingers to make desserts like charlotte russe. And their small, flaky pastry shells were the vessels for a variety of fillings, which were the mainstay at cocktail parties, teas, and wedding receptions all over the city.

In the New Orleans vernacular, these filled pastry shells are called "patties." Although all of McKenzie's bakery recipes have remained locked in a vault since the bakeries closed, this savory recipe continues to circulate. The company passed it out to keep sales brisk for their pastry shells.

{MAKES 1 DOZEN LARGE OR 3 DOZEN
  MINIATURE PATTIES}

4 dozen oysters with their liquor

2 tablespoons butter, melted

1 medium onion, coarsely grated

1 tablespoon all-purpose flour

½ cup chopped canned mushrooms with
   their juice (optional)

Salt

Black pepper

Dash of cayenne pepper

2 tablespoons chopped fresh parsley

¼ teaspoon fresh lemon juice

1 dozen large or 3 dozen miniature pastry shells

Preheat the oven to 375 degrees F.

Cook the oysters in their liquor by bringing the liquor to a boil in a medium saucepan, and then simmering the oysters for 10 minutes. (If you are using miniature pastry shells, finely chop the oysters before cooking.)

Melt the butter in another medium saucepan over medium heat and sauté the onion until soft. Blend in the flour, stirring until the mixture is smooth. Add the mushrooms and their juice (if using), salt and black pepper to taste, cayenne, parsley, lemon juice and the oysters. Cook for 5 minutes. Spoon the mixture into the pastry shells and bake for 5 to 8 minutes until lightly browned. Serve warm. ❧

Monica's Goat Cheese Appetizer

MONICA DAVIDSON IS the namesake of Crawfish Monica, the popular dish invented by her husband, Pierre Hilzim. Pierre is the trained chef in the family, but in 2007, Monica gave the newspaper the recipe for this delicious and unusual appetizer from her Chilean mother. This is one of those recipes that's perfect for little dinner parties, because it's so interactive. Put out several spreaders. Just be sure everybody eats garlic!

{MAKES 10 TO 12 SERVINGS}

2 (8-ounce) packages goat cheese
1 red bell pepper, cut into thin 1-inch-long strips
6 to 12 cloves garlic, minced
1 cup olive oil
Sliced French bread for serving

Spread out the goat cheese evenly in a long, shallow ceramic platter. Cover with the red bell pepper strips, then sprinkle with the minced garlic.

Warm the olive oil in a saucepan just until it begins to smoke. Pour the hot olive oil evenly over the garlic, red bell pepper, and goat cheese. The oil will take away the raw taste of the garlic. Serve with the French bread slices. ❧

Oysters Bienville

COUNTLESS VERSIONS OF Oysters Bienville exist. The dish is named in honor of Jean-Baptiste Le Moyne, Sieur de Bienville—the French colonial governor of Louisiana, who founded New Orleans in 1718. This version, attributed to Louisiana's Seafood and Marketing Promotion Board, was published in 1998 to accompany a story by Dale Curry, who was the food editor of *The Times-Picayune*.

Bake the oysters on either the half shell or on ovenproof plates, or transfer after baking to regular oyster plates.

{MAKES 6 SERVINGS}

½ cup (1 stick) butter
¼ pound mushrooms, chopped
2 dozen freshly shucked oysters with their liquor
Rock salt
¼ cup chopped green onions (white and green parts)
¼ teaspoon minced garlic
6 tablespoons all-purpose flour
2 large egg yolks
½ cup chopped fresh parsley
1 cup heavy cream
½ pound Parmesan cheese, grated
1 teaspoon salt
6 tablespoons seasoned bread crumbs
Lemon wedges for serving

Preheat the oven to 450 degrees F.

In a small skillet, melt 2 tablespoons of the butter over medium heat and sauté the mushrooms until tender. Drain and set aside.

Drain the oysters, reserving 1 cup of the liquor (or substitute milk or chicken broth). Cover a large baking dish (or as many baking dishes as you need) with rock salt. Fit as many oyster shells as you can in each dish. Place an oyster in each shell. (You may also use ramekins, placing 4 oysters in each one.)

Melt the remaining 6 tablespoons of butter in a 9-inch skillet over medium heat. Sauté the green onions and garlic for 5 minutes. Slowly add the flour and stir to make a smooth mixture. Remove from the heat.

In a small bowl, beat the egg yolks, and stir in the parsley and cream. Stir the yolk mixture into the green onion and flour mixture, blending them well. Add the 1 cup of oyster liquor and cook over low heat, stirring, until it becomes a thick, creamy sauce.

To the sauce, add the drained chopped mushrooms, cheese, and salt. Stir until the cheese is melted and well blended.

Spoon this sauce over the oysters and sprinkle with bread crumbs. Bake for 15 minutes, or until browned. Serve immediately with lemon wedges. ❧

Oysters in Snail Butter Sauce

"I DON'T HAVE the exact date this recipe was published, but I believe it is one of the late Myriam Guidroz's wonderful recipes, and it's one of my very favorites," says reader Jane Adams. Guidroz, a native of Belgium, was a cooking teacher in New Orleans and the author of *Adventures in French Cooking*. She wrote the recipe exchange column for *The Times-Picayune* during the 1980s and early 1990s. This was one of Guidroz's favorite recipes, too.

The recipe was originally published under its French title, Huîtres à l'Escargot. "Don't let the name fool you," Guidroz wrote. "Escargot means snail, but there aren't any in the recipe. The name comes from the sauce."

{MAKES 4 TO 6 SERVINGS}

4 dozen freshly shucked oysters with their liquor
1 cup finely chopped fresh parsley
4 large cloves garlic, minced
1 cup (2 sticks) butter
Salt
Black pepper
Sliced French bread for serving

Put the oysters and their liquor in a large skillet and heat slowly to a simmer. As the oysters plump, transfer them to a bowl with a slotted spoon.

When all the oysters are done, add to the skillet any juice that has accumulated at the bottom of the bowl and cook down the juice until it becomes almost syrupy. Add the parsley, garlic, and butter to the skillet and heat, stirring until the butter has melted. Return the oysters to the pan. Taste, add salt if necessary (reduced oyster juice can be very salty), and cover with plenty of black pepper. Spoon into ramekins and serve with plenty of French bread for dipping.

If you are not serving immediately, refrigerate, well covered. Reheat the oysters in a skillet or chafing dish before serving.

Variation: The oysters may also be spooned into 2 dozen small pastry shells. Follow the recipe, and add about ¼ cup fresh bread crumbs to the oyster mixture at the end to thicken it. ❦

Roosevelt Hotel Shrimp Remoulade

THERE ARE VARIOUS versions of this New Orleans standard. Some are so spicy they will make your eyes water, while others are mild. Here is a good basic remoulade sauce. You can experiment: Add hot sauce if you want a bit more heat, or reduce the amount of Creole mustard for a milder version. You can certainly add prepared horseradish to give it a good kick. Make it to please your own palate.

{MAKES 12 SERVINGS}

2 large egg yolks

1 cup Creole mustard, homemade (page 341) or store-bought, or any coarse, grainy brown mustard

¼ cup distilled white vinegar

Juice of 1 lemon (about 3 tablespoons)

Salt

Black pepper

2 cups vegetable oil

1 bunch green onions, minced (white and green parts)

½ stalk minced celery

4 pounds small to medium shrimp, boiled, peeled, and deveined

6 cups shredded lettuce (about ½ cup per serving)

In a large mixing bowl, blend the egg yolks, mustard, vinegar, lemon juice, and salt and pepper to taste. Add the oil slowly, beating constantly, as if you were making mayonnaise. When the sauce has thickened, add the green onions and celery. Combine the sauce with the shrimp and chill for 4 hours in the refrigerator. Serve on a bed of shredded lettuce. ❧

Stuffed Artichoke alla Sicilian

STUFFED ARTICHOKES HAVE long been popular in the Italian community in New Orleans. And, of course, everyone has a favorite version. Nancy Tregre Wilson included this recipe in *Louisiana's Italians, Food & Folkways.* She writes that it was printed years ago in a *Times-Picayune* newspaper story about the Sam Romano family's St. Joseph's altar on Magazine Street.

Artichokes are often overstuffed with bread crumbs, cheese, and seasonings. This old recipe suprised readers when it was printed in the paper because the artichokes are stuffed with only garlic and parsley.

{MAKES 2 SERVINGS}

1 artichoke
1 head (about 12 cloves) garlic, peeled and minced
1 cup finely chopped fresh parsley
½ teaspoon salt
1 teaspoon black pepper
1 teaspoon olive oil
1 lemon, sliced
3 to 4 cups water

Cut the stem off the artichoke and trim ½ inch off the tops of the leaves. Open and spread the leaves as much as possible. Wash under running water, then turn upside down and drain for 10 minutes.

Mix the garlic, parsley, salt, and pepper in a medium mixing bowl. Salt the artichoke lightly. Spread the artichoke leaves again and pack the stuffing between them. Pour the olive oil on top of the artichoke and top with a lemon slice. Place the artichoke upright in a saucepan with a tight-fitting lid. Pour water into the pot, about 1 inch deep, around the artichoke. Cover and simmer over low heat for about 45 minutes, adding more water if necessary. When a leaf can be easily removed, the artichoke is done. Season with additional lemon if desired. Cut the artichoke in half with a sharp knife to make 2 servings.

Rosemary Walnuts

THIS LITTLE RECIPE is much more than the sum of its parts. One taste and you'll be hooked.

{MAKES 2½ CUPS}

2½ cups walnuts
3 tablespoons chopped fresh rosemary
2 tablespoons canola oil
¼ teaspoon cayenne pepper
2 tablespoons sugar
1 teaspoon salt

Preheat the oven to 300 degrees F.

Toss the nuts and rosemary in a medium mixing bowl. Heat the oil in a small heavy saucepan over medium-low heat until warm. Add the cayenne and stir until it is dissolved. Pour the oil mixture over the nut mixture. Sprinkle on the sugar and salt, and toss to coat everything evenly.

Bake in a single layer on an ungreased baking sheet, stirring often, until the nuts are toasted and fragrant, about 20 minutes. Cool and store in an airtight container for up to 2 weeks. ❧

SOUPS, GUMBOS & CHOWDERS

When the weatherman warns of a cold front moving in from the west, locals scramble to their nearest grocery store or supermarket for ingredients to make gumbo. Marcelle always says that by the time the temperature drops, there isn't a chicken to be found south of Interstate 10. Packages of andouille fly off the shelves. Shopping baskets quickly fill with onions, bell peppers, celery, and bags of rice. Those living along the Gulf of Mexico and its bays may favor a gumbo of crabs, oysters, and shrimp, such as our delicious recipe for Seafood Gumbo (page 71). We are pleased to have a mirliton gumbo (page 52) from the late Austin Leslie, one of New Orleans most beloved chefs. For those who want to make use of the turkey carcassses after Thanksgiving or Christmas dinner, Marcelle suggests that you try the Turkey Bone Gumbo (page 74). The recipe has become a holiday tradition in the region.

However, if gumbo doesn't tickle your taste buds, then you might choose to make a velvety, rich crab and corn bisque (page 64) or one of the chowders (pages 53, 57, and 70). We are also proud to share the Masson's Restaurant Francais recipe for Oyster and Artichoke Soup (page 66).

SOUPS, GUMBOS & CHOWDERS

Austin Leslie's Mirliton Gumbo

SEVERAL READERS ASKED for this mirliton gumbo recipe that was in the newspaper in November 1991. Chef Austin Leslie, "the Face of Creole Soul," rose to international prominence in the 1970s and 1980s at Chez Helene, the restaurant upon which the critically acclaimed TV series *Frank's Place* was based.

Leslie and Chef Susan Spicer of Bayona were judges at the mirliton festival in the Bywater neighborhood, where restaurants sold mirliton gumbo, stuffed mirlitons, mirliton pie, and other mirliton-inspired dishes. In most other cities, the green, pear-shaped squash is called a "chayote," but in New Orleans, it's a mirliton, sometimes pronounced "MEL-ee-tawn."

Tragically, Austin Leslie was one of the many elderly victims who died of stress following Hurricane Katrina. When his home flooded, he spent two days in his attic, then four days at the Convention Center, before he wound up in Atlanta, where he died of a heart attack on September 29, 2005. Leslie lives on in his recipes, including this one.

{MAKES 6 SERVINGS}

6 mirlitons
¼ teaspoon dried thyme leaves, plus an extra pinch
2 bay leaves
Salt
Black pepper
2 tablespoons margarine or butter
1 medium onion, diced
1 stalk celery, diced
1 green bell pepper, diced
5 sprigs fresh parsley, chopped, plus extra for garnish
¼ cup all-purpose flour
½ pound ham, chopped
½ pound hot smoked sausage such as andouille, cut into slices
½ pound hot fresh pork sausage, cut into slices
½ pound small to medium shrimp, peeled and deveined
4 gumbo crabs, cleaned (see Note)
1 teaspoon filé
Pinch of garlic powder
Hot cooked rice for serving

Peel the mirlitons unless the skin is soft, in which case you can leave it on. Dice the mirlitons into 1-inch cubes and transfer to a large pot. Cover with water and add the ¼ teaspoon of thyme, the bay leaves, and salt and pepper to taste. Bring to a simmer and simmer for 30 minutes. Remove the mirlitons with a slotted spoon and save the broth.

In a 4-quart pot, melt the margarine and sauté the onion, celery, bell pepper, and parsley. Add the flour to make a roux, stirring constantly, and simmer slowly for about 10 minutes. Add the mirliton broth and about 4 cups of water and bring to a simmer.

Add the ham to the pot and simmer for 5 minutes. Add the smoked sausage, and cook for another 5 minutes. Add the pork sausage and cook for yet another 5 minutes. Add the shrimp, crabs, filé, a pinch of thyme, and garlic powder, and simmer over medium heat for 30 minutes. Add the diced mirlitons when you are ready to serve, and simmer until heated through. Remove the bay leaves. Serve the gumbo in bowls with cooked rice on top, garnished with parsley. ⅜

NOTE: *Gumbo crabs are small whole blue crabs, which are cut in half to use in gumbos and soups. In Louisiana you can buy them fresh or frozen.*

Bacon and Corn Chowder

WHEN WE ASKED readers which recipes they wanted to see in this cookbook, this request came from M.F: "A few years ago, y'all had a recipe for a chowder and I was wondering if y'all could find it and possibly put it in the cookbook," she wrote. "The chowder had corn, instant potato flakes (which you put in at the very end), and bacon. If y'all would include it I would greatly appreciate it."

This is a thick, hearty soup. Its thickness can be adjusted to your preference by stirring in more or less of the potato flakes.

{MAKES 2 TO 3 SERVINGS}

1 cup chopped bacon
½ cup finely chopped onion
½ cup finely chopped celery
1 teaspoon minced garlic
2 cups chicken broth
1½ cups heavy cream
1 cup milk
1 cup frozen corn kernels (not thawed)
½ teaspoon kosher salt
¼ teaspoon black pepper
½ to ¾ cup mashed potato flakes
2 tablespoons butter
Sliced French bread for serving

In a large pot, sauté the bacon on medium-high heat until slightly crisp, then drain well. Add the onion, celery, and garlic and sauté until the vegetables are translucent, about 5 minutes. Add the chicken broth and cook for an additional 3 minutes, stirring occasionally. Add the cream and milk. Reduce the heat to medium and let the soup reduce, stirring occasionally, 10 to 15 minutes.

Add the corn, salt, and pepper. While the soup is bubbling lightly, slowly add the potato flakes, stirring constantly. When the flakes are incorporated, take the soup off the heat. Add the butter and stir until melted. Serve hot with the bread. ❧

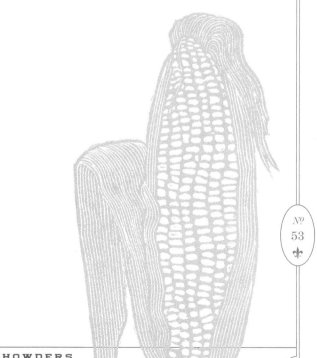

Black Bean Soup with Cilantro Cream

WHEN THE CALL went out for recipes to be collected in this book, Carol L. Kirkland from Mandeville submitted this recipe, which is a favorite of her family. The spiciness of the soup is cooled by the Cilantro Cream.

{MAKES 4 SERVINGS}

4 slices bacon, chopped
½ cup chopped onion
½ cup chopped sun-dried tomatoes
1 (15-ounce) can black beans, drained and rinsed
1 (14-ounce) can chicken broth
1 large clove garlic, chopped
½ teaspoon ground cumin
¼ teaspoon hot sauce
¼ cup chopped fresh cilantro

CILANTRO CREAM

¼ cup sour cream
1 tablespoon chopped fresh cilantro
1 teaspoon ground coriander

Cook the bacon and onion in a large heavy pot over medium heat until the onion is tender. Drain off the excess fat.

Add the tomatoes, beans, chicken broth, garlic, cumin, and hot sauce. Bring the mixture to a boil over high heat. Reduce the heat to medium-low and simmer for 5 minutes.

Remove from the heat and add the cilantro leaves. Purée the mixture in a blender and return to the pot, or use an immersion blender to purée it in the pot. Keep warm.

For the Cilantro Cream: Combine the sour cream, cilantro, and coriander in a small bowl and whisk to blend.

Serve the soup in bowls drizzled with the Cilantro Cream. ❧

Chicken and Sausage Gumbo

EVEN MORE THAN jambalaya or red beans and rice, gumbo is Louisiana's signature dish. There are as many recipes as there are bayous that twine through the state. Those living along the Gulf of Mexico tend to cook seafood gumbo, since crabs, shrimp, and oysters are readily available. The Acadians who live on the prairies in southwestern Louisiana favor gumbo made with chicken and sausage.

If andouille sausage is not available, another smoked sausage, such as kielbasa, is perfectly acceptable to use.

{MAKES ABOUT 8 SERVINGS}

1 (4- to 5-pound) hen (stewing chicken), cut into
  serving pieces
Salt
Cayenne pepper
1 cup vegetable oil
1 cup all-purpose flour
2 cups chopped yellow onions
1 cup chopped green bell peppers
½ cup chopped celery
About 2½ quarts chicken broth
2 bay leaves
½ teaspoon dried powdered or leaf thyme
1 pound andouille sausage, sliced ¼ inch thick
¼ cup chopped green onions (white and green parts)
2 tablespoons chopped fresh parsley
Hot cooked rice for serving

Season the hen generously with salt and cayenne, and set aside.

In a large Dutch oven, make a roux by combining the oil and flour over medium heat. Stirring constantly, cook for about 30 minutes, or until the roux is dark brown. Add the onions, bell peppers, and celery and cook for 5 to 10 minutes, or until the vegetables are very soft.

Add the broth and stir to blend well. Add the chicken, bay leaves, and thyme. Bring to a boil, then reduce the heat and simmer, partially covered, for about 2 to 3 hours, or until the chicken is fork-tender. Add the andouille and cook for another 30 minutes. Adjust the seasonings and add the green onions and parsley. Remove the bay leaves. Serve immediately over rice. 🦐

Crabmeat Higgins Soup

C.L. OF HOUMA mailed in a recipe for the creamy Crabmeat Higgins Soup from the St. Charles Restaurant, which operated at 333 St. Charles Avenue, next to One Shell Square. "I obtained the recipe from a neighbor, who worked in One Shell Square and frequented the restaurant," C.L. explained. We are not sure of the exact origin of this soup's name, but Higgins is a famous name in New Orleans. On the lakefront, Andrew Jackson Higgins, the owner of Higgins Industries, developed and manufactured the Higgins boat, which played an important role in the Western Allies' landing in Normandy on D-Day, during World War II.

The recipe was requested by a New Orleans resident, M.G., who wrote, "*Comfort food* has never been so true a term as post-you-know-who." It contains liquid crab boil, as do many local seafood soup recipes. In fact, cooks in south Louisiana season everything from red beans to the liquid for boiling hot dogs with a drop or two of liquid crab boil. This soup also contains evaporated milk, which adds its own unique flavor. Zatarain's Liquid Crab Boil Concentrate is available from the company's Web site. Be careful; it's potent!

{MAKES 8 SERVINGS}

½ cup (1 stick) butter

½ cup chopped onion

3 tablespoons minced green bell pepper

3 (10¾-ounce) cans Campbell's tomato soup

1 pound white crabmeat, picked over for shells and cartilage.

2 drops liquid crab boil, or to taste

Salt

Black pepper

3 (12-ounce) cans evaporated milk, or 2¼ cups milk and 2¼ cups cream

Garlic French bread for serving

Melt the butter in a large soup pot. Add the onion and bell peppers and sauté until soft, about 5 minutes. Add the tomato soup and crabmeat, bring to a simmer, and cook for about 30 minutes over low heat. Season with the crab boil, and salt and pepper to taste. Add the milk, stir, and heat through. Serve with garlic French bread. ❧

Crawfish and Corn Chowder

AFTER MARDI GRAS 2003, Constance Snow offered this recipe in a column for the Lenten season. She noted, "The chowder adds some spark to Southern-style corn soup with the addition of Louisiana crawfish in place of the usual ham. It's another dish we share with our Caribbean neighbors, in this case Cubans, who would season theirs with spicy chorizo sausage and top each bowl with a chopped hard-boiled egg. Vegetarians could just leave out the meat altogether. Whatever method you choose, it's a satisfying mix of textures and colors for a flavorful and thrifty supper."

{MAKES 6 SERVINGS}

3 tablespoons olive oil

1 medium onion, chopped

1 green bell pepper, chopped

1 stalk celery, chopped

1 carrot, peeled and chopped

1 bay leaf

1 teaspoon chopped fresh thyme, or
   ¼ teaspoon dried thyme leaves

2 cloves garlic, sliced

1 (14-ounce) can stewed tomatoes with their juice

3 cups chicken or vegetable broth

6 to 8 small new potatoes, quartered

Fresh kernels from 3 large ears corn, or 1½ cups
   frozen corn (not thawed)

1 pound peeled crawfish tails

Salt

Black pepper

2 tablespoons minced fresh parsley for garnish

Warm the oil over medium heat in a 3-quart saucepan and sauté the onion, bell pepper, celery, and carrot until the onion is golden. Add the bay leaf, thyme, and garlic and continue cooking for 1 or 2 minutes, until the garlic is fragrant. Add the tomatoes and broth and bring to a boil; then reduce the heat and simmer for 15 minutes. Add the potatoes and continue cooking until tender, about 20 minutes.

Stir in the corn and crawfish and simmer until the corn is tender, but still crisp, about 5 minutes. Remove the bay leaf. Adjust the seasoning with salt and pepper to taste.

To serve, garnish each bowl with parsley. ❧

Easy Spinach Soup

COUNTLESS READERS WHO love New Orleans and New Orleans food followed the recipe restoration process every week via the Internet, through our affiliated Web site, NOLA.com. Many of them were part of the great diaspora that scattered the city's citizens across the country after their homes were destroyed.

One former New Orleanian, who had left years before the storm, even e-mailed us from New Zealand. "I read your column (on NOLA.com) regularly, particularly watching for requests for recipes that I might have," J.J. wrote from Te Aroha, which is not far from Auckland. "There have never been any. It's disappointing that I've not been able to make even that small contribution to rebuilding my dearly loved home city, but I will continue to look."

J.J. married a Kiwi, as New Zealanders call themselves, and moved there in 1999. After we let J.J. know that readers could contribute to the rebuilding project by contributing their own favorite recipes, she sent this, saying, "Here's a recipe that no one has asked for that I really like, and it couldn't be easier."

{MAKES 4 SERVINGS}

2 tablespoons olive oil

2 cloves garlic, finely chopped

1 small onion, finely chopped

2 (14-ounce) cans chicken broth

1 (14-ounce) can sliced, stewed tomatoes with their juice

¼ cup small dried pasta, such as orzo

1 (10-ounce) package frozen chopped spinach, thawed and drained

¼ cup grated Parmesan cheese

Salt

Black pepper

In a 3-quart saucepan, heat the olive oil and sauté the garlic and onion for 3 to 5 minutes, until soft. Add the broth and tomatoes, and bring to a simmer. Add the pasta and simmer for 10 minutes. Add the spinach and cheese and stir well.

Heat until the soup is serving temperature. Season with salt and pepper to taste, and serve. ❧

Greek-Style Vegetable and Pasta Soup

C.D. WANTED THIS recipe for Greek vegetable soup. This would be a fine hearty soup to make in advance for football-watching. Serve it with toasted pita bread and a tossed green salad.

{MAKES 6 SERVINGS}

1 medium eggplant, peeled

2 tablespoons olive oil

1 medium onion, chopped

1 red bell pepper, chopped

1 tablespoon minced garlic

¼ teaspoon dried thyme leaves

½ teaspoon dried oregano leaves

1 bay leaf

6 cups chicken or vegetable broth

2 (14-ounce) cans chopped tomatoes with their juice

1 zucchini, halved lengthwise and thinly sliced into half-moons

1 yellow squash, halved lengthwise and thinly sliced into half-moons

1 cup orzo (rice-shaped pasta)

2 tablespoons fresh lemon juice

Salt

Black pepper

2 tablespoons minced fresh mint, for garnish

¼ pound feta cheese, crumbled, for garnish

Slice the eggplant thickly, salt both sides, and drain in a colander for 30 minutes. Rinse the slices well and pat them dry with paper towels. Cut into ½-inch cubes and set aside.

Heat the oil in a large pot, and sauté the onion and bell pepper until the onion is translucent. Stir in the garlic, thyme, oregano, and bay leaf. Continue cooking just until the garlic releases its fragrance, about 1 minute. Stir in the chicken broth and tomatoes and simmer for 15 minutes. Add the zucchini, squash, eggplant, and orzo and cook until the vegetables are tender, 6 to 8 minutes. Remove the bay leaf, stir in the lemon juice, and season to taste with salt and pepper.

To serve, garnish each bowl with chopped mint and crumbled feta cheese. ❧

Johnny Becnel's Daddy's Okra Gumbo

MARCELLE BIENVENU BECAME a fan of farmer Johnny Becnel around 1970, when she discovered his vegetable stand on the Belle Chasse Highway, south of New Orleans. She called him several times when writing about Creole tomatoes and citrus. Johnny explained to her the mystique of those tomatoes, grown in the alluvial soil of Plaquemines Parish. He also knew a lot about okra, and raised the hybrid developed by Louisiana State University—Gold Coast split leaf.

Marcelle and Johnny's many friends were saddened to learn of his death in the spring of 2004. His gumbo recipe first appeared in the newspaper in July 1995, at the height of Louisiana okra season. The recipe is "unbelievably fabulous," he had told the writer Carolyn Kolb. "This is as good as you ever ate in your life. My Daddy was a Cajun, and this recipe goes back a long, long way."

{MAKES ABOUT 8 SERVINGS}

4 tablespoons butter

2 medium onions, cut into ½-inch pieces

3 green bell peppers, cut into into ¾-inch chunks

¾ teaspoon chopped garlic

1½ pounds Creole tomatoes (or plum or other local tomatoes), peeled

Salt

Cayenne pepper

4 pounds okra, chopped

Tomato juice, as needed

1½ pounds small to medium shrimp, peeled and deveined

Hot cooked rice for serving

In a large gumbo pot, melt the butter over medium-high heat and sauté the onions and bell peppers until tender. Add the garlic, tomatoes, and salt and cayenne pepper to taste.

Simmer over medium-low heat, stirring occasionally, for 45 minutes, then add the okra. "You may have to add tomato juice if the mixture gets too thick," Becnel advised. Continue simmering, stirring occasionally, for about 1 hour. "The okra should be absolutely melted, like a thick paste," Becnel said. Then, add the peeled shrimp and cook just until they turn pink, about 5 minutes. Serve over steaming bowls of rice.

Variation: Becnel's family also made this with fresh corn off the cob instead of the okra. "Then we call it corn stew," he said. Substitute 4 cups of corn kernels for the okra. ❧

Sweet Potato, Corn, and Jalapeño Bisque

In November 2005, we heard from two readers craving the exact same recipe. One wrote: "Funny how when life is in a turmoil, the debris pile in front of your house has been 15 feet high, and you haven't slept in your own bed for three months, you can't stop thinking about a soup recipe that got flooded! It is Sweet Potato, Corn, and Jalapeño Bisque."

"I would *love* to have the sweet potato soup with jalapeño peppers recipe that appeared on the front page of the Food section some time last winter," wrote the second reader. "Alas, my copy didn't make it, and if ever I need some comfort food, it's now." The recipe appeared in the newspaper in 2004.

{MAKES ABOUT 12 SERVINGS}

1 tablespoon peanut oil

1 cup chopped yellow onion

1 tablespoon minced garlic

6 medium sweet potatoes (about 5 pounds), peeled and cut into 1-inch cubes

8 cups vegetable or chicken stock

1 to 2 fresh jalapeño peppers, stemmed, seeded, and finely chopped

2 cups fresh or frozen corn kernels

¼ cup molasses

1 tablespoon kosher salt

½ teaspoon cayenne pepper

½ teaspoon black pepper

Pinch of ground cinnamon

Finely chopped green onions (green part only) for garnish

Heat the oil for about 1 minute in a 6-quart saucepan or Dutch oven over medium heat. Add the onion and garlic, and sauté until soft, 2 to 3 minutes. Add the sweet potatoes and stock, and bring the mixture to a boil. Reduce the heat and simmer until the potatoes are soft, about 10 minutes.

Remove from the heat, and use an immersion blender to purée the mixture in the pot, or purée the soup in batches in a food processor and return the mixture to the pan. Add the jalapeños, corn, and molasses, stirring well. Season with the salt, cayenne, and black pepper, and add the cinnamon. Bring the soup to a simmer and serve immediately, garnished with green onions. ❧

Pho, Traditional Vietnamese Beef Soup

OUTSIDERS AND NEWCOMERS to New Orleans are sometimes surprised to discover the Asian flavor in modern New Orleans cuisine. The Vietnamese community in New Orleans East has been known for years for creating a little slice of Vietnam on the levee. At one time, hundreds of individual garden plots, filled with greens and vegetables unfamiliar to most Americans, were tended by residents who lived in the nearby Versailles Arms apartments.

The informally organized Saturday morning Vietnamese farmers' market in the area survived Katrina. The hardy local residents, many of whom had already undergone one great upheaval in their lives (the Vietnam War), were some of the first to return to this area of the city, which had been hit especially hard. And several Vietnamese restaurants on the West Bank of New Orleans were among the first to reopen after the storm.

Pho, one of the national dishes of Vietnam, is a favorite in several local restaurants. This recipe was published in *The Times-Picayune* in 1995 with a story about the Vietnamese market.

{MAKES 6 SERVINGS}

4 pounds beef soup bones

1 pound chuck roast, trimmed of fat

2½ quarts water

1 medium onion, sliced

1 thumb-sized chunk fresh ginger, bruised

1 cinnamon stick

2 star anise pods

½ teaspoon bottled fish sauce (*nuoc nam*)

Black pepper

½ pound dried rice sticks (flat noodles)

½ pound beef tenderloin, sliced paper thin

Lime wedges for garnish

Nuoc Cham (facing page)

Basic Vegetable Platter (facing page)

Put the soup bones and chuck roast (in one piece) in a large Dutch oven or stock pot with the water, onion, ginger, cinnamon, and star anise. Bring to a boil and continue boiling for 10 minutes, skimming often to remove the scum from the surface. Reduce the heat and simmer, covered, for about 2 hours. Add the fish sauce and black pepper to taste.

Strain and degrease the stock, reserving the chuck roast and the meat from the soup bones. The easiest way to degrease the stock is to store it overnight, covered, in the refrigerator, and lift the congealed fat from the surface. Alternatively, use a spoon to skim fat from the stock. About 1 quart of rich stock should remain. Shred the chuck roast before serving.

Drop the rice sticks into 2 quarts of boiling water. Return to a boil and continue boiling for 4 minutes. Drain and rinse well with cold water to prevent sticking. (This may be done just before serving, or in advance).

To serve, return the stock to a boil. Distribute the noodles among large individual bowls, along with shreds of the cooked chuck roast and soup bone meat. Top each with a few slices of raw tenderloin, then ladle the boiling stock (which blanches the uncooked beef) over all.

Allow diners to customize their own bowls with lime juice, Nuoc Cham, and garnishes from the vegetable platter. ❧

Nuoc Cham

{MAKES ABOUT ½ CUP}

¼ lime
2 cloves garlic
2 tablespoons sugar
3 tablespoons bottled fish sauce
6 tablespoons water
3 hot red chile peppers, seeded and thinly sliced

Juice the lime over a food processor, and scrape in the pulp. Add the garlic, sugar, fish sauce, and water and process until smooth. Pour into a small serving bowl and stir in the thinly sliced peppers. ❧

Basic Vegetable Platter

{MAKES 6 SERVINGS}

2 cups soft lettuce leaves, such as Boston or red leaf (not iceberg)
1 cup fresh mint leaves
1 cup fresh cilantro
½ pound bean sprouts
½ cup sliced green onions (green part only)
1 cucumber, halved lengthwise and cut into paper-thin half-moons

Mound the lettuce in the center of the platter, and arrange mounds of the herbs, sprouts, and green onions around the lettuce. Surround with overlapping slices of cucumber. ❧

Louisiana Crab and Corn Bisque

THIS RICH SOUP is an ideal dish to serve during the summer because it combines fresh corn from the garden and delicate lump crabmeat from the Gulf of Mexico. Our recipe files contain many versions of this favorite, but we decided this particular recipe, from Marcelle Bienvenu, is one you'll love. If you prefer, you can substitute shrimp for the crabmeat

{MAKES 4 TO 6 SERVINGS}

2 tablespoons butter

1 cup chopped yellow onion

¼ cup chopped red bell pepper

½ cup chopped green bell pepper

½ cup chopped celery

1 tablespoon minced garlic

2 cups shrimp or chicken stock

½ cup dry white wine

½ teaspoon dried thyme leaves

¼ cup vegetable oil

¼ cup all-purpose flour

3½ cups heavy cream

1 teaspoon salt

1 teaspoon hot sauce

1 cup fresh or frozen corn kernels

1 pound lump crabmeat, picked over for shells and cartilage, or 1 pound medium shrimp, peeled and deveined

1 tablespoon chopped fresh parsley

1 tablespoon chopped green onions (green part only)

Heat the butter in a large saucepan over medium heat. Add the onion, bell peppers, celery, and garlic and sauté for 1 minute. Add the stock, wine, and thyme and bring to a boil.

In a skillet, combine the oil and flour over medium heat. Make a blond roux, stirring constantly for about 2 to 3 minutes. Add the roux to the mixture in the saucepan and mix well to combine thoroughly.

Reduce the heat to medium, and add the cream in a steady stream, whisking with a wire whisk to combine the mixture. Add the salt, hot sauce, and corn. Simmer for 5 minutes. Add the crabmeat, parsley, and green onions and cook for about 5 minutes, or until the soup is heated through. Serve immediately. ✇

Margie's Oyster Soup

When *the times-picayune* resumed publication following Katrina, the first several cover stories of the Food section featured comfort food, comfort food, and more comfort food. A story on soup for the holidays included this recipe from a beloved chef, the late Warren Leruth (see page 142).

The source was his mother-in-law, the late Marie Margarite Huet Rizzuto. Leruth included the recipe in a booklet that was privately printed and given away at the 20th anniversary of his restaurant in 1983.

{MAKES 10 SERVINGS}

4 dozen freshly shucked salty oysters, with their liquor

½ cup (1 stick) butter

2 bunches green onions, chopped (white and green parts)

1 medium yellow onion, chopped

1 clove garlic, chopped

1 celery heart, finely chopped

¾ cup all-purpose flour

1 cup heavy cream

½ bunch fresh parsley, chopped

Salt

White pepper

Cayenne pepper

Poach the oysters gently in their own liquor for 5 to 10 minutes, until they are plumped. Drain the oysters, reserving the liquor. Add enough water to the liquor to get 2 quarts of liquid.

Heat the butter in a large soup pot and sauté the green onions, yellow onion, garlic, and celery until they are tender. Stir in the flour to make a smooth paste. Slowly whisk in the oyster liquor and water and the cream. Heat until barely boiling. Add the parsley and poached oysters, and season to taste with the salt, white pepper, and cayenne pepper. Serve immediately. 🦋

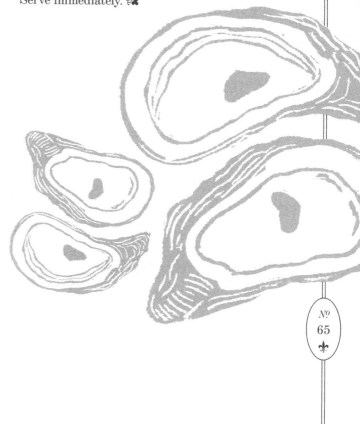

Masson's Oyster and Artichoke Soup

In August 2006, Judy Walker wrote a story about tea towel–recipe calendars. (These were calendars given out by Masson's in the form of a linen dish towel. Each year, there was a different recipe printed with the calendar on the towel.) Y.R. of Metairie had written that she lost a tea towel–calendar with Masson's Oyster and Artichoke Soup recipe on it. After her home flooded, it was thrown out in the chaos.

Another reader we'll call W., whose home in Lake Terrace did not flood, had the towel and sent it to Y.R. "We were very good friends with the Masson family, and I have quite a few tea towel–calendars," wrote W. She also delivered to *The Times-Picayune* a color photocopy of the 1984 Masson's Restaurant Français towel, so the recipe could be shared with other readers.

We will never know all the endless kindnesses that were bestowed in the wake of the storm. W.'s generosity is one of countless examples of how New Orleans residents helped each other heal.

{MAKES 4 SERVINGS}

⅓ cup (⅔ stick) butter

1 bunch green onions, chopped (white and green parts)

Pinch of dried thyme leaves

Small pinch of cayenne pepper

3 bay leaves

2 tablespoons all-purpose flour

1 (14-ounce) can chicken broth

2 cups extra oyster liquor (purchased from your fishmonger)

1 pint small freshly shucked oysters

1 (14-ounce) can artichoke hearts, cut up

3 sprigs fresh parsley, chopped

½ cup heavy cream

Salt

In a large saucepan, melt the butter over medium heat and sauté the green onions, thyme, cayenne, and bay leaves until the green onions are soft. Add the flour and stir well with a wire whisk to blend. Add the chicken broth and oyster liquor, stir well, and simmer for 15 minutes. Add the oysters, artichoke hearts, and parsley. Simmer for 10 minutes more, add the cream, and heat through. Remove the bay leaves. Season with salt and serve. 🦐

Meaty Gumbo over
Warm Spicy Potato Salad

A SPECIAL REQUEST was made to include this recipe from *The Times-Picayune*'s Cookbook and Recipe Contest, which the newspaper sponsored annually until 1993. The winning recipes were published in the Easter Sunday edition of *The Times-Picayune*. This was one of the winners in 1992, and is the creation of Thomas Lee Snakenberg of Metairie. His recipe for the "must-have" potato salad, to accompany the gumbo, is included.

{MAKES 10 TO 12 SERVINGS}

1 tablespoon salt

1 teaspoon black pepper

¼ teaspoon cayenne pepper

1 (3- to 4-pound) fryer chicken, cut into
    serving pieces

¼ cup vegetable oil

½ pound andouille sausage, sliced into ½-inch pieces

½ pound fresh pork sausage, sliced ½ inch thick

½ pound smoked ham, coarsely chopped

¼ cup all-purpose flour

¼ cup chopped yellow onion

½ cup chopped green bell peppers

½ cup chopped celery

1 (10-ounce) can Ro-Tel diced tomatoes and
    green chile

2 cloves garlic, chopped

6 cups warm chicken stock

2 bay leaves, crushed

1 teaspoon dried thyme leaves

½ teaspoon dried basil leaves

½ cup chopped fresh parsley, plus more for garnish

Warm Spicy Potato Salad (facing page)

Chopped green onions (green part only) for garnish

Filé for serving

Combine the salt, black pepper, and cayenne in a shallow dish. Sprinkle the chicken pieces with the mixture. (Reserve the remaining seasoning mixture, if any.)

Heat the oil in a large heavy pot or Dutch oven over medium heat and brown the chicken pieces evenly, in batches if necessary. Using a slotted spoon, transfer to a platter and set aside. Add the sausages and ham to the same pot, and brown evenly. Using a slotted spoon, transfer to a platter and set aside.

Slowly add the flour and, stirring constantly, make a dark brown roux. Add the onion, bell pepper, celery, tomatoes, and garlic. Cook, stirring, until the vegetables are tender. Slowly add the stock and bring to a boil.

Add the browned chicken, sausages, and ham. Simmer for 1 hour. Add the leftover seasoning mixture, if any, of salt, black pepper, and cayenne, as well as the bay leaves, thyme, and basil. Simmer for 15 minutes. Add the ½ cup of parsley and simmer for 10 minutes.

Serve the gumbo over a scoop of potato salad. Garnish with parsley and green onions and allow people to add filé to taste. 🌿

Warm Spicy Potato Salad

{MAKES 6 SERVINGS}

¼ cup Creole seasoning, such as Zatarain's

4 medium potatoes, peeled

1 teaspoon celery salt

½ teaspoon chopped fresh parsley

1 teaspoon seasoned pepper

½ teaspoon seasoned salt

½ to ¾ cup mayonnaise

½ teaspoon Creole mustard, homemade
   (page 341) or store-bought, or any
   coarse, grainy brown mustard

½ teaspoon white wine vinegar

2 warm hard-boiled eggs

Combine the Creole seasoning with 3 cups of water in a medium saucepan. Add the potatoes. Boil over high heat until tender, then drain.

Combine the celery salt, parsley, seasoned pepper, and seasoned salt in a large mixing bowl. Add the mayonnaise to taste, Creole mustard, and vinegar. Dice the potatoes and eggs and add to the mixture. Mix well. ✒

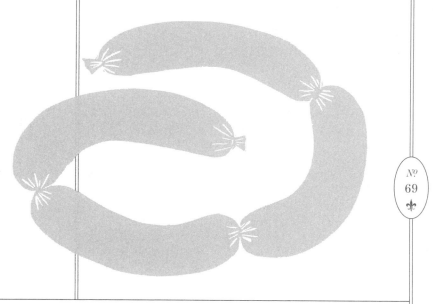

Mrs. Francis Toomy's
Fresh Corn and Shrimp Chowder

THIS RECIPE COMES from one of Sue Baker's columns, which appeared in the *Dixie-Roto* magazine, probably in the late 1960s or early 1970s. *Dixie-Roto* was a Sunday supplement to the newspaper.

The day we received a request for it, we also received the recipe from someone who thought it should be included in the book! Several such coincidences have punctuated our recipe-restoration efforts.

{MAKES 6 TO 8 SERVINGS}

½ cup (1 stick) margarine or butter

½ cup chopped green onions (white and green parts)

½ cup chopped celery, including the tops

½ cup chopped fresh parsley

¼ chopped green bell peppers

2 pounds medium fresh shrimp, peeled and deveined

2 cups fresh corn kernels

1 (17-ounce) can cream-style corn

4 cups water or fish stock

½ teaspoon Worcestershire sauce

Dash of ground nutmeg

Salt

Black pepper

Melt the margarine in a Dutch oven or large heavy pot over medium heat. Add the green onions, celery, parsley, and bell peppers. Cook, stirring, until the vegetables are softened. Add the shrimp and cook over low heat until they turn pink. Add the fresh corn and simmer for 5 minutes. Add the cream-style corn, water, Worcestershire, nutmeg, and salt and pepper to taste. Simmer for 30 minutes, and serve.

Seafood Gumbo

A READER SENT this message: "God bless the staff member who gave birth to this marvelous idea [of restoring lost recipes]. Ever since Katrina I have lamented over my one and only gumbo and étouffée recipes that I clipped from the T-P many years ago, at least twenty. My copy was soiled and taped, but it produced the best gumbo I ever had. Hope you can still find it that far back. [The recipes] were part of a series from the Saints football players. The article included a roux, the best I ever tasted, okra seafood gumbo and étouffée. Just getting those recipes back would make my subscription worthwhile."

Even though several of us spent hours searching, we could not find the Saints recipe series. However, we did find a recipe from 1986 for this excellent seafood gumbo.

{MAKES 6 TO 8 SERVINGS}

10½ tablespoons margarine or vegetable oil

1 medium white onion, chopped

3 green onions, chopped (white and green parts)

4 cloves garlic, minced

2 green bell peppers, chopped

2 bay leaves

3 gumbo crabs, cleaned and broken into pieces (see Note)

1 (14- to 16-ounce) can whole tomatoes with their juice

½ pound okra, sliced

1 pound medium shrimp, peeled and deveined

¼ cup salad oil

½ cup all-purpose flour

1 pint oysters with their liquor

Salt

Black pepper

Hot cooked rice for serving

In a soup pot, melt the margarine and add the white onion, green onions, garlic, bell peppers, and bay leaves. Cook over medium heat until the onions brown evenly. Add the crabs, tomatoes, and okra and cook for 10 minutes. Cover the cooked ingredients with water, then add 1 quart more. Add the shrimp, increase the heat, and bring to a slow boil.

In a skillet, preferably cast-iron, heat the salad oil over medium heat. Add the flour and stir until brown. Add this roux to the soup pot, a little at a time, until the desired thickness is obtained. Add the oysters and return to a boil. Remove the bay leaves. Season to taste with salt and pepper. Serve over rice in large soup bowls. 🦐

NOTE: *Gumbo crabs are small whole blue crabs, which are cut in half to use in gumbos and soups. In Louisiana you can buy them fresh or frozen.*

Sicilian Lentil Soup

J.D. OF INDEPENDENCE, Louisiana, wrote, "My most memorable recipe, which I have lost, is a recipe for Sicilian lentil soup. I am not sure how it was labeled. I have tried to pick it up on the Internet but it is not listed. I think this recipe was in the Food section five to seven years ago."

While we couldn't find that particular recipe, we did come across one from Constance Snow, which appeared in the paper in April 2005. She usually makes a double or triple recipe in a big pot, seasons it different ways, and then freezes it in portions in plastic zipper-top bags.

{MAKES 6 TO 8 SERVINGS}

¼ cup olive oil
2 medium onions, finely chopped
2 stalks celery, finely chopped
3 carrots, peeled and finely chopped
2 to 4 cloves garlic, minced
1 pound lentils, picked over and rinsed
2 bay leaves
3 quarts vegetable or chicken stock, or water
Salt
Black pepper
Cayenne pepper
Lemon wedges for serving

Warm the olive oil in a large soup pot or Dutch oven over medium-high heat. Add the onions, celery, and carrots. Cook, stirring, until the onions are lightly browned, 3 to 4 minutes. Add the garlic and continue cooking until fragrant, about 1 minute. Stir in the lentils, bay leaves, and stock. Bring to a boil, then reduce the heat and simmer until the lentils are very tender, about 1 hour.

Discard the bay leaves and, if necessary, thin the soup to the desired consistency with water. Season to taste with salt, black pepper, and cayenne. If you prefer a perfectly smooth blend, purée the soup in a food processor or blender and reheat. Serve hot, with lemon wedges, or just before serving, stir in 1 pound of cooked and drained small pasta, such as tubettini or macaroni. Drizzle each serving with olive oil and top with grated Romano cheese. ❧

VARIATIONS:

Indian Lentil Soup— Omit the celery. Lightly brown 1 tablespoon of minced fresh ginger, 1 tablespoon of ground coriander, and 2 teaspoons of ground cumin with the onions. Increase the garlic to 8 cloves and proceed with the recipe. Omit the black pepper and season with ¼ to ½ teaspoon of cayenne pepper.

Sephardic Lentil Soup— Lightly brown 2 teaspoons of ground cumin with the onions. Add 2 or 3 peeled and seeded ripe tomatoes, chopped, during the final 30 minutes of cooking. Just before serving, stir in ¼ cup of chopped fresh mint. Drizzle additional olive oil over each bowl.

Greek Lentil Soup— Increase the olive oil to ⅓ cup. Add 1 tablespoon of tomato paste with the stock. Just before serving, stir in ¼ cup of minced fresh parsley and 3 tablespoons of lemon juice.

French Lentil Soup— Add 1 teaspoon of herbes de Provence with the garlic. Just before serving, stir in ¼ cup of chopped fresh parsley.

Southwestern Lentil Soup— Lightly brown 2 teaspoons of ground cumin and ½ teaspoon of dried oregano (preferably Mexican oregano) with the onions, celery, and carrots. Instead of lemon wedges, serve with lime wedges, and set out bowls of fresh cilantro, crisp tortilla strips, sour cream, and chopped fresh chiles, so everyone can garnish the soup as desired.

Dutch Split Pea Soup— Substitute green or yellow split peas for the lentils, and water for the stock. Add a meaty ham bone (or chunks of ham) with the water. Cook for about 30 minutes longer. Omit the lemon wedges. 🐝

Turkey Bone Gumbo

In November 2001, Ronnie Foreman's recipe for Turkey Bone Gumbo became an instant favorite after the Lafayette resident was featured in Marcelle Bienvenu's column, "Cooking Creole." Readers have demanded the recipe every Thanksgiving since.

For years, Foreman has gathered turkey carcasses from family, friends, and neighbors the day after Thanksgiving. The carcasses are simmered in flavored water to make a stock. He uses the stock, along with any leftover turkey meat, to make a delectable gumbo, which he serves to his friends while they play poker.

Ronnie says it's a must to have potato salad, baked sweet potatoes, rice (of course), and lots of French bread to go along with the gumbo. We have cut back the turkey broth recipe to just one turkey carcass, so you don't have to collect them!

{MAKES 8 TO 10 SERVINGS}

¾ cup vegetable oil

¾ cup all-purpose flour

1½ cups chopped yellow onions

1 cup chopped green bell peppers

½ cup chopped celery

1 teaspoon salt

½ teaspoon cayenne pepper

½ pound smoked sausage, such as andouille, chopped (optional)

1 recipe Turkey Broth (facing page)

1½ pounds cooked turkey meat, chopped, plus any reserved meat from the carcass in the broth

Reserved onions and celery from broth

2 tablespoons chopped fresh parsley

2 tablespoons chopped green onions (green part only)

Hot cooked rice for serving

Potato Salad with Garlic Mayonnaise for serving (facing page)

In a large cast-iron pot or enameled cast-iron Dutch oven over medium heat, combine the oil and flour. Stirring constantly and slowly for 20 to 25 minutes, make a dark brown roux, the color of chocolate. Add the onions, bell peppers, celery, salt, and cayenne. Cook, stirring often, until the vegetables are soft, about 5 minutes. Add the sausage (if using) and cook for 5 minutes, stirring often. Add the broth and bring to a boil. Reduce the heat to medium-low and simmer for 45 minutes.

Add the turkey meat and the reserved onions and celery from the broth and cook for 15 minutes. Add the parsley and green onions. Serve in soup bowls with steamed rice, and accompany with the potato salad. ✺

Turkey Broth

{MAKES ABOUT 2 QUARTS}

1 turkey carcass
3 stalks celery, cut into 4-inch pieces
2 medium onions, quartered
1 gallon water, or enough to cover the carcass
2 teaspoons salt
1 tablespoon whole black peppercorns
4 bay leaves

Put the carcass in a large stockpot. Add the celery, onions, water, salt, peppercorns, and bay leaves. Bring to a boil, then reduce the heat to medium and simmer, uncovered, for 2 hours. Remove from the heat.

Skim any oil that has risen to the surface. Strain the broth through a large fine-mesh sieve. Reserve any meat that has fallen off the bones and pick off any meat that may still remain on the carcass to add to the gumbo. Reserve the onions and celery for the gumbo. ❧

Potato Salad with Garlic Mayonnaise

{MAKES 8 TO 10 SERVINGS}

4 pounds small boiling potatoes
3 cloves garlic, minced
1 teaspoon salt
3½ tablespoons fresh lemon juice
½ cup mayonnaise, or more to taste
½ teaspoon Creole mustard, homemade (page 341) or store-bought, or any coarse, grainy brown mustard
⅓ cup chopped green onions (green part only)
Black pepper

Boil the potatoes in lightly salted water until just tender. Drain and cool.

Mash the garlic with the salt in a small bowl to make a paste. In a large bowl, combine the garlic paste, lemon juice, mayonnaise, and Creole mustard, whisking to blend well. When the potatoes are cool, peel and cut in half. Add the potatoes and the green onions to the mayonnaise mixture and toss to coat evenly. Season with salt and black pepper. ❧

SALADS & SALAD DRESSINGS

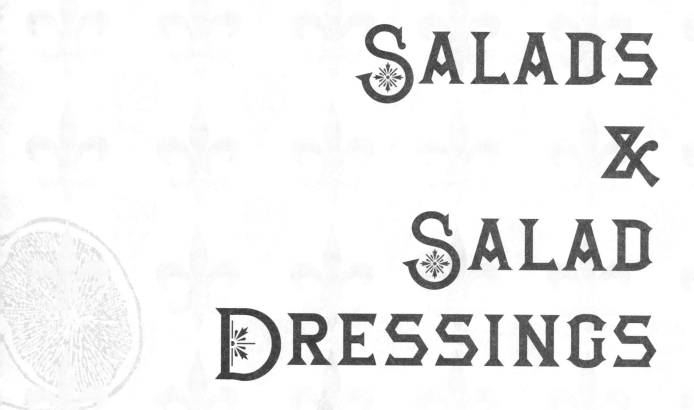

In New Orleans, a salad can be anything from a wedge of iceberg lettuce dripping with Roquefort dressing to greens or pasta combined with olive salad. There are many versions of Caesar salad, but ours, with its Green Chile Dressing (page 81), has a definite South-of-the-Border flavor. Everyone should have a recipe for chicken salad in his or her files and the one on page 82 is a classic, as is the Sensation Salad (page 87). Of course, anyone who has ever dined at Galatoire's Restaurant in New Orleans knows about their Godchaux Salad (page 84)—superb.

In more recent years, sweet and spicy-hot Thai and Vietnamese salads have become more popular here, especially during our steamy summers. A Thai chef who goes by only one name, Nappowan, shared her recipe for neam sohd, *a refreshing and delicious Thai chicken salad (page 85). No mundane salads here!*

Salads & Salad Dressings

Bon Ton Salad Dressing

A READER WHO identified herself as "a New Orleanian living in Texas who misses all the good food" commented on the recipe handout from the Bon Ton Restaurant, discussed at length in the newspaper the previous week. The handout features luscious bread pudding (page 322), but this reader noted that the Bon Ton salad dressing, on the back side of the handout, is even better.

Both of the Bon Ton's recipes are credited to one of the original owners, Alzina Pierce. The recipe calls for "dark vinegar." Since this is doubtless from the pre-balsamic era, we're guessing it refers to cider vinegar, which looks dark when compared with white vinegar.

{MAKES ABOUT 1 QUART}

1 large egg

2 teaspoons Creole mustard, homemade (page 341) or store-bought, or any coarse, grainy brown mustard

2 teaspoons salt

2 teaspoons black pepper

1 teaspoon Tabasco sauce

1 teaspoon Worcestershire sauce

½ teaspoon chopped garlic

2 teaspoons grated Parmesan cheese

1 teaspoon horseradish

1 cup dark vinegar, such as cider vinegar

1½ cups olive oil

Combine all the ingredients except the olive oil in a mixing bowl. Whip until thoroughly mixed. Pour the olive oil in slowly while whipping vigorously. Store, covered, in the refrigerator for up to 1 week. ⚜

Caesar Salad with Cilantro and Green Chile Dressing

This is not a classic Caesar salad, but it is a popular one with our newspaper readers, several of whom asked for the recipe to be included here.

{MAKES 8 SERVINGS}

DRESSING

¾ cup pumpkin seeds

1 cup fresh cilantro leaves

¾ cup mayonnaise

¾ cup vegetable oil or herb-flavored oil

1 (4-ounce) can diced green chiles, well drained

¼ cup red wine vinegar

¼ cup crumbled cotija (Mexican cheese) or feta cheese

1 clove garlic, crushed

½ teaspoon sea salt

⅛ teaspoon black pepper

SALAD

1 large head romaine or red romaine lettuce

1½ cups seasoned croutons

½ cup crumbled cotija or feta cheese

For the dressing: Toast the pumpkin seeds in a dry skillet over medium heat until lightly browned. Set aside ½ cup.

Combine the remaining ¼ cup seeds in a blender or food processor with all the other dressing ingredients, and process until coarsely chopped. Chill for at least 1 hour to allow the flavors to blend. Store in a glass container.

For the salad: In a salad bowl, combine all the ingredients for the salad with the ½ cup of toasted pumpkin seeds reserved from the dressing. Toss the salad with the dressing and serve immediately. ❧

Classic Chicken Salad

CHICKEN SALAD IS ideal for making finger sandwiches, plopping on the top of thick slices of Creole tomatoes, or stuffing into half an avocado. This one is a classic.

{MAKES ABOUT 6 SERVINGS}

1 (3-pound) fryer chicken
1 large carrot, peeled and coarsely chopped
1 stalk celery, coarsely chopped
1 medium onion, peeled and quartered
2 bay leaves
1 teaspoon whole black peppercorns
1 teaspoon salt
2 sprigs fresh parsley, plus 2 tablespoons chopped
1 cup mayonnaise
3 hard-boiled eggs, finely chopped
2 tablespoons fresh lemon juice
1 tablespoon Dijon mustard
¼ cup chopped celery
2 teaspoons sweet pickle relish
Salt
Black pepper

Put the fryer in a large deep pot and cover with water. Add the carrot, celery, onion, bay leaves, peppercorns, salt, and parsley sprigs. Bring to a boil, then reduce the heat and simmer, partially covered, until the meat begins to fall off the bones, about 1½ hours.

Remove the chicken from the pot. Strain the broth and set a little aside in case you want to moisten the salad. (The rest can be cooled and stored in containers in the freezer to use for soups or sauces.) Let the chicken cool, then pick the meat off the bones. Coarsely chop or shred the chicken.

In a large mixing bowl, combine the chicken with the mayonnaise, eggs, lemon juice, mustard, celery, chopped parsley, and relish. Season with salt and pepper and toss to mix well. If you like it a little moister, add a few tablespoons of the reserved chicken broth. Cover and chill the salad in the refrigerator for at least 1 hour before serving.

Country Club Chicken Salad

P.B. SENT THE recipe exchange column a summery recipe she thought others might enjoy. "On my first trip to the Colonial Country Club in Harahan in 1998, I first ate this wonderful chicken salad," she wrote. "I remember thinking what an odd combination of ingredients to serve with honey mustard dressing. I made it for my crew at home and they loved it too."

{MAKES 6 SERVINGS}

6 cups dark salad greens, such as spinach, watercress, or arugula

5 skinless chicken breasts

Salt

Black pepper

½ cup garlic-flavored croutons

2 tomatoes, cut into wedges

10 slices bacon, fried until crisp and crumbled

5 hard-boiled eggs, chopped

⅓ cup grated Parmesan cheese

1 to 1½ cups honey mustard salad dressing

Arrange the salad greens on plates.

Season the chicken with salt and pepper. Coat a skillet with vegetable cooking spray, heat the skillet, and pan-grill the chicken just until cooked through. Let cool for 1 or 2 minutes. Cut into ¼-inch strips.

Arrange the chicken on top of the greens. Toss on a few croutons and put 2 or 3 tomato wedges on each plate. Sprinkle with bacon bits and eggs, then dust with Parmesan cheese. Pour about ¼ cup of salad dressing over each salad and serve. ❧

Galatoire's Godchaux Salad

NAMED FOR LEON GODCHAUX, the founder of the once-illustrious department store on Canal Street, this salad is a favorite of the regular old-line customers of Galatoire's Restaurant. By all means, use fresh lump crabmeat and shrimp for this incredibly delicious dish. The recipe is from *Galatoire's Cookbook*, by Melvin Rodrigue with Jyl Benson.

{MAKES 6 SERVINGS}

1 medium head iceberg lettuce, washed, dried, and torn into bite-size pieces

2 tomatoes, cored and cut into large bite-size pieces

1 pound jumbo lump crabmeat, picked over for shells and cartilage

30 large shrimp, boiled and peeled

Creole Mustard Vinaigrette (recipe follows)

3 hard-boiled eggs, chopped, for garnish

12 anchovy fillets for garnish

In a large bowl, combine the lettuce, tomatoes, crabmeat, and shrimp. Gradually add the dressing to the salad, according to your preference, and toss gently until all the ingredients are well coated. Divide the salad among six chilled plates. Garnish each one with chopped egg and 2 anchovy fillets.

Extra dressing can be served on the side. 🐚

Creole Mustard Vinaigrette

{MAKES 1½ CUPS}

⅓ cup red wine vinegar

½ cup Creole mustard, homemade (page 341) or store-bought, or any coarse, grainy brown mustard

Salt

Freshly ground black pepper

⅔ cup vegetable oil

In a small bowl, combine the vinegar and mustard, and season with salt and pepper to taste. Add the oil in a slow drizzle, while whisking to incorporate and create an emulsion. 🐚

Thai Chicken Salad

IN THE SWELTER that is a New Orleans summer, refreshing Asian salads are increasingly popular. This quickly made one, called *neam sohd* in Thai, comes from the kitchen of Nappowan, the chef/owner at the Siamese Restaurant in Metairie. The restaurant serves this dish, similar to *larb* (a meat salad), with lots of dressing.

{MAKES 2 SERVINGS}

7 tablespoons fresh lime juice

1 tablespoon sugar

7 tablespoons bottled fish sauce

8 to 10 ounces boneless skinless chicken breast, cut into chunks

¼ cup chopped fresh cilantro

¼ cup minced green onion (white part only)

½ red onion, thinly sliced

2 teaspoons minced ginger, or less to taste

10 to 20 roasted peanuts

Cucumber slices for serving

Tomato wedges for serving

Iceberg lettuce leaves for serving

In a small bowl, combine the lime juice, sugar, and fish sauce to make the dressing. Set aside.

Bring a saucepan of water to a boil. Mince the chicken, or pulse it in a food processor until it is coarsely ground. Put the chicken into the boiling water. When it turns white and is cooked through, drain it well.

In a medium bowl, mix the chicken with the cilantro, green onion, red onion, ginger, peanuts, and the dressing. Serve with the cucumber, tomato, and lettuce on the side. Diners can fold the iceberg lettuce around bites of *neam sohd*. ❧

Poppy Seed Salad Dressing

"I AM LOOKING for the poppy seed dressing that the restaurant in the D.H. Holmes Department Store used to serve on their salads," wrote L.H. of Harahan. "Holmes would give the recipe away on request."

No one came forward with the vintage recipe, but the one below is a version that was originally published in an old New Orleans Public Service, Inc. (NOPSI) flier. NOPSI employed home economists to develop recipes for the fliers given away on street-cars and in other locations. Residents treasure the fliers that survived Katrina. Serve this dressing with fruit salads.

{MAKES 4 CUPS}

1½ cups sugar

2 teaspoons dry mustard

2 teaspoons salt

⅔ cup red wine vinegar

1 tablespoon onion juice

1 tablespoon poppy seeds

2 cups salad oil

In a blender or food processor, combine the sugar, dry mustard, salt, vinegar, onion juice, and poppy seeds and whir until thoroughly blended, about 5 seconds. Without stopping the blender, remove the cover and gradually pour the oil into center of the container. Store, covered, in the refrigerator for up to 1 week. ❧

Sensation Salad

Sensation salad, which originated at the old Bob and Jake's Restaurant in Baton Rouge, is still popular around the capital and in the St. Francisville area. Bob and Jake's is no more, but this recipe is similar to the one served there.

{MAKES ABOUT 6 SERVINGS}

1 tablespoon fresh lemon juice

3 tablespoons wine vinegar or apple cider vinegar

⅓ cup olive oil, or more to taste

4 cloves garlic, crushed

Salt

Freshly ground black pepper

1 medium head iceberg lettuce, torn into
    bite-size pieces

1 bunch fresh parsley, finely chopped

½ cup grated Romano cheese

Combine the lemon juice and vinegar in a small bowl, whisking to blend. Gradually add the oil, whisking constantly. Add the garlic, and season with salt and pepper to taste.

Put the lettuce in a large salad bowl and add the parsley and grated cheese. Add the dressing, a little at a time and add only enough to coat the lettuce evenly. Cover and refrigerate for 15 minutes before serving.

Any leftover dressing can be stored in an airtight container in the refrigerator for up to 2 weeks. 🐜

Shrimp and Orzo Salad

THE COMBINATION OF Gulf shrimp, orzo (rice-shaped pasta), fresh herbs, and tomatoes makes this a great salad to serve during the summer for a picnic or a casual supper.

{MAKES 4 TO 6 SERVINGS}

6 cups water

2 teaspoons salt, or more to taste

1½ teaspoons cayenne pepper

2 pounds large shrimp

½ cup orzo pasta

2 cups mayonnaise

¼ cup Creole mustard, homemade (page 341) or store-bought, or any coarse, grainy brown mustard

1 teaspoon finely chopped fresh dill

2 tablespoons finely chopped fresh parsley

3 tablespoons fresh lemon juice

½ pint cherry tomatoes

Freshly ground black pepper

Hot sauce to taste (optional)

Combine the water, salt, and cayenne in a large pot and bring to a boil. Add the shrimp, allow water to return to a boil, and cook until they turn pink, about 3 to 5 minutes. Remove the shrimp from the pot with a slotted spoon and spread them out on a large platter to cool.

Add the orzo to the water in the pot and bring to a boil. Cook, stirring occasionally, until tender, about 10 minutes. Drain and cool.

Shell and devein the shrimp, and cut into bite-size pieces. Combine the mayonnaise, mustard, dill, parsley, and lemon juice in a large bowl and whisk to blend. Fold in the shrimp, the orzo, and the cherry tomatoes. Season with more salt if needed, the black pepper, and the hot sauce (if using). Cover and chill well before serving. ❧

Spring Potato Salad

Since it opened in 1995, the Crescent City Farmers Market has had a huge impact on the New Orleans food scene, and beyond. The Market's innovations, such as a system to turn food stamps into tokens to use at the markets, have been adopted elsewhere, too.

This CCFM recipe came to the newspaper from Kay Roussell, one of many local chefs who have worked with Paul Prudhomme.

{MAKES 4 SERVINGS}

1½ pounds new potatoes (with skins on), scrubbed and quartered

⅓ cup olive oil

2 to 3 cloves garlic, minced, or to taste

3 tablespoons Creole mustard, homemade (page 341) or store-bought, or any coarse, grainy brown mustard

1 tablespoon sherry vinegar or white wine vinegar

3 tablespoons chopped fresh herbs, such as thyme, basil, or parsley, or a combination

Salt

Black pepper

Crumbled crisp bacon for serving (optional)

Crumbled feta or Roquefort cheese for serving (optional)

Cook the potatoes in a large saucepan in boiling salted water until tender, but still firm, 10 to 15 minutes.

Meanwhile, heat the olive oil in a small saucepan and sauté the garlic until tender and fragrant, but not at all browned, 2 to 3 minutes. Whisk in the mustard and vinegar to make a hot vinaigrette. Toss with the potatoes and herbs and season to taste with salt and pepper. Sprinkle with the bacon and cheese (if using). Serve hot or at room temperature. ॐ

Breakfast & Brunch

While you may want to have dinner at Antoine's, you most certainly would not want to miss having breakfast at Brennan's. In 1946, Owen Brennan and his siblings opened up Brennan's in the French Quarter and began offering a breakfast that featured glorious egg dishes such as Eggs Sardou (page 100), eggs Hussarde, and of course, eggs Benedict. Who would have thought lowly eggs could be transformed into such lofty delights?

A hearty breakfast or brunch in New Orleans is a tradition. Marcelle's choice on a lazy Saturday morning is a stack of pain perdu (page 112), more commonly known as French toast, drizzled with pure cane syrup or topped with fig preserves, and accompanied with bacon or sausage. For a hearty brunch, she always chooses Grillades and Grits (page 102), a New Orleans favorite.

A visit to New Orleans without beignets (page 95) liberally sprinkled with powdered sugar and washed down with café au lait is unthinkable. And if you want a taste of the past, by all means try a Calas (page 97), a rice cake that is best eaten hot right out of the skillet. Of course, just about everyone who lives in and around New Orleans enjoys omelets, fluffy biscuits, and cornbread, which are also included here.

BREAKFAST & BRUNCH

Banana Fritters

Fritters, which are much like beignets, are a favorite breakfast item in and around New Orleans. Be sure to use clean, fresh vegetable oil when frying.

{MAKES ABOUT 20 FRITTERS}

2 medium bananas, ripe but firm, peeled and coarsely chopped

1 cup all-purpose flour

1 large egg, lightly beaten

¼ teaspoon salt

2 teaspoons baking powder

About ½ cup milk

3 cups vegetable oil

Confectioners' sugar for sprinkling

½ teaspoon ground cinnamon

Combine the bananas, flour, egg, salt, and baking powder in a medium mixing bowl. Add enough milk to achieve the consistency of a thick pancake batter.

Heat the oil in a large deep pot or deep fryer to 360 degrees F. Drop the batter by spoonfuls into the hot oil, a few at a time, and fry until the fritters rise to the surface of the oil and are golden brown, turning 2 or 3 times.

Drain on paper towels and sprikle with confectioners' sugar and cinnamon. Serve immediately.

Beignets

In NEW ORLEANS we enjoy the classic, traditional beignets: square sweet doughnuts dusted with confectioners' sugar. But in the country, the old-time cooks make beignets that resemble fritters. Fruit, such as bananas, apples, or sometimes even sweet potatoes, is incorporated into the batter. Savory beignets can be made with crawfish and cheese, or eggplant and shrimp, to serve at cocktail parties.

Beignets are quite easy. Just make a batter, sweet or savory, and add whatever you like. They fry up quickly, so it's best to make them right before serving. Be sure you have clean, fresh oil and make sure it's hot when you drop in the batter. This is a basic recipe, which you can embellish.

{MAKES ABOUT 2 DOZEN}

1 cup water

1 cup milk

1 large egg

3 cups all-purpose flour

2 tablespoons baking powder

1 teaspoon salt

2 teaspoons sugar

Pinch of nutmeg

4 to 6 cups vegetable oil

Confectioners' sugar for sprinkling

Combine the water, milk, and egg in a large mixing bowl and mix well. Add the flour, baking powder, salt, sugar, and nutmeg, and mix until the batter is smooth.

Heat the oil in a large deep pot or deep fryer to 360 degrees F. Drop the batter by spoonfuls into the hot oil, a few at a time, and fry until they are golden brown, turning 2 or 3 times. Drain on paper towels and sprinkle with confectioners' sugar. ❧

Brunch Loaf

WHEN SEVERAL REQUESTS were received for this make-ahead breakfast casserole recipe, a thorough search ensued, but to no avail. Then Judy Walker put out a call in her "Exchange Alley" column, and a reader came through with it. Thanks go to B.D.B. of Harvey!

{MAKES ABOUT 8 SERVINGS}

4 cups cubed day-old French bread

2 cups shredded cheddar cheese

10 large eggs, lightly beaten

1 quart milk

1 teaspoon dry mustard

1 teaspoon salt

¼ teaspoon onion powder

¼ teaspoon cayenne pepper

8 to 10 slices bacon, cooked until crisp, crumbled

½ cup sliced mushrooms

½ cup chopped tomatoes

Generously grease a 9-by-13-inch baking pan. Put the bread on the bottom and sprinkle with the cheese.

In a large mixing bowl, combine the eggs, milk, mustard, salt, onion powder, and cayenne and pour over the cheese. Sprinkle with the bacon, mushrooms, and tomatoes. Cover the pan and chill overnight.

Preheat the oven to 375 degrees F. Uncover the pan and bake for about 1 hour, or until the mixture sets. After the first 30 minutes, check the top to make sure it's not browning too quickly. If it is, tent the pan with foil. Cut into squares and serve hot. ❦

The Picayune's Creole Cook Book Calas

CALAS ARE AN old tradition in New Orleans that were nearly lost. Although a few Creole families still made them on Mardi Gras morning and for other special occasions, the rice fritters had almost disappeared from public consciousness when the local chapter of the international Slow Food movement, under the guidance of cooking teacher Poppy Tooker, revived them in the late 1990s. There are many local anecdotes about adults who were moved to tears when they tasted calas again.

This recipe, from the 1901 edition of the seminal *Picayune's Creole Cook Book*, probably predates the Civil War. It was given to the cookbook editors by one of the last of the olden Cala women, one who has walked the streets of the French Quarter for fifty years and more.

Modern cooks who want to experiment with the recipe may substitute ½ packet of active dry yeast for the compressed cake, and shortening for the lard. This recipe shows why New Orleans is a world capital of the delicate art of frying.

{MAKES 6 CAKES}

3 cups water

½ cup rice

½ cake of compressed yeast, dissolved in ½ cup hot water

3 eggs

½ cup granulated sugar

3 tablespoons flour

About ½ teaspoon grated nutmeg

Lard for frying the Calas

Confectioners' sugar

In a saucepan, bring the water to a hard boil. Wash the rice thoroughly, drain, and put into the boiling water. Let it boil until very soft and mushy. Drain the rice and set it aside to cool. When cold, mash well and mix with the dissolved yeast.

Set the rice to rise over night. In the morning beat the eggs thoroughly and add to the rice, mixing and beating well. Add the granulated sugar and flour to make the rice adhere. Mix well and beat thoroughly, to make a thick batter. Set to rise for 15 minutes longer. Then add the nutmeg, and mix well.

In a frying pan, bring to a boil enough lard for the rice cakes to "swim" without touching the bottom of the pan. Test the lard by dropping in a small piece of bread. If it becomes golden brown, the lard is ready, but if it burns or browns instantly, it is too hot. The golden brown color is the true test.

Take a large, deep spoon, and drop the rice batter a spoonful at a time into the boiling lard, remembering always that the cake must not touch the bottom of the pan. Let it fry to a nice brown.

The old "Cala women" used to take the Calas piping hot, in a clean towel, basket, or bowl, and rush through the streets with the welcome cry "Belle Cala! Tout Chaud!" But in families the cook simply takes the calas out of the frying pan and drains off the lard by laying them in a colander or on heated pieces of brown paper. They are then placed in a hot dish, sprinkled with confectioner's sugar, and eaten hot with café au lait. 🐝

Cheese and Potato Omelet

For a twist on a traditional omelet, try this one. It's more like a savory tart, because the potatoes and cheese are incorporated into the egg mixture.

{MAKES 2 TO 4 SERVINGS}

¼ cup vegetable oil
2 medium potatoes, peeled and cut into 1-inch dice
Salt
Cayenne pepper
6 large eggs
Black pepper
¾ cup finely grated Gruyère or Swiss cheese
2 tablespoons snipped fresh chives
2 tablespoons butter

Heat the oil in a skillet over medium heat. Add the potatoes and season with salt and cayenne to taste. Cook, shaking the skillet to allow the potatoes to cook evenly, until they are golden brown, 8 to 10 minutes. Drain the potatoes on paper towels.

Beat the eggs in a small mixing bowl and season with salt and pepper. Add the cheese, potatoes, and chives.

Melt the butter in a nonstick skillet or omelet pan over medium heat. Add the egg mixture. Stir a few times and let the omelet set. Cook until the omelet is done on the bottom. Invert the omelet onto a warm round platter and cut into wedges to serve. ❧

Easy Processor Biscuits

"A FEW WEEKS ago you had some biscuit recipes in the paper," wrote a reader from New Orleans. "I just had to give you this recipe. If you use real butter, it will come out perfectly every time. If you use margarine, you will have to add about one-fourth cup more flour, or the dough will be too sticky."

{MAKES 12 TO 15 BISCUITS}

2½ cups self-rising flour
½ cup (1 stick) cold butter, cut into 1-inch pieces
¾ cup buttermilk

Preheat the oven to 450 degrees F.

Position the metal blade in the bowl of a food processor. Add the flour and butter. Pulse 5 to 7 times, until mixture resembles coarse meal. With the processor running, slowly add the buttermilk through the feed tube until the dough forms a ball, leaving the sides of the bowl. Turn out the dough onto a floured surface and knead lightly 3 or 4 times.

Roll the dough to ½ inch thickness. Cut into rounds with a sharp 2½-inch biscuit cutter. Place rounds on an ungreased baking sheet about 2 inches apart and bake for 10 minutes, or until lightly browned. ❧

Eggs Sardou

EGGS SARDOU WAS created in 1908 at Antoine's Restaurant for a dinner honoring the French playwright Victorien Sardou. The dish later became a popular breakfast offering at Brennan's. There are many versions. The original dish served at Antoine's consisted of artichoke hearts criss-crossed with anchovy fillets and topped with poached eggs. The eggs were sauced with hollandaise, sprinkled with chopped ham, and garnished with truffle slices. In more contemporary recipes like this one, artichoke bottoms sit in a pool of creamed spinach and are topped with poached eggs, which are then sauced with the hollandaise.

{MAKES 2 SERVINGS}

1½ tablespoons butter

1 (10-ounce) package frozen spinach, cooked according to the package directions

1 tablespoon all-purpose flour

¼ cup heavy cream

1 tablespoon chopped green onions (green part only)

¼ teaspoon salt

¼ teaspoon cayenne pepper

Pinch of grated nutmeg

1 teaspoon white distilled vinegar

4 large eggs

HOLLANDAISE SAUCE

3 large egg yolks

½ cup (1 stick) butter, melted and kept warm

1 tablespoon fresh lemon juice

Pinch of cayenne pepper

4 artichoke bottoms, warmed in salted water

Melt the butter in a saucepan over medium heat. Add the spinach and cook for 3 minutes, or until warmed. Sprinkle in the flour, stir, and then add the cream. Cook, stirring occasionally, for about 5 minutes over low heat, or until the mixture thickens. Add the green onions and mix well. Add the salt, cayenne, and nutmeg. (You can make the creamed spinach ahead of time and refrigerate it until ready to use. Reheat gently when ready to assemble the dish.)

To poach the eggs, bring 2 inches of water to a simmer in a 10-inch skillet. When the water starts to shimmer, add the vinegar. Crack each egg into an individual saucer and gently slip them into the simmering water. With a large spoon, gently lift the white over the yolk. Repeat until the white has enclosed the yolk. Poach until the whites are set and the yolks are filmed over, about 3 minutes. The eggs can be used immediately, or transferred to a shallow bowl of cold water. When ready to serve, slip the eggs into simmering water for 15 to 20 seconds to rewarm.

For the Hollandaise Sauce: Put the egg yolks in a small saucepan over very low heat and whisk until they thicken just a bit. Add the melted butter, a little at a time, removing the saucepan from the heat from time to time to prevent curdling. Add the lemon juice and cayenne, and whisk to blend.

Divide the creamed spinach equally between two dinner plates, spooning it into the center of each one. Place 2 artichoke bottoms on top of the spinach and top with the eggs. Spoon the Hollandaise Sauce generously over all. 🍤

Nº 100

COOKING UP A STORM

Grillades and Grits

THIS NEW ORLEANS favorite is the quintessential choice for breakfast or brunch. Pieces of beef or veal are cooked long and slow in a gravy made with that ubiquitous trio—onions, bell peppers, and celery—plus tomatoes, and seasoned just right, until the meat literally melts in your mouth. Always served with smooth, rich, cheesy grits and fluffy biscuits, it's a dish that can set you straight on the morning after a big night on the town.

{MAKES ABOUT 10 SERVINGS}

4 pounds boneless beef or veal round steak, about ¼ inch thick

1 tablespoon salt

1 teaspoon cayenne pepper

½ teaspoon black pepper

½ teaspoon garlic powder

½ cup all-purpose flour

½ cup vegetable oil

3 medium yellow onions, chopped

2 medium green bell peppers, chopped

3 stalks celery, chopped

3 cups whole canned tomatoes, crushed, with their juice

2 cups beef broth

½ cup dry red wine

2 bay leaves

½ teaspoon dried tarragon leaves

½ teaspoon dried basil leaves

½ cup finely chopped green onions (green part only)

3 tablespoons finely chopped fresh parsley

Baked Grits for serving (facing page)

Remove any fat from the beef or veal. Cut the meat into 2-inch squares. Combine the salt, cayenne, black pepper, and garlic powder in a small bowl. Have the flour at hand.

Lay several pieces of the meat on a cutting board and sprinkle with the seasoning mix and a little of the flour. With a meat mallet, pound each piece of meat until slightly flattened. Flip the pieces over and repeat the process. Do this with all of the meat.

In a large heavy pot, heat the oil over medium-high heat. Add the meat, several pieces at a time, and brown evenly on both sides. As the meat is cooked, transfer it to a platter. When all the meat is browned, return it to the pot. Add the onions, bell peppers, and celery and cook, stirring, until the vegetables are soft and golden, 8 to 10 minutes.

Add the tomatoes and reduce the heat to medium-low. Add the broth, wine, bay leaves, tarragon, and basil. Stir to blend and simmer, uncovered, stirring occasionally, until the meat is very tender, about 1½ to 2 hours. If the mixture becomes dry, add a little water or more broth.

When ready to serve, remove the bay leaves and add the green onions and parsley. Serve with the grits. 🌿

Baked Grits

{MAKES 10 TO 12 SERVINGS}

2 cups yellow grits, cooked according to the
  package directions
3 large eggs, lightly beaten
½ pound cheddar cheese, grated
1 cup milk
½ cup (1 stick) butter

Preheat the oven to 350 degrees F.

After the grits are cooked, add the eggs, cheese,
milk, and butter and stir until well blended and
the cheese and butter are completely melted. Pour
into a 2-quart baking dish and bake for about
45 minutes, until the mixture sets. ❧

Ida's Biscuits

THIS RECIPE IS from the files of Marcelle's mother. It may have come from a friend of hers who lived down the road, Ida Robichaux. Ms. Ida and her husband lived with their nine children on their dairy farm.

Hot from the oven and light as a cloud, these biscuits are fantastic when bathed in cane syrup, or spread with fig or strawberry preserves. The dough can also be frozen and baked later.

{MAKES ABOUT 2 DOZEN BISCUITS, DEPENDING ON THE SIZE}

4 cups buttermilk biscuit mix
1 heaping tablespoon sugar
1 teaspoon salt
½ teaspoon cream of tartar
1 teaspoon baking powder
1 cup shortening
1½ cups milk

Preheat the oven to 400 degrees F.

Sift together the dry ingredients in a large bowl. Drop the shortening in the middle of the dry ingredients and pour the milk over it. With your hands, squeeze the mixture and mix everything together, working in the dry ingredients. Continue working with your hands until you have a slightly sticky ball of dough.

To roll out the dough, dust a work surface heavily with flour. Pat the dough into a round and then use a rolling pin to roll out the dough to about ¼ inch thickness. Then cut out rounds with a sharp-edged biscuit cutter. Or, make hand-molded biscuits: Dust your hands with flour or biscuit mix, break off pieces of dough, and pat them into small rounds.

Place the biscuits about ½ inch apart on an ungreased baking sheet and bake until golden brown, 12 to 15 minutes. ❧

Jolene Black's Cream Biscuits

"I HAVE MISPLACED a biscuit recipe that was one of the easiest biscuit recipes I have ever tried," N.P.G. wrote to the recipe exchange column. "There were two ingredients, self-rising White Lily flour and heavy cream. [They were] the most incredible and delicious biscuits I have made."

This recipe was a minor sensation after Jolene Black shared it with readers in April 2005. The trick to the recipe is using these exact ingredients. The biscuits won't be as light if you use any other kind of self-rising flour. The fat in the heavy cream replaces the shortening or butter in comparable recipes.

Black's inspiration for creating the perfect biscuit recipe was Velia Black, her husband's grandmother and a great country cook from Jasper, Alabama, a small town outside of Birmingham. Jolene Black recommends the use of heavy cream that is not ultra-pasteurized, if you can find it. White Lily is a low-gluten brand beloved by Southern biscuit-makers. It can be ordered by mail from King Arthur Flour.

{MAKES 10 TO 12 BISCUITS}

2½ cups White Lily self-rising flour
1½ cups heavy cream

Preheat the oven to 450 degrees F. Lightly grease a baking sheet.

Put the flour in a medium mixing bowl and add the cream. Stir until a soft, sticky ball forms. (The dough will seem wet at first.) On a very lightly floured surface, knead lightly with your well-floured hands about 3 times, just until the dough comes together.

Pat the dough to about ½ -inch thickness. Cut out biscuits with a 2½-inch round cutter. Bake on the prepared baking sheet for 10 to 12 minutes, until the biscuits are golden brown. ✺

Leon's Skillet Cornbread

AFTER "EXCHANGE ALLEY" published a request for a cornbread recipe made in a cast-iron skillet, a reader in Mandeville sent this one. The result is cornbread that is crunchy on the outside and moist on the inside.

If you don't have buttermilk on hand, it's easy to remember the old substitution trick: For every cup of buttermilk called for in the recipe, use 1 tablespoon of lemon juice or vinegar plus enough milk to make 1 cup. Let it sit for a few minutes before using.

{MAKES 6 TO 8 SERVINGS}

2 cups yellow cornmeal

¼ cup all-purpose flour

4 teaspoons baking powder

1 teaspoon salt

2 tablespoons sugar

2 large eggs, lightly beaten

About 2 cups buttermilk

3 to 4 tablespoons vegetable oil

Preheat the oven to 425 degrees F.

Sift the cornmeal, flour, baking powder, salt, and sugar into a large glass or metal mixing bowl (not plastic). Mix in the eggs and enough buttermilk to make a loose, soupy batter.

On the stove top, heat the vegetable oil in a 10-inch cast-iron skillet until smoking slightly. Carefully swirl the skillet to coat the interior with oil, then carefully pour the hot oil into the batter and stir until the oil is blended into the batter.

Pour the batter into the hot skillet. Place the skillet in the hot oven and bake the cornbread for about 25 minutes, or until a few brown spots appear on the top. Serve hot. ❧

Monkey Bread

MONKEY BREAD, EASILY made with canned biscuits, butter, cinnamon, and sugar, is a delicious breakfast offering. Children love it!

{MAKES ABOUT 10 SERVINGS}

½ cup (1 stick) butter, melted

1 cup granulated sugar

½ cup brown sugar, dark or light

1 to 2 teaspoons ground cinnamon

1 cup chopped nuts, such as pecans or walnuts (optional)

30 refrigerated biscuits (3 packages), or 30 frozen sweet rolls, thawed

Preheat the oven to 350 degrees F. Generously grease a 10-inch tube pan.

Pour the melted butter into a shallow bowl or soup plate. In a small bowl, mix the sugars and cinnamon thoroughly and spread out on a plate or a square of wax paper or foil. Have the chopped nuts (if using) at hand in a bowl.

Take the biscuits or rolls, one at a time, and roll into a ball about the size of a golf ball. Dip 4 or 5 at a time in the melted butter and roll in the sugar mixture. Arrange in the tube pan a scant ½ inch apart. Sprinkle with nuts (if using). Repeat, layering the sugared balls of dough and sprinkling with some of the nuts (if using) over each layer. (Keep an empty plastic bag handy: You can stick your hand in it to answer the phone or open the door without spreading sugar all over.) Sprinkle any leftover sugar mixture on top of the rolls.

Bake until golden brown, 45 minutes to 1 hour. If the top gets brown too quickly, cover loosely with foil. Turn the bread out of the pan as soon as it is removed from the oven, or the sugar may stick to it. To remove from the pan, place a platter on top of the tube pan and, using oven mitts, invert both.

Pull apart the bread and serve warm. ❧

Basic Omelet

As any omelet lover knows, there are endless ingredients to fold into this egg concoction. Crumbled sausage, lump crabmeat, and lightly grilled vegetables, such as zucchini and yellow squash, are fabulous. And if you have a sweet tooth, try preserves, jellies, and jams.

Omelets are ideal to offer on Sundays before the long afternoon of football watching or for a leisurely family gathering. Set up your own omelet station. Have some nonstick 8-inch skillets or omelet pans at the ready, as well as various ingredients from which to choose. And don't forget the eggs—large ones. You'll also need butter, small mixing bowls, salt, and other seasonings, as well as hot sauce. Encourage guests to try to make their own. It's fun!

There is some debate over whether to add a bit of water or cream to the egg mixture before cooking an omelet. Marcelle has been taught to add about a tablespoon of cool water to the egg mixture to help fluff it up. On the other hand, one of her chef friends says he adds about 2 tablespoons of heavy cream to a three-egg omelet to give it a bit of richness.

How to fold an omelet is equally controversial. There are those who feel that an omelet folded once—in half—is perfectly acceptable, while others adhere to the traditional French method of folding a third of the omelet over on itself (and any filling) and then flipping it over for a second fold, making the omelet long and narrow. This is how Marcelle likes to prepare it. At posh French restaurants, the chef will carefully "roll" a cooked omelet with a clean towel so that the seam side is on the bottom and it's positioned just so on the plate before serving.

{MAKES 1 SERVING}

3 large eggs, lightly beaten
1 tablespoon cool water
Salt
Black pepper
1 tablespoon butter

Combine the eggs and water in a small mixing bowl, whisking gently. Season with salt and pepper. Heat an 8-inch nonstick skillet or an omelet pan over medium-high heat. Add the butter and after it foams, add the egg mixture and shake the skillet to spread it evenly over the bottom of the skillet. Push the edges of the omelet toward the center and tilt the pan so the uncooked egg reaches the edge of the pan. Cook until the bottom firms up and the omelet is slightly runny in the middle. Tilt the skillet slightly so that the omelet slides down to the bottom curve.

Spoon some of the filling on top of the egg mixture, then fold the omelet over the mixture. Cook for a few seconds to set the omelet. Slide out of the skillet onto a serving plate. Don't worry if it breaks. This is not a beauty contest. It will still taste the same. 🐚

Omelet with Mascarpone and Herbs

IN THIS OMELET, fresh herbs are paired with mascarpone, a buttery-rich double cream cheese. The combination is wonderful.

{MAKES 2 SERVINGS}

5 large eggs

Salt

Freshly ground black pepper

2 heaping tablespoons mascarpone

3 teaspoons total finely chopped fresh herbs, such as chervil, parsley, chives, and tarragon

1 tablespoon butter

Lightly beat the eggs in a small mixing bowl and season with salt and pepper. Fold in the mascarpone and the herbs.

Melt the butter in a nonstick skillet or omelet pan over medium-high heat. When the foam just subsides, pour in the egg mixture. Use a fork or chopsticks to pull the sides of the egg mixture into the center several times and tilt the pan to let the mixture run underneath and set. As the eggs set, fold the omelet onto itself and cook for 30 seconds or so. Slide onto a plate, cut the omelet in half, and serve. ❧

Omelet à la Creole

THE CREOLE FILLING makes this omelet special.

{MAKES 4 SERVINGS}

FILLING

2 tablespoons olive oil
1 cup finely chopped onions
1 cup finely chopped green bell peppers
1 tablespoon minced garlic
1 cup chopped tomatoes
¼ cup finely chopped ham
Salt
Cayenne pepper

OMELET

12 large eggs, lightly beaten
4 tablespoons water
Salt
Freshly ground black pepper
4 tablespoons butter

For the filling: Heat the oil in a skillet over medium heat. Add the onions, bell peppers, and garlic. Cook, stirring often, for 2 minutes, or until the vegetables are softened. Add the tomatoes and ham, season to taste with the salt and cayenne, and cook for about 1 minute. This will make enough filling for 4 omelets. Set aside.

For each omelet: Combine 3 of the eggs, 1 tablespoon of the water, and salt and pepper to taste in a small mixing bowl. Melt 1 tablespoon of the butter in an 8- or 9-inch skillet, preferably nonstick, over medium heat. Add the egg mixture and shake the skillet to allow it to spread out evenly. Use a fork or chopsticks to pull the sides of the egg mixture into the center several times and tilt the pan to let the mixture run underneath and set. Cook until the bottom firms up and the omelet is slightly runny in the middle. Tilt the skillet slightly so that the omelet slides down to the bottom curve. Spoon some of the filling on top of the egg mixture, then fold the omelet over the mixture. Cook for a few seconds to set the omelet. Slide out of the skillet onto a serving plate. Make 3 more omelets in the same way. 🍳

Pain Perdu

PAIN PERDU, WHICH, translated literally from French, means "lost bread," is known as French toast everywhere else in the country. It is an old Creole and Acadian favorite. For a festive touch during the Christmas holidays, substitute eggnog for the milk.

Depending on personal taste, pain perdu can be drizzled with syrup, topped with preserves or jelly, or sprinkled with confectioners' sugar.

{MAKES 4 SERVINGS}

2 large eggs, beaten

1 cup milk

½ cup sugar

¼ teaspoon vanilla extract

½ cup (1 stick) butter

8 slices stale bread (some prefer French bread)

Blend the eggs, milk, sugar, and vanilla together in a shallow bowl. Melt the butter in a large heavy skillet. Meanwhile, dip a few slices of bread in the mixture.

Make sure the bread is soaked through to the center. Fry the soaked bread in the butter, turning once, until golden brown on both sides. Remove from the pan and soak and fry the remaining bread in the same way. Serve immediately as they come out of the pan. ✤

Mr. Vincett's Banana Bread

"I'M LOOKING FOR a recipe that was in the Food section of *The Times-Picayune*. It was Mr. Vincett's banana bread," G.G. of Chalmette wrote to the newspaper. She lost the recipe, and many more, in the floodwaters. In St. Bernard Parish, where G.G. lives, only a handful of structures didn't flood.

We found the recipe for her. In 2003, Nancy Bell had shared her recipe for a cakelike banana bread with Food section readers. The recipe originally came from her college suite-mate's father, Mr. Vincett. Bell always keeps a stash of bananas in her freezer to make this bread. The buttermilk is the secret ingredient that makes it so special and light.

{MAKES 2 LOAVES}

¾ cup (1½ sticks) butter, softened, plus more for serving (optional)

1½ cups sugar

2 large eggs, lightly beaten

2 cups all-purpose flour

1 teaspoon baking soda

½ cup buttermilk

¾ cup chopped pecans

1 cup mashed ripe bananas, preferably frozen and then thawed

1 teaspoon vanilla extract

Preheat the oven to 325 degrees F. Grease and flour two 8½-by-4¼-by-2½-inch loaf pans.

In a large mixing bowl, beat together the butter and sugar with an electric mixer until fluffy, then mix in the eggs.

In a separate medium bowl, mix together the flour and baking soda. Add these dry ingredients to the creamed mixture alternately with the buttermilk, beginning and ending with the dry ingredients. Stir in the pecans, bananas, and vanilla.

Pour the batter into the loaf pans, and bake until golden brown and a cake tester or wooden toothpick inserted in the middle of each loaf comes out clean, about 1 hour. Remove from the oven and let cool in the pans for 10 minutes. Serve warm, with a little butter if desired.

Store leftovers at room temperature and serve them toasted for breakfast. Or let the loaves cool thoroughly and freeze, wrapped in heavy-duty aluminum foil. ❧

SEAFOOD

*L*ike most of those who have lived in and around New Orleans, Marcelle Bienvenu has enjoyed seafood in all manner of preparations. She remembers her Papa and Mama taking her to Fitzgerald's on Lake Pontchartrain for platters piled with perfectly fried shrimp, oysters, and soft-shell crabs. She fondly recalls her first stuffed flounder at Broussard's in the French Quarter and the oysters Mosca (page 130) at Elmwood Plantation.

Marcelle also remembers her mother admonishing her, "Don't eat boiled crawfish in front of people you don't know. They will think we are uncivilized." (She also told Marcelle not to speak French to strangers because Cajun patois sounded harsh to those who spoke "good" French.) Now, eating boiled crawfish is not only acceptable in public, but also the thing to do when crawfish are in season in Louisiana.

Most of the seafood to which we have access from the Gulf of Mexico and the inland bays along the coast can be baked, boiled, fried, broiled, or grilled. The Barbecued Shrimp, which are not really barbecued at all (page 120), is a New Orleans classic. Thankfully, we were able to find the recipes for Crawfish in Saffron Cream (page 126) as well as Crawfish Patrick (page 127), both of which had been lost in the floodwaters of Katrina.

We also have the recipe for stuffed crabs (page 142) from the late, great chef Warren Leruth. For those Jazzfest fans, we offer recipes for Crawfish Braid (page 125) and Jerry's Crawfish Bread (page 133).

SEAFOOD

Baked Shrimp and Potatoes

In 1998, FOOD EDITOR Dale Curry visited Bayou Loutre in Yscloskey, a shrimping village in St. Bernard Parish, where Katrina later caused havoc. The Islenos had settled in this community along the lower Mississippi River in 1778. The Islenos were Spanish colonists from the Canary Islands, and traces of the Castilian Spanish language still remain.

Curry talked with Selina Gonzales, a native of the community, who shared some of her mother's recipes, including this one. Many of the recipes were Spanish, relying heavily on olive oil and lots of garlic. Fish and shrimp were naturals for this kind of cooking.

A spectacular dish to feed a crowd can be made by adding a whole redfish to this recipe. Place the cleaned, deheaded fish, with fins removed, in the center of a large pan, surround it with the shrimp and potato mixture, and bake.

{MAKES 6 SERVINGS}

3 dozen large shrimp, peeled and deveined

Salt

Black pepper

2 cups sliced red potatoes (cut into rounds about ¼ inch thick)

¾ cup (1½ sticks) butter, melted

½ cup olive oil

1 whole head garlic, peeled and minced

1 large green bell pepper, chopped

1 (10-ounce) can Ro-Tel diced tomatoes and green chiles

Preheat the oven to 400 degrees F. Combine all the ingredients in a large mixing bowl and transfer to a large baking pan. Cover with foil and bake for 45 minutes to 1 hour, or until the potatoes are soft and tender. ❧

Baked Stuffed Oysters

MANY READERS SENT in their favorite recipes to be included in this book. This one comes from Patti Ohlsen of Carrierre, Mississippi, who told us, "This recipe was in the newspaper about two decades ago. It is written exactly as the paper printed it (because I still have the clipping) but I added the eggplant when I cooked it."

{MAKES 6 SERVINGS}

1½ dozen medium-size oysters and their shells

½ cup cooking oil

6 tablespoons all-purpose flour

2 to 3 cups oyster liquor

2 medium yellow onions, chopped

1 cup chopped white button mushrooms

2 cloves garlic, minced

1 stalk celery, chopped

1 green bell pepper, chopped

4 green onions, chopped (white and green parts)

1 tablespoon fresh lemon juice

½ teaspoon Tabasco sauce

1 teaspoon paprika

1 teaspoon Worcestershire sauce

4 tablespoons butter

½ medium eggplant, boiled in water to cover, peeled, and mashed

1¼ cups bread crumbs

Preheat the oven to 350 degrees F.

Scrub the oyster shells for serving. In a medium saucepan, boil the oysters in their own liquor for 5 minutes, then drain, reserving the liquid. When they are cool enough to handle, chop the oysters into coarse pieces.

In a large skillet, heat the oil over medium heat. Add the flour and cook, stirring, to make a light brown roux. Stir in the oysters, enough oyster liquid to make a thick smooth mixture, and all the remaining ingredients except the bread crumbs. Reduce the heat to low and cook, stirring occasionally, for 10 minutes. Remove about ½ cup of the mixture to be used as a sauce. To the remainder, add 1 cup of the bread crumbs.

Fill each oyster shell with the stuffing mixture and place on a baking sheet. Sprinkle the remaining ¼ cup of bread crumbs evenly over the stuffed shells, and bake for 15 minutes.

Remove the stuffed shells from the oven and place on individual plates. In a small saucepan, warm the reserved ½ cup of the sauce for 2 or 3 minutes over low heat (or microwave it in a glass measuring cup) and spoon some over each oyster shell. ❧

Barbecued Shrimp

Barbecued shrimp, which originated at Pascal's Manale in New Orleans, is a popular dish with locals and visitors alike. And there are almost as many versions as there are cooks. This one, sent in by Maria Vicknair of LaPlace, is her take on it.

Barbecued shrimp always contains copious amounts of butter, and head-on shrimp are always used in southeast Louisiana. The fat in the heads melts and becomes the secret ingredient in the sauce.

{MAKES 8 TO 10 SERVINGS}

1 to 1½ pounds butter

1 cup olive oil

¾ cup Worcestershire sauce

3 tablespoons cayenne pepper

½ teaspoon hot sauce

6 cloves garlic, coarsely chopped

¼ cup Italian seasoning

4 teaspoons paprika

¼ cup seasoned salt

6 bay leaves

4 lemons, cut in half

6 to 8 pounds medium or large shrimp with shells and heads on

French bread for serving

Preheat the broiler.

Put all the ingredients except the lemons and shrimp in a large saucepan. Squeeze the lemons and then put in the rinds, too. Heat and stir the sauce ingredients together over medium heat until the butter is melted and everything is well blended.

Place the shrimp in a single layer on one or two large shallow baking or broiling pans, and pour the sauce mixture over them. Discard the lemon halves and bay leaves. Broil for 4 to 5 minutes on each side. When done, the shells should pull away from the shrimp.

Serve with warm French bread to soak up the sauce. ❧

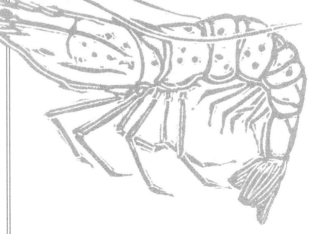

Bubby's Stuffed Flounder

Since 1984, Frank "Bubby" Graff Jr. of River Ridge has been giving away copies of his own cookbook, which he titled *Southern Comfort,* after his CB handle (his name on citizens band radio). When he was interviewed in 2006 for a story on creating individual cookbooks, he said he adds more of his and his wife's recipes every couple of years. He went from stapling the pages to a spiral binding, and then a volunteer put his recipes on computer. He now puts them in three-ring binders.

Graff said he has given away "tons—I have no idea how many copies" of his cookbook, which he continues to have printed at a local print shop, a dozen at a time, two or three times a year, at a cost of about twelve to fifteen dollars per copy.

Graff came up with this recipe at his fishing camp when somebody gave him a dozen flounder. "Just take your time and you can get all that stuffing in that little pocket," he said.

{MAKES 4 SERVINGS}

4 medium flounder

Salt

Black pepper

½ cup (1 stick) butter, 1 tablespoon melted butter, plus more for drizzling

1 green bell pepper, finely chopped

1 medium yellow onion, finely chopped

½ cup chopped green onions (white and green parts)

3 cloves garlic, minced

2 slices white bread, soaked in water and squeezed dry

2 tablespoons chopped fresh parsley

1 large egg, beaten

1 cup chopped cooked shrimp

1 cup lump or claw crabmeat, picked over for shells and cartilage

¼ teaspoon cayenne pepper

4 dashes of Tabasco sauce

Plain bread crumbs for sprinkling

1 tablespoon fresh lemon juice

1 lemon, sliced

Place the fish, dark-side up, on a cutting board. With a sharp boning knife, cut along the center bone of the fish. Make another slit perpendicular to the first one, then carefully peel open the fish, pulling the flesh back to form pockets. Season the inside of each pocket with salt and pepper and set aside. Repeat with the remaining fish.

In a heavy saucepan, melt the ½ cup butter over medium heat and sauté the bell pepper and yellow onion until soft, 5 to 10 minutes. Add the green onions and garlic and mix well, an cook for another minute or two, until the garlic is fragrant. Remove from the heat and add the bread, parsley, egg, shrimp, and crabmeat. Add the cayenne and Tabasco. Mix well, but gently.

Preheat the oven to 350 degrees F. Butter a shallow baking pan.

Fill the pockets of the fish with the stuffing mixture. Sprinkle a few bread crumbs on top of the stuffing and drizzle with a little butter.

Place the fish in the prepared pan and bake for about 30 minutes, or until the fish flake. As the fish bake, every 10 minutes put a teaspoonful of lemon juice and a teaspoonful of melted butter over the fish and stuffing to keep them moist. Serve garnished with lemon slices. ❧

Commander's Tasso Shrimp with Five-Pepper Jelly

SOME OF THE READERS who lost their recipes in the storm requested the late chef Jamie Shannon's recipe from Commander's Palace. You might want to experiment with the pepper jelly for other applications, such as dabbing it on roast pork or lamb, or using it to dress a cold chicken sandwich. Tasso is a heavily seasoned smoked ham used for flavoring many south Louisiana dishes.

{MAKES 6 SERVINGS}

½ pound tasso, cut into 30 matchsticks
30 jumbo shrimp, peeled, deveined, and butterflied
2 large eggs
2 cups milk
2 cups all-purpose flour
Vegetable oil for deep-frying
Five-Pepper Jelly (recipe follows)
Crystal Butter Sauce (recipe follows)
Red oak leaf lettuce or watercress sprigs for garnish

Place a piece of tasso inside the slit in each shrimp, and secure with a toothpick. In a large mixing bowl, beat the eggs and milk together until blended. Put the flour in a shallow bowl. Dip each shrimp into the egg mixture and then dredge in the flour.

Heat the oil to 350 degrees F in a deep fryer or large heavy pot. Deep-fry the shrimp in batches, 3 to 4 minutes, or until golden brown. Remove with a slotted spoon.

To serve, arrange ¼ cup of the pepper jelly on each of 6 salad plates. Place the butter sauce in a small bowl and dip the shrimp into the sauce to coat them evenly. Place 5 shrimp on each plate in a circular design and garnish with the greens. ✺

Five-Pepper Jelly

{MAKES ABOUT 3 CUPS}

1½ cups white distilled vinegar
2 tablespoons balsamic vinegar
¾ cup corn syrup
1 yellow bell pepper, finely diced
1 red bell pepper, finely diced
1 green bell pepper, finely diced
1 jalapeño pepper, finely diced
⅛ teaspoon cayenne pepper

Combine the white and balsamic vinegars and the corn syrup in a large saucepan and bring to a boil. Reduce the heat and boil slowly until reduced by half, about 10 to 15 minutes. Add the peppers and cayenne and simmer for 10 minutes. Remove from the heat and let cool. ✺

Crystal Butter Sauce

{MAKES ABOUT 2 ½ CUPS}

½ cup Crystal hot sauce or another pepper sauce
½ cup dry white wine
1½ teaspoons minced shallots
¾ teaspoon minced garlic
2 cups (4 sticks) butter

Combine the hot sauce, wine, shallots, and garlic in a small saucepan and cook over medium heat until the mixture is reduced by half. Let cool to warm, then slowly add the butter, 4 tablespoons at a time, stirring constantly.

The key to this sauce, like all butter sauces, is to keep it warm at all times, not too hot or too cold. Periodically place the pan over low heat to keep the sauce just warm enough to melt the butter. ✺

Courtbouillon

UNLESS YOU'RE FROM south Louisiana, court-bouillon is a seasoned broth for poaching fish or seafood. Here, it's a dish. In New Orleans, order "COO-be-yon," as it's pronounced, and you're likely to get a baked whole fish with a tomato-based sauce. But in Acadiana, a courtbouillon is a thick, tomato-based stew made with a roux, in which fish fillets or chunks of fish are cooked. This is a very flavorful Cajun version.

{MAKES 8 SERVINGS}

⅔ cup all-purpose flour

⅔ cup vegetable oil

2 medium yellow onions, chopped

1 medium green bell pepper, chopped

2 stalks celery, chopped

3 cloves garlic, minced (optional)

1 (1-pound) can whole tomatoes,
  with their juice, chopped

1 (10-ounce) can Ro-Tel diced tomatoes
  and green chiles (mild version)

6 cups warm fish stock or water

1 tablespoon salt

1 teaspoon cayenne pepper

2½ pounds firm fish fillets, such as redfish, speckled
  trout, or sea bass, cut into 3-inch chunks

1 bunch green onions (green part only), chopped

¼ cup finely chopped fresh parsley

Hot cooked rice for serving

Warm French bread for serving

Combine the flour and oil in a large heavy pot, such as a Dutch oven, over medium heat. Stirring slowly and constantly, make a roux the color of chocolate. Add the onions, bell peppers, celery, and garlic. Cook, stirring, until the vegetables are soft, about 5 minutes. Add the whole tomatoes and Ro-Tel and stir to blend. Reduce the heat to medium-low and cook, stirring occasionally, until the oil forms a paper-thin layer over the top of the mixture, about 30 minutes.

Add the fish stock, salt, and cayenne and cook, stirring occasionally, for 1 hour. The mixture should be slightly thick. (If the mixture becomes too thick, add more stock or water.) Add the fish, cover, and cook (do not stir) until the fish flakes easily with a fork, about 10 minutes. Add more salt and cayenne if necessary.

Add the green onions and parsley, and serve immediately in soup bowls with steamed rice. Pass plenty of warm French bread at the table. ❦

Crab Chops

Crab cakes, crab chops, or crab patties—whatever you want to call them, they are delicious! This is Marcelle Bienvenu's version. Dab them with tartar sauce or your favorite cocktail sauce.

{MAKES 6 SERVINGS}

3 tablespoons butter

3 green onions, chopped

2 tablespoons all-purpose flour

1 cup milk

1 pound lump crabmeat, picked over for shells and cartilage

20 saltine crackers, finely crumbled

1 large egg, lightly beaten

½ teaspoon salt

¼ teaspoon cayenne pepper

⅛ teaspoon Tabasco sauce

Cracker meal or bread crumbs for dredging

Melted butter for frying

Vegetable oil for frying

Tartar sauce for serving

Melt the 3 tablespoons of butter in a large skillet over medium heat. Add the green onions and cook, stirring, for about 1 minute. Alternate adding the flour and milk, stirring constantly, to make a smooth, thick white sauce. Remove from the heat.

Add the crabmeat, cracker crumbs, egg, salt, cayenne, and Tabasco. Gently mix together and set aside to cool completely. (If you wish, you can chill it in the refrigerator.)

Gently shape the mixture into 6 patties. Dredge them in the cracker meal, coating completely and evenly.

Put about ½ inch of equal parts of butter and vegetable oil in a large nonstick skillet over medium heat. Fry the patties, 2 to 3 minutes on each side, until golden brown. Drain on paper towels and serve warm with tartar sauce. 🦀

Crawfish Braid

ONE READER WROTE shortly after the storm, "I am looking for your help. Due to Hurricane Katrina, I lost my recipe for crawfish bread."

Many favorite foods are served every year at the New Orleans Jazz and Heritage Festival, also known as Jazzfest, and crawfish bread is one of them. Seldom are these dishes available the rest of the year, and vendors protect their recipes like the precious jewels they are. Therefore, many people create their own versions of favorite Jazzfest recipes, and this is one. If you have a bread machine, you can easily adapt this recipe to make it in your appliance.

{MAKES 8 TO 10 SERVINGS}

3 to 3½ cups all-purpose flour

1 package active dry yeast

1 tablespoon sugar

1 teaspoon salt

½ teaspoon dried thyme leaves

½ teaspoon dried oregano leaves

½ teaspoon dried basil leaves

½ teaspoon onion powder

1 cup warm water (120 to 130 degrees F)

1 tablespoon olive oil

1 pound peeled crawfish tails, coarsely chopped

1 (4-ounce) jar pimientos, drained and chopped

¾ cup chopped green onions (white and green parts)

1 cup grated pepper Jack cheese

1 large egg, lightly beaten

Sesame seeds for sprinkling

In a large mixing bowl, combine 1½ cups of the flour, the yeast, sugar, salt, thyme, oregano, basil, and onion powder. Gradually stir in the warm water and oil, then beat for 2 minutes with an electric mixer at medium speed, scraping the bowl occasionally. Then beat for 2 minutes at high speed.

Stir in enough of the remaining flour to make a soft dough. Knead on a floured work surface until smooth and elastic, about 5 minutes. Place in a large greased bowl, turning to grease the top. Cover and let rise in a warm, draft-free spot until doubled in size, 30 to 45 minutes. Punch the dough down. Place on a floured work surface and roll into a 14-by-10-inch rectangle.

Scatter the crawfish lengthwise over the center third of the dough. Top with the pimientos, green onions, and cheese. With a sharp knife, make slashes from the filling to the dough edges along the length of the rectangle at 1-inch intervals. Alternating sides, fold strips of dough at an angle across the filling for a braided effect. Place the bread on a greased baking sheet. Cover and let rise in a warm, draft-free spot until doubled in size, 30 to 45 minutes.

In the meantime, preheat the oven to 400 degrees F (allow about 20 minutes). Brush the loaf with the beaten egg and sprinkle with sesame seeds. Bake for 30 to 35 minutes, until golden. 🦞

Crawfish in Saffron Cream

THE CALL WENT out that K.P. in Washington, D.C., was trying to find a crawfish with saffron cream recipe for her father, who lives Uptown and lost all his *Times-Picayune* recipes in the storm.

This turned out to be a prizewinner in the paper's recipe contest held a long time ago. L.P. of New Orleans sent it to us for K.P. and her dad with the notation, "A very tasty dish, indeed."

{MAKES 4 SERVINGS}

4 tablespoons butter
¼ cup minced shallots
4 to 6 mushrooms, sliced
Pinch of saffron
¼ cup dry sherry
¼ cup white vermouth
½ cup heavy cream
1 teaspoon dill weed
2 tablespoons minced fresh parsley
1 pound peeled crawfish tails
Salt
Black pepper
Hot cooked rice for serving

Melt the butter in a large skillet and add the shallots. Sauté over medium heat for 2 minutes, then add the mushrooms. Cook for 5 minutes, stirring occasionally.

Meanwhile, put the saffron in the sherry and stir. Let stand for a few minutes, then add to the pan with the vermouth. Cook and stir for 4 minutes, or until the liquid has reduced by half. Add the cream, dill, and parsley. Increase the heat to medium-high, and reduce the sauce until slightly thickened. Add the crawfish tails and season to taste with salt and pepper. Heat through and serve over rice.

Crawfish Patrick

"I LOST ALL of my recipes in the post-Katrina flood. Can you locate the recipe for crawfish Patrick?" wrote K.C. of Algiers.

This recipe was sent to us by D.D. of Goodbee, who said it was incredibly easy to make and was "one of [her] most requested meals when out-of-town relatives come to visit." The recipe doubles and even quadruples easily for a crowd.

{MAKES 4 TO 6 SERVINGS}

½ cup (1 stick) butter
1 medium yellow onion, chopped
2 stalks celery, chopped
2 tablespoons all-purpose flour
½ teaspoon Creole seasoning, preferably Tony Chachere's, or to taste
⅛ teaspoon Kitchen Bouquet
1 pound peeled crawfish tails
¾ cup chicken broth
2 to 3 chopped green onions (green part only)
Hot cooked rice or pasta for serving

In a large skillet, melt the butter, and then cook the onion and celery over medium heat until soft and golden, about 10 minutes. Slowly and thoroughly stir in the flour with a wire whisk. Stir in the Creole seasoning and Kitchen Bouquet. Add the crawfish tails and broth, bring to a simmer, and cook on low heat for 20 minutes. Stir often, because the mixture tends to stick to the pan at this point. Remove from the heat and add the green onions. Serve over rice or pasta. ❧

Crawfish Pie

P. Smith of Marrero nominated this recipe, from Marcelle Bienvenu's column, for inclusion in the cookbook. She said, "I have given away countless copies of the crawfish pie recipe. In fact, many people compliment me on MY crawfish pie."

{MAKES 6 SERVINGS}

4 tablespoons butter

1 cup chopped yellow onions

½ cup chopped green bell peppers

¼ cup chopped celery

1½ teaspoons salt

½ teaspoon cayenne pepper

½ cup chopped canned tomatoes

1 pound peeled crawfish tails

2 tablespoons cornstarch

½ cup water

2 tablespoons chopped green onions (green part only)

1 tablespoon chopped fresh parsley

1 unbaked 9-inch pie shell

Preheat the oven to 375 degrees F.

Melt the butter in a large skillet over medium heat. Add the onions, bell peppers, and celery, and cook, stirring, until the vegetables are soft and golden, 6 to 8 minutes. Add the salt, cayenne, and tomatoes and cook, stirring occasionally, for 5 minutes. Add the crawfish tails and cook for about 5 minutes more, stirring occasionally, until they give off some liquid.

In a small bowl, dissolve the cornstarch in the water then add to the pan. Stir for 2 to 3 minutes, or until the mixture thickens. Add the green onions and parsley and stir to mix. Remove from the heat and let cool for about 30 minutes.

Pour the crawfish mixture into the pie shell. Place the pie on a baking sheet and bake for about 45 minutes, or until the edges of the pie shell are golden. Cool for several minutes before cutting into wedges to serve.

Crawfish Stew-Fay

This oddly named dish, which originated with Marcelle Bienvenu's mother, is a classic étouffée from south Louisiana. It's called a "stew-fay" simply because it has a slurry (the combination of water and cornstarch) added to thicken it up a bit.

{MAKES ABOUT 8 SERVINGS}

½ cup (1 stick) unsalted butter

2 cups chopped yellow onions

1 cup chopped green bell peppers

½ cup chopped celery

2 pounds peeled crawfish tails

1 tablespoon cornstarch dissolved in 1 cup water

Salt

Cayenne pepper

2 tablespoons chopped green onions (green part only)

1 tablespoon chopped fresh parsley leaves

Hot cooked long-grain rice for serving

Melt the butter in a large, heavy pot over medium heat. Add the onions, bell peppers, and celery and cook, stirring, until the vegetables are soft and pale gold, 6 to 8 minutes. Add the crawfish and cook, stirring occasionally, until they begin to throw off a little liquid, about 5 minutes.

Add the cornstarch mixture, reduce the heat to medium-low, and cook, stirring occasionally, until the mixture thickens, 3 to 4 minutes. Season with salt and cayenne to taste. Remove from the heat and stir in the green onions and parsley. Serve in bowls over rice. 🦐

Elmwood Oysters Mosca

WE RECEIVED TWO requests for the same very popular recipe. The first came from D.F., formerly of Meraux, who wrote, "About a year ago, I requested Elmwood Plantation's recipe for Oysters Mosca. . . . Unfortunately, like so many, I lost my recipes in Katrina." The other request came from a resident of Grand Isle, who also lost most of her recipes.

Nick Mosca, formerly the master chef at Elmwood Plantation, had developed the recipe with his father at Mosca's restaurant in Avondale. Nick was master chef at Elmwood Plantation from 1962 to 1978, when the restaurant burned down.

{MAKES 2 ENTRÉE OR 4 APPETIZER SERVINGS}

4 tablespoons butter

¼ cup olive oil

¼ cup finely chopped green onions (white and green parts)

2 tablespoons finely chopped fresh parsley

1 tablespoon minced garlic

⅔ cup seasoned Italian bread crumbs

¼ cup grated Parmesan cheese

½ teaspoon salt

¼ teaspoon black pepper

⅛ teaspoon cayenne pepper

½ teaspoon dried basil leaves

½ teaspoon dried oregano leaves

About 8 freshly shucked oysters

Preheat the oven to 425 degrees F.

Melt the butter with the olive oil in a large skillet over medium heat. Sauté the green onions, parsley, and garlic until the green onions are soft and translucent. Stir in the bread crumbs, cheese, salt, pepper, cayenne, and herbs.

Place all the oysters (or as many as you can fit) in an ovenproof baking and serving dish. Spoon the bread crumb mixture over the oysters and bake for 15 minutes, or until golden. Serve immediately. ❧

Garlic Shrimp

KELLY HAMILTON, a history professor, runs the excellent culinary history tours in the French Quarter. About a year after Katrina, she sent a recipe to the newspaper. "I have a story to share," she wrote. "Our home in Gentilly flooded, and the kind people from a Presbyterian church in Oregon gutted the house. Well, word got out back in Oregon that I lost my cookbook collection. So these amazing people, total strangers, have been sending me cookbooks! One man even sent his grandma's 1942 cookbook he inherited called *Woman's Home Companion Cook Book*.

"I believe I have the largest Oregon/Pacific Northwest collection in Louisiana! Food speaks a universal language and I have enjoyed reading the recipes, particularly the seafood ones as there are similarities. I can't begin to describe how touched I am by their generosity. For the rebuilding recipe collection, here's one of my favorite ways to prepare shrimp."

{MAKES 2 TO 4 SERVINGS}

2 dozen large shrimp, peeled and deveined

3 tablespoons chopped fresh parsley (fresh basil is a nice summer substitute)

3 cloves garlic, minced

½ teaspoon red pepper flakes

½ cup fresh bread crumbs

½ cup Parmesan cheese

3 tablespoons olive oil

2 tablespoons butter, melted

Preheat the oven to 350 degrees F.

Put the shrimp in a shallow baking dish and set aside. In a medium mixing bowl, combine all the remaining ingredients except the butter. Cover the shrimp with the bread crumb mixture, then drizzle with the melted butter. Bake for 15 minutes or until golden. 🦐

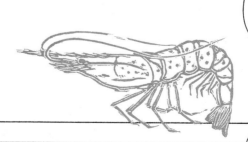

Herbsaint's Grilled Tuna with Bagna Cauda

CHEF DONALD LINK, named Best Chef of the South by the James Beard Foundation in 2007, makes this popular grilled tuna salad at Herbsaint, his mainstay restaurant on St. Charles Avenue. Link shared this recipe for a story about the region's beloved Creole tomatoes.

There will be bagna cauda left over; serve it warm with raw vegetables for dipping, or use to dress other salads.

{MAKES 2 SERVINGS}

2 (6- to 8-ounce) tuna steaks, 2 to 4 inches thick
Olive oil for coating fish
Salt
Black pepper
Red pepper flakes
½ to 1 pound fresh spinach or arugula
½ red onion, thinly sliced
1 Creole tomato (or plum or another local tomato), diced
2 hard-boiled eggs
¼ cup Bagna Cauda (recipe follows)

Coat the tuna with olive oil and sprinkle with salt, pepper, and red pepper flakes. Heat a grill pan over high heat and oil it lightly, or prepare a hot charcoal fire and oil the grill.

Grill the tuna for 1 to 2 minutes for medium-rare. Cut into 1-inch cubes and in a large mixing bowl, toss with all the remaining ingredients. ❧

Bagna Cauda

{MAKES 1 CUP}

2 anchovy fillets
Zest and juice of 1 lemon
4 cloves garlic
¼ cup red wine vinegar
¼ cup extra-virgin olive oil
4 tablespoons butter, melted
1 teaspoon chopped fresh rosemary
Salt
Black pepper

With a mortar and pestle, smash the anchovies, lemon zest, and garlic into a paste. Transfer the paste to a mixing bowl and add the lemon juice and vinegar. Whisk in the oil, melted butter, and rosemary. Season with salt and pepper to taste. Use immediately. Store leftovers for up to 2 days in an airtight container in the refrigerator. ❧

Jerry's Crawfish Bread

"I THOUGHT YOU would be interested in my version of crawfish bread," wrote Jerry H. of Destrehan. It was almost time for Jazzfest, the New Orleans Jazz and Heritage Festival, where crawfish bread is a favorite food served every year. (See page 125 for the yeast version, Crawfish Braid.) "This is fantastic and as good as anything served at any festival," he continued. "I was moved to create this recipe after my wife and I, who are volunteers at the Destrehan Plantation Festival, ate the wonderful crawfish bread served there by one of the vendors."

{MAKES 8 TO 10 SERVINGS}

4 tablespoons butter

¼ cup olive oil

1 cup chopped green onions (white and green parts)

½ cup finely chopped celery

½ cup finely chopped green bell pepper

4 cloves garlic, minced

½ cup dry white wine

1 pound peeled crawfish tails with fat

1 (8-ounce) package cream cheese, cut into small squares

½ teaspoon Creole seasoning, such as Tony Chachere's, Zatarain's, or Paul Prudhomme's Seafood Magic, or to taste

1 (11-ounce) roll refrigerated French bread dough

½ pound shredded pizza mix cheese or mozzarella

Preheat the oven to 350 degrees F. Grease a baking sheet.

In a large skillet, melt the butter with the olive oil over medium heat. Sauté the green onions, celery, bell pepper, and garlic until wilted. Add the wine and the crawfish tails with their fat. Stir well and add the cream cheese. Stir until melted. Add the Creole seasoning and cook until the mixture is thickened, just a few minutes. Remove from the heat and let the flavors blend.

Carefully roll out the French bread dough to a thickness of ½ inch on the baking sheet. Spoon the crawfish mixture down the center of the dough, and sprinkle with the shredded cheese. Fold the dough over the mixture to make a loaf. Cut 2 small slits in the top of the dough.

Bake for about 20 minutes, or until the loaf is golden brown. Let set for a few minutes before slicing into serving-size pieces. ⁓

Lasserre's Magic Crawfish

WHEN MARCELLE BIENVENU first published this recipe in one of her columns, a lot of people were skeptical about the cream of shrimp soup. It has since been asked for repeatedly by readers, and was one of the most requested recipes for this cookbook. Lasserre is Marcelle's husband, Rock Lasserre, and this is one of his favorite dishes.

{MAKES ABOUT 6 SERVINGS}

6 tablespoons butter
2 medium yellow onions, chopped
2 cloves garlic, minced
½ green bell pepper, chopped
1 stalk celery, chopped
1 pound peeled crawfish tails
1 (10.75-ounce) can condensed cream of shrimp soup
½ cup water
⅓ cup dry white wine
Salt
Cayenne pepper
¼ teaspoon hot sauce, or to taste
Minced green onions for garnish (green part only)
Hot cooked rice for serving

Melt the butter in a large heavy pot, preferably cast-iron, over medium heat. Add the onions, garlic, bell peppers, and celery and cook, stirring, until lightly browned and soft, about 6 minutes. Add the crawfish tails and cook, stirring, for 10 minutes. Add the soup, water, and wine and stir. Bring to a simmer and continue simmering for 30 minutes.

Season with salt, cayenne, and hot sauce and simmer for another 10 minutes. Add the green onions and serve over rice.

Oyster Dressing

ONE OF THE first requests we received for this cookbook was to include this recipe from the Elmwood Fitness Center. This is a lighter, healthier version of the oyster dressings enjoyed all over southern Louisiana during the holidays, which usually feature French bread crumbs and sometimes ground beef.

If you want the dressing less spicy, reduce the amount of cayenne.

{MAKES 12 SERVINGS}

2 tablespoons olive oil

1½ cups chopped green onions
   (white and green parts)

1½ cups diced yellow onions

1½ cups chopped celery

1½ cups chopped green bell peppers

2 quarts oysters with their liquor

1 tablespoon salt

1 tablespoon cayenne pepper, or less to taste

1 tablespoon garlic powder

1 tablespoon thyme leaves

3 cups coarse fresh whole-wheat bread crumbs

Preheat the oven to 350 degrees F. Coat a 9-by-13-inch baking pan or casserole dish with nonstick cooking spray.

In a large skillet, heat the olive oil over medium heat and sauté the green onions, yellow onions, celery, and bell peppers. Add the oysters and oyster liquor. Cook until the yellow onions and celery are translucent, 5 to 6 minutes. Stir in the salt, cayenne, garlic powder, thyme, and bread crumbs.

Pour the mixture into the pan and bake for about 20 minutes, or until the top is golden brown. ❧

Salt and Pepper Shrimp

OUR FOOD EDITOR, Judy Walker, received a note from J.C. asking about a salt and pepper shrimp recipe that she lost to the floodwaters that followed Hurricane Katrina and the failure of the levees. The recipe, previously published in the Food section, came from the kitchen of Gavin MacArthur, a local man who grew up in the San Francisco area, eating his mom's Chinese food. It is his take on a Chinese favorite.

{MAKES 2 TO 4 SERVINGS}

1 pound medium shrimp with shells and heads on
¾ teaspoon salt
1½ teaspoons rice wine or dry sherry (not sake)
3 cups vegetable oil
3 tablespoons cornstarch
3 cloves garlic, minced
1 (1-inch) piece ginger, peeled and minced
½ teaspoon red pepper flakes, or to taste (see Note)
2 green onions, minced (white and green parts)

With kitchen shears, cut through the shrimp shells about halfway down the length of the back of the shrimp. Cut off the legs and the sharp spines of the shrimp, then devein them, leaving the shells on.

Rinse the cleaned shrimp under cold water and use paper towels or a clean kitchen towel to pat them very dry. In a medium mixing bowl, toss the shrimp with ½ teaspoon of the salt and the rice wine and set aside for 10 minutes, but no longer.

Heat the oil to 375 degrees F in a medium saucepan. Toss the shrimp with the cornstarch, then carefully add them to the hot oil, in batches if necessary. Cook for 45 seconds to 1 minute, just until they turn bright orange. Use a slotted spoon to remove the shrimp from the oil, and drain on paper towels. Remove the oil from the heat and set aside to cool.

Heat a heavy skillet over high heat until hot, but not smoking. Add 2 tablespoons of the reserved frying oil, along with the garlic and ginger. Sauté until fragrant, about 30 seconds. Add the shrimp, the remaining ¼ teaspoon of salt, and the red pepper flakes. Sauté until the shrimp are just cooked through, about 1 minute. Add the green onions and toss to combine. Serve immediately. Eat them, shells and all. 🦐

NOTE: *Use more or less red pepper flakes, to your taste. About 1 teaspoon is pretty spicy. You also can use different kinds of pepper, such as white pepper, black pepper, Sichuan pepper, or Chinese five-spice powder.*

Shrimp and Grits

"I HOPE YOU can help me find a recipe," one reader wrote. Her best friend's mother, who had passed away two weeks before the hurricane, had given her a recipe for shrimp and grits. She continued, "As with many of your followers, I lost my entire recipe collection. . . . This was a dish I loved to share annually at Christmas brunch. Thanks for all your help."

The specific recipe the reader was seeking was the creation of Davis Lew Bremenstul Jr., who was inspired by South Carolina versions of the dish. New Orleanians love their Grillades and Grits (page 102), while South Carolinians love their grits with shrimp. In his recipe, reproduced here, the grits are firmed up like polenta and served with a sauce.

{MAKES 6 SERVINGS}

Butter for greasing, plus 3 tablespoons
About 4 cups chicken broth
1 cup quick-cooking or instant hominy grits
1½ cups grated Jarlsberg cheese (preferred) or Swiss cheese
½ pound white button mushrooms, sliced
¾ cup finely chopped green onions (white and green parts)
1 clove garlic, minced
1½ pounds medium shrimp with heads, peeled
½ cup dry white wine

Butter an oval 2-quart casserole dish, such as a 13-by-11-by-1½-inch dish.

In a 2-quart saucepan, bring the chicken broth to a boil and add the grits. Cook until thick but still pourable, 5 to 7 minutes. Stir in 1 cup of the cheese. Remove from the heat, and pour the mixture into the prepared dish, smoothing it out to make it uniformly thick. Set aside, or cover and refrigerate until ready to use. (The dish can be assembled up to 1 day ahead; return to room temperature before baking.)

Preheat the broiler or preheat the oven to 500 degrees F.

In a large skillet, melt the 3 tablespoons of butter over medium-high heat and sauté the mushrooms, green onions, and garlic for 2 minutes. Add the shrimp, and cook for 4 minutes. Leave the shrimp slightly undercooked because they'll cook more under the broiler. Transfer the shrimp to a plate, and in the same skillet cook the wine until it reduces by half, about 2 minutes. Add the remaining ½ cup of cheese and continue cooking just until the cheese melts, 2 to 3 minutes more, stirring constantly.

Spoon the shrimp evenly over the grits and drizzle with the cheese sauce. Broil or bake, uncovered, until the top just starts to brown and the cheese bubbles, 2 to 10 minutes, depending on whether you're broiling or baking and how far the heat element is from the food. Serve warm, cut into wedges or slices. ❧

Shrimp Burgers

SHRIMP BURGERS WERE a staple on Fridays during Lent when Marcelle Bienvenu was growing up. If you don't want to tuck them into a bun, that's fine. Serve them with French fries and coleslaw for a delightful meat-free supper.

{MAKES 4 TO 6 PATTIES}

2 pounds medium shrimp, peeled, deveined, and chopped

½ cup finely chopped yellow onions

¼ cup finely chopped green bell peppers

½ cup finely chopped celery

1 large egg, beaten

1 teaspoon salt

½ teaspoon cayenne pepper

3 tablespoons finely chopped green onions (green part only)

3 tablespoons finely chopped fresh parsley

1 teaspoon baking powder

4 slices stale white bread, cut into small cubes

All-purpose flour for dredging

3 to 6 tablespoons vegetable oil for frying

Toasted hamburger buns for serving

Tartar sauce for serving

Combine the shrimp, onions, bell peppers, and celery with the beaten egg in a mixing bowl. Add the salt, cayenne, green onions, parsley, baking powder, and cubed bread. Mix well. Cover and refrigerate for 2 hours.

Remove the mixture from the refrigerator and form into patties the size of a hamburger. Put the flour in a shallow bowl and dredge the patties in it. Heat the oil in a skillet over medium-high heat, and cook the shrimp burgers on both sides until golden brown and cooked through. Drain on paper towels.

To serve, spread a toasted hamburger bun with tartar sauce and tuck in the shrimp burger. The burgers are best served warm. ❧

Shrimp Creole

FROM A COLUMN by Marcelle Bienvenu in January 1997:

Shrimp Creole, or Shrimp à la Creole, was for years a mainstay on most restaurant menus in New Orleans. It was often served in homes on Fridays during the Lenten season, in keeping with the Catholic rules of fast and abstinence. . . . I embarked on a week-long research project. . . . This is the result. It's quite simple and quick to prepare. You can make it your own by adding personal touches, so use it as a basic recipe.

{MAKES 4 TO 6 SERVINGS}

4 tablespoons butter

2 tablespoons all-purpose flour

1½ cups chopped onions

1 cup chopped green bell peppers

¾ cup chopped celery

3 cloves garlic, minced

2 bay leaves

2 cups chopped fresh tomatoes or chopped canned tomatoes with their juice

1 cup shrimp or chicken stock

1 teaspoon salt

¼ teaspoon cayenne pepper

2 pounds medium shrimp, peeled and deveined

2 teaspoons chopped fresh parsley

Hot cooked rice for serving

Melt the butter in a medium heavy pot over medium heat and add the flour. Cook, stirring, to make a blond roux, 5 to 6 minutes. Add the onions, bell peppers, celery, and garlic. Cook, stirring, until the vegetables are soft and lightly browned, about 6 minutes.

Add the bay leaves, tomatoes, shrimp stock, salt, and cayenne. Simmer, uncovered, for 30 minutes, stirring occasionally. Add the shrimp and cook until they turn pink, 3 to 4 minutes.

Remove the bay leaves and add the parsley. Serve over rice. 🦐

Spicy Cajun Shrimp

B.M. SENT THIS, her favorite shrimp recipe, to include in the cookbook. It's a great one!

"I cut this recipe out of the paper many years back," she wrote, "and we have enjoyed it ever since. We like spicy food, but the 1 teaspoon of cayenne was entirely too much. Don't use more crushed red pepper flakes either."

As a variation, you may use half shrimp and half scallops instead of all shrimp, or substitute other fish or shellfish.

{MAKES 2 TO 3 SERVINGS}

2 dozen large fresh or frozen shrimp, or 1 pound medium fresh or frozen shrimp, thawed if frozen, peeled, and deveined

¼ teaspoon to 1 teaspoon cayenne pepper

½ teaspoon black pepper

½ teaspoon salt (optional)

½ teaspoon red pepper flakes

½ teaspoon dried thyme leaves, crushed

1 teaspoon dried basil leaves, crushed

½ teaspoon dried oregano leaves, crushed (optional)

⅓ cup butter

1½ teaspoons minced garlic

1 teaspoon Worcestershire sauce

1 cup diced tomatoes

¼ cup beer, at room temperature

Hot cooked rice for serving (optional)

Rinse the cleaned shrimp under cold running water. Drain well, then set aside. In a small bowl combine the cayenne, black pepper, salt (if using), red pepper flakes, and herbs.

Combine the butter, garlic, Worcestershire, and the pepper-herb mixture in a large skillet over high heat. When the butter is melted, add the tomatoes, and then the shrimp. Cook for 2 minutes, stirring well. Add the beer, cover, and cook for 1 minute longer. Remove from the heat. Serve over rice, if desired. 🍤

Stuffed Crabs Leruth

THE LATE WARREN LERUTH was an excellent chef and some of his recipes, such as this one, remain quite popular. This recipe was sent to us during crab season by B.B, a frequent correspondent who lives in Baton Rouge. "I have had this [recipe]—Stuffed Crabs Leruth—for at least 30 years," B.B. wrote. "Since crabmeat is plentiful now, this would be a good time to make this excellent and easy recipe."

{MAKES 6 SERVINGS}

½ cup (1 stick) butter

1 medium yellow onion, chopped

1 bunch green onions, chopped (white and green parts)

½ green bell pepper, chopped

¼ stalk celery, chopped

½ loaf French bread, soaked in milk and squeezed dry

¼ cup chopped fresh parsley

Salt

Black pepper

1 pound white or lump crabmeat, picked over for shells and cartilage

Bread crumbs for sprinkling

Preheat the oven to 375 degrees F. Coat 6 ramekins or cleaned crab shells with nonstick cooking spray.

In a large ovenproof skillet, melt the butter over medium heat and sauté the yellow onion, green onions, bell pepper, and celery until the vegetables are tender, 5 to 6 minutes. Add the bread and parsley and season with salt and pepper to taste. Stir to mix, and remove from the heat. Allow the stuffing to cool and gently stir in the crabmeat. Divide the crabmeat mixture evenly among the ramekins. Top with bread crumbs and bake until browned, about 20 minutes.

Café Reconcile's White Beans and Shrimp

CAFÉ RECONCILE OPENED in 2002 in New Orleans to serve social justice as well as lunch. At-risk teens and young adults from the juvenile detention system and Louisiana Rehabilitation Services, as well as students in high school vocational training programs, work here and receive training for jobs in restaurants, catering, and hotel businesses. Many former employees are now valued workers in the city's restaurants.

White beans and shrimp, from founding chef Don Boyd, has become one of the restaurant's most-loved dishes.

{MAKES 6 SERVINGS}

1 pound dried great Northern beans

2 cups chopped onion

1 cup chopped celery

1 cup chopped green bell peppers

¼ cup chopped fresh parsley

⅓ cup chopped garlic (about 1½ heads)

1 tablespoon dried thyme leaves

1½ teaspoons granulated garlic

1½ teaspoons granulated onion

½ teaspoon black pepper

Dash of cayenne pepper

Dash of white pepper

Salt

2 to 2½ quarts chicken or vegetable stock

1 tablespoon olive oil

1½ pounds medium shrimp, peeled and deveined

2 cups heavy cream

Hot cooked rice for serving

Jalapeño cornbread for serving

Put the beans in a large bowl, cover with about 3 inches of water, and soak overnight.

Drain the beans. Combine them in a large pot with the onions, celery, bell peppers, parsley, 2 tablespoons of the chopped garlic, the thyme, granulated garlic and onion, black pepper, cayenne, white pepper, and salt to taste. Add the stock. Bring to a boil and then lower the heat. Simmer, covered, for 2 to 3 hours, until the beans are tender. Skim the scum off the surface of the liquid during the first 15 minutes of cooking.

In a large skillet, heat the olive oil over medium heat and sauté the remaining chopped garlic until it starts to brown. Add the shrimp and cook, stirring, until they turn pink.

Add the cream to the beans and then add the shrimp and garlic mixture. Bring to a simmer, being careful not to boil. Serve over white rice with jalapeño cornbread. ✌

POULTRY

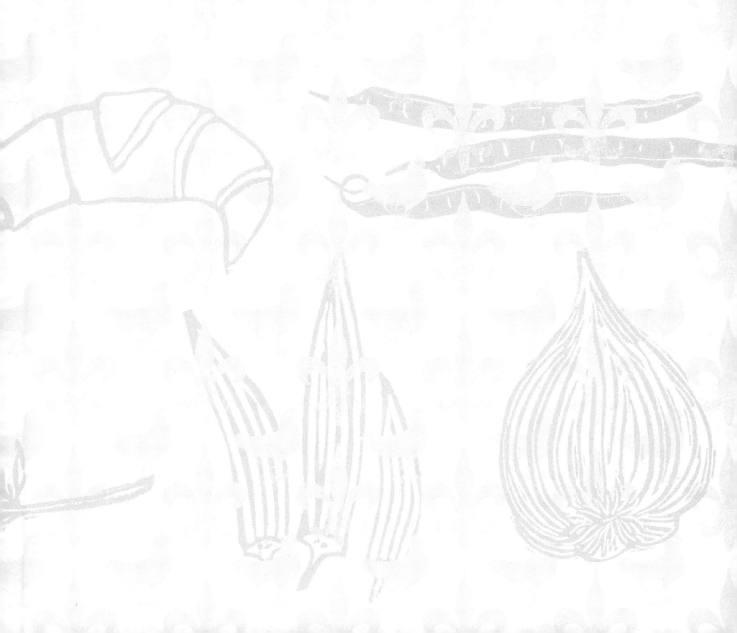

Most of the recipes in this section are treasures from the past. One of the first letters that arrived after The Times-Picayune *began this cookbook project asked for Chicken with Apricots (page 152), which appeared years ago in a column by Myriam Guidroz. Although the newspaper editors couldn't find it, another reader supplied us with one she brought over from Romania, which we hope will suffice. We did find a recipe for Poulet aux Fines Herbes (chicken with herbs, page 159) and for Ultimate Turkey Poulette à la Roosevelt (page 161), two of Guidroz's recipes, which we know readers will enjoy.*

From another Times-Picayune *columnist, Leon Soniat, comes his recipe for Marinated Fried Chicken (page 156), which took us a while to find because the person who asked for it couldn't remember the exact name of the dish. But we found it and it's here!*

The Creole Chicken with Okra (page 153) is a great example of how blending Creole with Italian is a good thing. For those of you who want to try Poor Al's Fried Turkey (page 154), just be careful and don't do it in your house or under the carport!

POULTRY

Beer-Barbecued Turkey Drumsticks

FOR MORE THAN a year after Katrina, the Food pages tried to provide recipes for microwaves and slow cookers, since so many people in our readership area were without access to ovens or more conventional ways of cooking. This recipe came to us from Mount Hermon, a small community in Washington Parish, north of Lake Pontchartrain. The sender said this recipe was made several times in a microwave hooked up to a generator after Hurricane Katrina knocked out power there. "We had to use a lot of meat in our freezers with simple recipes," the note said. The drumsticks were so popular they were put on the menu at a local cafe.

{MAKES 4 SERVINGS}

2½ to 3 pounds turkey drumsticks
1 cup barbecue sauce
½ cup beer
1 tablespoon packed dark brown sugar
1 teaspoon ground ginger
¼ teaspoon salt
¼ teaspoon black pepper

Arrange the drumsticks in a 10-inch round microwave-safe baking dish, with the meaty portions closer to the edge of the dish. Combine the remaining ingredients in a small mixing bowl and pour the mixture over the turkey. Cover the dish with wax paper or a lid or microwave-safe plate.

Microwave on high for 15 minutes. Turn the drumsticks over. Microwave on medium for 65 to 75 minutes, or until the meat is tender, turning the drumsticks once after 35 minutes of cooking time. Serve the drumsticks with the cooking sauce. ❧

Chicken Baked Royally

F.A. LOST HER favorite baked chicken recipe during Hurricane Katrina. Thanks to *The Times-Picayune*'s head librarian, Nancy Burris, we can put this one in the "found" column.

{MAKES 6 SERVINGS}

4 tablespoons butter

1 tablespoon vegetable oil

6 boneless chicken breast halves or boneless thighs

½ pound mushrooms, sliced

1 tablespoon all-purpose flour

1 (10.75-ounce) can cream of chicken soup

1 cup dry white wine

1 cup water

½ cup heavy cream

1 teaspoon salt

¼ teaspoon dried tarragon leaves

¼ teaspoon black pepper

1 (14-ounce) can artichoke hearts, drained

6 green onions, chopped (green parts only)

2 tablespoons chopped fresh parsley

Hot cooked rice or noodles for serving

Preheat the oven to 350 degrees F. Coat a 3-quart casserole dish with nonstick cooking spray.

In a large skillet, melt the butter with the oil over medium-high heat and brown the chicken on all sides, about 10 minutes. Transfer to the prepared casserole dish.

In the same skillet, sauté the mushrooms until tender, about 5 minutes. Stir in the flour, then the soup, wine, and water and continue stirring until smooth. Simmer until the sauce thickens, about 10 minutes, stirring frequently and scraping the bottom of the pan well. Add the cream, salt, tarragon, and pepper, and pour the sauce over the chicken.

Bake, uncovered, for 1 hour. Add the artichokes, green onions, and parsley, and bake for 5 minutes more, or until the chicken is fork-tender. Serve with rice or noodles. ❧

Chicken Cacciatore

A METAIRIE RESIDENT asked for this recipe, which she had lost in the hurricane. It was contributed by Mary Jo and Johnny Mosca to H. Leighton Steward et al's *The New Sugar Busters!* cookbook, published in 2003. The couple are the owners of Mosca's, a fabled restaurant on Highway 90 in Avondale. And, yes, ten cloves of garlic for six servings is correct.

{MAKES 6 SERVINGS}

¾ cup olive oil

2 (3-pound) chickens, each cut into serving pieces

½ teaspoon salt

1 teaspoon black pepper

10 cloves garlic, mashed

1 teaspoon dried rosemary leaves

1 teaspoon dried oregano leaves

½ cup dry white wine

1½ cups tomato sauce, or 1 (16-ounce) can peeled, crushed tomatoes

Whole-wheat pasta for serving (optional)

Heat the olive oil in a large skillet over medium-high heat. Brown the chicken pieces in batches, turning them often, about 10 minutes for each batch. Return the chicken pieces to the skillet and sprinkle the chicken pieces with the salt and pepper. Add the garlic, rosemary, and oregano, stirring to distribute the seasonings.

Remove the pan from the heat. Pour the wine over the chicken. Add the tomato sauce, return to the heat, and simmer until the juices of the chicken run clear and the wine and sauce blend and thicken, 20 to 30 minutes.

Serve warm with whole-wheat pasta, if desired. 🐓

Chicken with Apricots

ONE OF THE recipes sought for this cookbook was one for chicken with apricots, which was requested by B.C.W. She remembered that the recipe came from the column of Myriam Guidroz. While that exact recipe still has not surfaced, this one was sent by J. d'A. of Metairie.

"I only have an old Romanian recipe for 'chicken with apricots' which I brought from my home country," J. d'A. wrote. "I assure you it is delicious and a big hit with all my friends." She said her mother wrote a voluminous Romanian cookbook (it was never published and probably included this recipe). "The emphasis," J. d'A. wrote, "is on the freshness of the ingredients to give the food an intense flavoring. We use hardly any spices." She keeps the skin on the chicken for a richer taste, but the health-conscious may remove it.

{MAKES 8 SERVINGS}

1 (11- to 12-ounce) package dried apricots

1 cup water

2 tablespoons vegetable oil

½ large onion, thinly sliced into ½-inch-long strips

4 bone-in chicken breast halves and 4 legs, with skin on (1½ to 2 pounds total)

2 tablespoons dry white wine

1 teaspoon tomato paste

2 to 3 teaspoons sugar

2 lemon wedges

Hot rice pilaf for serving

Soak the apricots in the water for 20 to 30 minutes until soft and plump. Remove and set aside. Save the soaking water.

Coat a large skillet at least 2 inches deep with nonstick cooking spray. Add the oil and warm over medium heat. Sauté the onions until transparent, 5 to 10 minutes. Remove from the pan and set aside. Raise the heat to high and quickly brown all the chicken pieces on both sides in batches. Do not allow them to burn.

Pour the wine into the pan immediately. Add the tomato paste and the soaking water from the apricots, stirring until the tomato paste is dissolved. Add the onions, apricots, sugar to taste, and the juice from the lemon wedges, setting aside the rinds. Bring to a boil, then lower the heat and cover. Simmer for 10 minutes, then turn over the chicken pieces and apricots, cover again, and simmer for 10 more minutes.

Meanwhile, using a small sharp paring knife, remove the pulp and all the white pith from the lemon rind. Mince the yellow zest. Sprinkle over the chicken and continue simmering until the chicken is very tender, maybe another 10 minutes. The exact timing depends on the thickness of the breasts and drumsticks. Serve with rice pilaf. 🌺

Creole Chicken with Okra

DORIS LANDRY RECEIVED a first-place award for this creation in *The Times-Picayune*'s 1989 Cookbook and Recipe Contest. It is a culinary blend of two cultures that makes a satisfying one-dish meal when served over rice or pasta.

"My Creole mother taught me how to make the gravy," said Landry, "although we always prepared the seasonings in the roux rather than separately. And she always told me that a Creole gravy must never be red, always rusty. A red gravy looks more Italian. My Italian mother-in-law gave me the idea of combining the okra with the chicken and gravy."

Fresh thyme is best, if you can get it or grow it yourself, as Landry has. "If you can't get it fresh, dried will do, but get the leaves, not the ground thyme," she said. The leaves are tiny and appear granular when dried. Ground thyme is powdery.

{MAKES 6 SERVINGS}

½ cup (1 stick) butter or margarine

6 chicken leg quarters or breast quarters

¼ cup all-purpose flour

1 bunch green onions, finely chopped (white and green parts)

1 large yellow onion, finely chopped

5 cloves garlic, minced

1 (8-ounce) can tomato sauce

4 cups water

2 bay leaves

¼ teaspoon dried thyme leaves, or 1 teaspoon chopped fresh thyme

2 pounds whole fresh or frozen (thawed) small okra

Salt

Black pepper

Hot cooked rice or noodles for serving

Melt the butter or margarine in a Dutch oven. Add the chicken and cook over medium-high heat until golden brown on each side. Remove from the pan.

Stir the flour into the drippings over low heat. Cook for approximately 10 minutes until you have a light brown roux. Add the green onions, yellow onion, and garlic, and continue cooking over low heat until soft, 15 minutes. Add the tomato sauce and cook for 5 minutes, stirring frequently.

Add the water, bay leaves, and thyme. Bring to a boil, then lower the heat so the liquid simmers. Add the chicken to the pot and simmer for 15 minutes. Lay the okra across the top of the chicken. Continue cooking for about 30 minutes, or until both the chicken and the okra are tender. Stir lightly with a fork to avoid breaking the okra. Remove the bay leaves. Season with salt and pepper and serve over rice or noodles. ❧

Poor Al's Fried Turkey

THE TIMES-PICAYUNE published some of the first-ever fried turkey recipes in print, and has continued to publish many over the years. In November 1992, food editor Dale Curry wrote, "Even when it's not Thanksgiving, the most-requested recipe from *The Times-Picayune*'s files is that for deep-fried turkey."

In 1984, before many New Orleanians had heard of this Cajun-style dish, we published a recipe from Jim Chehardy with pictures of the hotel manager (later a restaurateur) hauling a lassoed twenty-five-pound turkey out of a crawfish-boiling pot filled with ten gallons of boiling peanut oil. We showed pictures of the hypodermic needle for horses used to shoot the turkey with crab boil, and the propane burner that fueled the fire to crisp Tom Turkey in less than two hours.

One cook tried the recipe under a carport and set his house on fire. The evening television news on Thanksgiving spotlighted the angry cook, flames raging from the house behind him.

From then on, the recipe was always printed with appropriate warnings, such as *Do not attempt to fry the bird in your kitchen or under a carport*. This recipe is from Marcelle Bienvenu's column. You can easily halve the recipe and fry one turkey instead of two.

These days you can buy all kinds of turkey-frying rigs in all sizes, from ten gallons and up. Some even have a hypodermic needle to inject the turkey and a thermometer for the oil. At the very least you need the pot, a fry basket, and a lid.

{MAKES 20 TO 24 SERVINGS}

2 (10- to 12-pound) turkeys

1 large onion, minced

8 cloves garlic, peeled

½ cup chopped peppers, such as green bell peppers, jalapeños, mild bananas, or a combination

¼ cup salt

¼ cup cayenne pepper

About 10 gallons peanut oil

Rinse the turkeys with cool water and pat dry with paper towels. Leave the skin flap at the neck intact.

In a small mixing bowl, combine the onion, garlic, peppers, 2 tablespoons of the salt, and 2 tablespoons of the cayenne.

With a sharp boning knife, make slits about 3 inches long and 1 inch deep in the breasts and upper thighs of the turkeys and stuff the onion mixture into the slits with your fingers. (You may want to use plastic gloves for this.) Pack it in well. Season the outside of the turkey with the remaining 2 tablespoons salt and 2 tablespoons cayenne, rubbing well. Place the turkeys in large plastic bags and refrigerate for 8 to 12 hours.

Remove the turkeys from the refrigerator and set them aside for about 30 minutes. Pour in oil to fill the turkey fryer about three-fourths full. Turn on the heat. When the oil is between 350 and 360 degrees F, grab a turkey by the neck flap and gently and carefully submerge it in the hot oil. Be careful—the hot grease may overflow and splatter. Cover the pot. Turn the turkey every 10 minutes, using long-handled forks. It will take 45 minutes to 1 hour to cook. When the legs begin to spread open and an instant-read meat thermometer reaches 170 to 180 degrees F when inserted in the thickest part of the thigh, the turkey is done.

Carefully lift the basket out of the hot oil. You can insert a broomstick through the handles and have two strong people lift the basket out of the pot. Using a long-handled fork, transfer the turkey to a large brown paper bag and let stand for about 15 minutes before carving. Repeat the process with the second turkey. ❧

Lemon and Garlic Chicken

CHRIS KERAGEORGIOU WAS born into poverty in a tiny port town near Marseilles. He was part of the French underground during World War II, traveled the world as a merchant mariner, and worked as a waiter in New Orleans before he opened his own French country restaurant, La Provence, on the north shore of Lake Pontchartrain. There, where Kerageorgiou cooked for more than thirty years, his quail gumbo, cod brandade, eggplant flan, lamb à la Grecque, braised rabbit, and other dishes won him thousands of devoted fans. They mourned his passing in 2007. This recipe is from the cookbook that Kerageorgiou and a chef pal, Goffredo Fraccaro, published in 1992, *Cooking with Chris and Goffredo: Louisiana and Mediterranean Cuisine.*

{MAKES 4 SERVINGS}

4 (3- to 4-ounce) boneless, skinless chicken
    breast halves

Juice of 1 lemon

2 tablespoons olive oil

10 cloves garlic, peeled and bruised

½ teaspoon dried oregano leaves

6 tablespoons dry white wine

Salt

Black pepper

Rinse the chicken with cold water, then pat dry. Put the chicken in a medium bowl. Combine the lemon juice, 1 tablespoon of the olive oil, the garlic, and oregano, and pour over the chicken. Cover the bowl and marinate in the refrigerator for at least 1 hour.

Heat the remaining 1 tablespoon of olive oil in a large skillet over medium-high heat. Lay the chicken in the hot oil. Sauté for 2 to 3 minutes on each side, or until the chicken is cooked through. Add the wine, marinade, and salt and pepper to taste; then cover the skillet and cook for 3 minutes.

Uncover the pan. Remove the chicken and keep it warm. Continue cooking the sauce, reducing it to the desired consistency. Place the chicken on a serving dish, apply the sauce, and serve. ❧

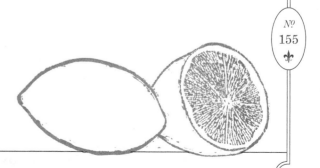

Leon Soniat's Marinated Fried Chicken

L.E.P. FROM JEFFERSON wrote, "I had a chicken recipe that Mr. Leon Soniat had put in the paper in either the late '70s or early '80s. I always kept it in a cookbook that we rarely used except for the above recipe. I remember that the chicken was marinated overnight [and] that the chicken came out really good."

The late Leon Soniat wrote a cooking column for *The Times-Picayune* for years, and his two cookbooks containing those recipes are still popular sellers. Serve this garlicky fried chicken with tossed salad and French bread or potatoes to round out the meal.

{MAKES 4 SERVINGS}

6 cloves garlic, minced
Dash of salt, plus ½ teaspoon
2 large eggs, well beaten
2 tablespoons olive oil
1 (3-pound) fryer chicken, cut into serving pieces
½ teaspoon black pepper
¼ teaspoon cayenne pepper
1 cup all-purpose flour
1 cup vegetable oil or shortening

In a small dish, mix the garlic with a dash of salt and mash with a fork. In a bowl large enough to hold the chicken pieces, mix the eggs, garlic mixture, and olive oil. Submerge the chicken pieces in the egg mixture, cover, and marinate in the refrigerator for 4 to 8 hours, turning occasionally.

Mix the ½ teaspoon salt, black pepper, cayenne, and flour in a shallow bowl or pie plate. After the chicken has marinated, remove it from the egg mixture and roll it in the seasoned flour.

Heat the oil in a heavy skillet over medium heat. Fry the chicken until golden brown on all sides. ✧

Maria's Creamed Chicken

A READER FONDLY remembered a dish called Maria's Creamed Chicken from Myriam Guidroz's column. She said it was one of those dishes that just made you feel good. We found it and agree that it's a dish to enjoy. In her column, Guidroz wrote, "Try it on a day when you want something good but not too rich or fancy—a grandmotherly sort of meal." She explained that Maria came to cook for her family when Guidroz was nine months old. "Some months later," she said, "my first complete sentence was 'More, please, this is good.'"

{MAKES 4 SERVINGS}

1 (3-pound) fryer chicken

3 to 4 tablespoons butter

Salt

Black pepper

2 medium onions, coarsely chopped

4 carrots, peeled and cut into 2-inch pieces

Pinch of thyme leaves

1 bay leaf

About 2 cups chicken stock or broth

2 tablespoons all-purpose flour

About ½ cup heavy cream

1 to 2 teaspoons fresh lemon juice

Hot parsleyed potatotes, rice, or noodles for serving

Cut up the chicken into serving pieces, pulling off as much fat as possible. Melt just enough butter to film the bottom of a large heavy pot, such as a Dutch oven. Add the chicken pieces, including the bony parts, such as the neck, back, and wings, which will flavor the sauce.

Season lightly with salt (the stock added later may already be salty) and pepper to taste. Cook over very low heat, turning the pieces of chicken frequently, until they are a very pale gold. Add the chopped onions, the carrots, thyme and bay leaf. Pour in just enough stock to come about halfway up the chicken and vegetables. Cover the pot, putting the lid at a slant so some of the liquid can evaporate. Cook until the pieces of chicken are very tender, but not falling off the bones, about 30 to 40 minutes.

Remove the pieces of chicken from the pot, discarding the bony parts and the skin that can be pulled off easily. Discard the bay leaf. There should be about 1½ cups of an almost syrupy sauce at the bottom of the pot. If there is more, boil it, uncovered to reduce. Or add a little more chicken stock if necessary.

In a small bowl or cup, mix the flour and cream into a thin paste. Add to the chicken juices, stirring hard, and simmer, uncovered, for about 10 minutes. If the sauce seems too thick, add a little more cream or chicken broth. Squeeze in a little lemon juice. Taste and correct the seasoning as needed. Return the chicken pieces to the sauce and heat them through.

Serve with parsleyed potatoes, rice, or noodles, as your fancy strikes you. ❧

Smothered Chicken

SMOTHERING IS A favorite down-home Southern technique similar to braising. The idea is to cook something in liquid in a covered pot until it falls apart in tender pieces. Vegetables are always involved. This is Justin Wilson's recipe, which he created for Baumer Foods. The recipe was included in a 1995 newspaper story about the regional foods featured at the annual Louisiana Foodservice and Hospitality Exposition in New Orleans.

Justin E. "Papa Justin" Wilson, a safety engineer, was a native of Roseland who became internationally known for his humor and cooking shows on local public television. He died on September 5, 2001, at the age of eighty-seven.

{MAKES 4 TO 6 SERVINGS}

1 (2- to 3-pound) chicken, cut into serving pieces
2 tablespoons soy sauce
Salt
Cayenne pepper
3 to 4 drops hot sauce
2 tablespoons vegetable oil
2 cups chopped onions
½ cup chopped green bell peppers
½ cup chopped fresh parsley
1 cup dry white wine
2 teaspoons chopped garlic
Hot cooked rice for serving

Rinse the chicken well, pat dry, and season with soy sauce, and salt, cayenne, and hot sauce to taste. Set aside.

In a large deep skillet, heat the oil. Sauté the onions, bell peppers, and parsley over medium-high heat until the onions are translucent. Add the wine and stir. Add the garlic and stir, and then add the chicken. Mix everything together and lower the heat to medium. Cover and cook for at least 2 hours, stirring occasionally. The chicken should be so tender that it falls apart. Serve over cooked rice. 🌶

Poulet aux Fines Herbes

THERE WERE SEVERAL requests for chicken with garlic and herbs. This one, published in *The Times-Picayune* in 1993, should fill the bill. It is another gem from the late Myriam Guidroz, a columnist for the newspaper.

The herb-butter mixture is pushed under the skin of the chicken, flavoring the meat as it roasts. You can stuff chicken breast parts or the breast of a whole chicken.

{MAKES 4 SERVINGS}

1 (3-pound) fryer chicken, or 4 large chicken breast halves with bones in and skin on

4 tablespoons butter, softened

1 to 2 cloves garlic

¼ cup chopped fresh parsley

1 to 2 teaspoons chopped fresh (or a pinch of dried) tarragon, rosemary, or basil

Salt

Black pepper

Olive or salad oil for brushing the chicken

1 cup water or cream (optional)

Rinse the chicken and pat it dry. In a small bowl, mix the butter, garlic, and chopped herbs into a paste. Season with a little salt and pepper.

With your fingers, loosen the skin from the meat on each side of the breast bone on a whole chicken, or, on each chicken breast. On a whole chicken, push half the herb-butter mixture on each side of the breastbone and, with your fingertips, press on the skin to spread the stuffing evenly all over the meat, including the tops of the drumsticks and thighs. Salt and pepper the chicken inside and out; tie the legs together and fold the wings under. Or, divide the herb-butter mixture in four, insert it under the skin of each breast, and sprinkle the chicken with salt and pepper.

Preheat the oven to 375 degrees F. Lightly oil a baking dish just large enough to hold the chicken. Place the whole chicken in it or arrange the pieces close together in one layer. Brush the skin with oil and sprinkle with salt and pepper.

Bake for about 1 hour for a whole chicken, or 30 to 40 minutes for the pieces, or until the chicken is golden and the juices run clear when it is pierced deeply in the thickest part.

Remove the chicken from the pan and keep warm in the turned-off oven. Make a gravy by adding the water or cream to the caramelized juices in the pan. Stir and scrape until the juices dissolve in the liquid (they will thicken if using cream), then pour over the chicken, and serve. ❧

Poulet Blanc

WE RECEIVED A request from L.P., who wanted the recipe for Poulet Blanc (white chicken) from the late Leon Soniat, a former columnist for *The Times-Picayune*.

"I remember the recipe," L.P. wrote, "but unfortunately not all the ingredients. However, I do remember the chicken was fried in butter and the shallots were sautéed and flour was added, and then milk, Tabasco, salt and pepper and all were simmered until the sauce thickened, then you added nutmeg and this was served over noodles or toast. Gee . . . for an old gal, the memory's better than I thought!" P.F. of New Orleans was kind enough to send in the recipe for her.

{MAKES 4 TO 6 SERVINGS}

6 boneless chicken breast halves, with skin on

¼ cup olive oil

3 cloves garlic, minced

2 tablespoons fresh lemon juice

½ teaspoon dried thyme leaves

1¼ teaspoon salt

½ cup (1 stick) butter

4 shallots, finely chopped

5 tablespoons all-purpose flour

3 cups whole milk

Black pepper

2 dashes of Tabasco sauce

Pinch of ground nutmeg

Hot cooked noodles or toast for serving

Place each breast between two pieces of wax paper. With the flat side of a cleaver or with a meat pounder, pound the meat hard until it spreads out and is almost double in size. Slice the flattened breasts into strips.

In a large mixing bowl, combine 3 tablespoons of the olive oil, the garlic, lemon juice, thyme, and 1 teaspoon of the salt. Stir a few times. Marinate the chicken strips in this mixture in the refrigerator for 1 hour.

After the meat has been marinated, melt the butter in a heavy skillet. Add the remaining 1 tablespoon of olive oil, and fry the strips of chicken over medium-high heat for 2 minutes on each side. (Do not overcook, as chicken breasts will get a little rubbery if cooked too long.)

Remove the chicken and add the shallots to the pan. Sauté until tender. Reduce the heat to medium, add the flour, and mix well. Cook for 4 minutes, stirring constantly. Add the milk slowly, stirring all the while and mixing well. Season with the remaining ¼ teaspoon of salt and the pepper to taste, and add the Tabasco. When the milk begins to simmer, return the chicken to the pan and simmer slowly for a few minutes, until the sauce is thickened and the chicken is heated through. Add the nutmeg, stir, and the dish is ready.

Serve over noodles or slices of toast. ❧

Ultimate Turkey Poulette à La Roosevelt

BERNICE S. PREIS was kind enough to provide this recipe from the late Myriam Guidroz, who was a food writer for *The States-Item* and then, when the papers merged, for *The Times-Picayune*, from 1967 until her death in 1994. She had many devoted readers.

This dish was a popular one at the old Roosevelt Hotel (later the Fairmont). A reader remembered it "being served on a sizzling steak platter. The toast was trimmed and there was a thin layer of ham over the turkey." This version of the recipe uses bacon instead of ham.

{MAKES 2 TO 4 SERVINGS}

½ cup (1 stick) butter

¼ cup all-purpose flour

1 pint heavy cream

1 bunch green onions, chopped (white and green parts)

6 mushrooms

Salt

Black pepper

4 to 8 slices toast (2 per serving)

4 to 12 strips bacon (2 or 3 strips per serving)

4 to 12 slices cooked turkey or chicken (2 to 3 slices per serving)

Grated Parmesan cheese

Preheat the oven to 350 degees F, or preheat the broiler.

Melt 4 tablespoons of the butter in a saucepan over low heat. Add the flour, stirring constantly until well blended, but being very careful not to let it brown. Add the cream, still stirring, and be sure all is well blended and there are no lumps. Simmer for 3 to 4 minutes.

In another saucepan, melt the remaining 4 tablespoons of butter and sauté the onions and mushrooms over medium heat until the onions are transparent, but not brown. Add this to the cream mixture. Correct the seasoning with salt and pepper.

Place the toast in a shallow baking pan and top each slice with 2 or 3 strips of bacon, then 2 or 3 slices of turkey or chicken. Cover entirely with the cream sauce. Sprinkle with Parmesan cheese and bake or broil until golden brown. Serve on individual plates or on one large platter.

BEEF, PORK & VEAL

Although New Orleans and its Mississippi Gulf Coast neighbors are located on the rim of the Gulf of Mexico, from which comes myriad seafood, the locals do enjoy meat in its various forms. Marcelle Bienvenu, for example, has a penchant for pork. Her mother, who came from a farming family, had access to fresh pork when Marcelle was growing up, so they often had pork smothered with home-grown turnips (page 177)— a country Cajun meal.

In New Orleans, the urban counterpart might be Osso Bucco (page 176), an Italian favorite made with veal shanks braised long and slow and accompanied by gremolata (minced parsely, lemon zest, and garlic). Calves liver (page 172) is enjoyed both in rural areas and in the city.

One of the recipes in this chapter is for Beef Daube Glace (page 166), an old Creole delicacy, which we felt should be included if for no other reason than to preserve a culinary tradition. Marcelle's fraternal grandmother made this dish during the Christmas holidays to give as gifts, which makes sense once you realize that it is a delicious but arduous dish to prepare. Marcelle learned to make daube from her Aunt Jenny many years ago, and it took them the better part of a day.

Beef, Pork & Veal

Beef Daube Glace

THE NEW ORLEANS Creoles of the eighteenth and nineteenth centuries observed Christmas Eve by attending midnight Mass at St. Louis Cathedral, followed by *la réveillon,* a meal served at their homes after the church service.

The tradition ceased for a time but was revived in the 1980s, when several New Orleans restaurants began hosting *réveillon* dinners during the holiday season. The special menus have become popular with both the locals and visitors, and continue to be an important part of the Christmas celebrations around the city.

Beef Daube Glace was one of the traditional dishes served by the old Creoles at their *réveillons.* A daube glace is a pot roast that is simmered until meltingly tender and then jellied in a terrine. In the early 1990s, Mr. B's Bistro in the French Quarter offered it on its *réveillon* menu. Gerard Maras, then the chef at the restaurant, and Ralph Brennan, the owner, did some research and developed a recipe. "I used a lot of old sources like the *Picayune's [Creole] Cook Book,* any old frail cookbooks," Maras said. "I looked for common denominators. I talked to people like Ralph's mom and dad, who've eaten it for years and years. We went back to the original as much as possible."

Maras's recipe calls for a full brisket because it's the easiest way to buy it. It makes one large or two small pans of daube glace. Serve it sliced with French bread as an appetizer or hors d'oeuvre, or at a luncheon or tea, as the Creoles did.

"You can eat it like a pâté with sour pickles and sprinkle vinegar on it or salt and pepper," Maras said. "Some people make a sandwich out of it. It's not hard to make. It's time-consuming, but it's worth the time if you enjoy that type of food."

{MAKES 8 TO 10 ENTRÉE OR 50 APPETIZER SERVINGS}

1 (3-pound) beef brisket

2 tablespoons Creole seasoning, such as Tony Chachere's or Zatarain's

6 tablespoons butter

4 stalks celery, chopped

2 medium onions, diced

2 carrots, peeled and diced

4 bay leaves

½ teaspoon red pepper flakes

1 tablespoon hot sauce

⅓ cup Worcestershire sauce

6 cups veal or beef stock

Salt

1 cup canned plum tomatoes with their juice

6 cloves garlic, crushed and chopped

2 tablespoons gelatin, dissolved in ½ cup water

Preheat the oven to 325 degrees F.

Rub the beef with the Creole seasoning. Melt the butter in a heavy braising pan, such as a Dutch oven over medium heat. Add the beef, and brown well on all sides. Add the celery, onions, carrots, bay leaves, red pepper flakes, hot sauce, and Worcestershire sauce, and cook for 5 minutes. Then add the stock, salt to taste, tomatoes, and garlic. Bring to a simmer on the stove top.

Cover the braising pan and place in the oven. Cook, turning the beef occasionally, for about 3 hours, until the beef is very tender, almost falling apart. Remove the meat from the pan, cut into small pieces, and set aside in a bowl. Discard the bay leaves. Remove most of the vegetables, and add to the meat. Strain the remaining broth and transfer to a saucepan. Over high heat, reduce the liquid to 3½ cups. Adjust the seasoning and stir in the dissolved gelatin. Put the meat and vegetables in an 11- or 12-inch terrine or a 5-by-10-inch loaf pan, or two small 5¾-by-3¼-inch loaf pans and cover with the broth. Place in the refrigerator and let the daube set up for 24 hours. To serve, slice the daube ½ inch thick and serve with crusty French bread and butter. ⚜

Beef Kabobs

SEVERAL READERS REQUESTED this recipe, which is easy to prepare for a summertime meal. One of Marcelle Bienvenu's columns featured this creation by her friend Percy Guidry, an extraordinary cook from Lafayette.

{MAKES ABOUT 4 SERVINGS (8 KABOBS)}

1 (1½-pound) sirloin steak, about 1 inch thick, cut into 2-inch cubes

1 tablespoon Creole seasoning

2 tablespoons balsamic vinegar

1 tablespoon Dijon or Creole mustard, homemade (page 341) or storebought

2 tablespoons Worcestershire sauce

1 teaspoon fresh lemon juice

1 teaspoon garlic powder

1 large red bell pepper, cut into 2-inch pieces

1 large green bell pepper, cut into 2-inch pieces

1 large purple onion, cut into 2-inch pieces

Put the meat in a shallow bowl. Combine the seasoning, vinegar, mustard, Worcestershire sauce, lemon juice, and garlic powder in a small bowl and then pour it over the meat. Cover and refrigerate for at least 2 hours.

Prepare a fire in a charcoal grill or preheat a gas grill.

Remove the meat from the marinade. Thread the meat and vegetables alternately on eight skewers, about ½ inch apart, to prevent the meat and vegetables from spinning. Place the kabobs on the heated grill, close the lid, and cook for 10 minutes. Turn, close the lid, and cook for another 10 minutes. Turn again, close the lid, and cook for 15 minutes more (a total of about 35 minutes) for well-done meat. Cook for less time if you like it medium-rare. ❧

Bruccioloni with Italian Sauce

SOME VERSIONS OF bruccioloni, or rolled stuffed meat, are filled with a mix of ground beef, veal, and pork. Others feature sweet Italian or hot sausage, or pine nuts and raisins, or all three. Doris Anderman Landry's bruccioloni is made with thin slices of veal or beef wrapped around sliced hard-boiled eggs and a blend of Parmesan, fresh garlic and parsley, bread crumbs, and olive oil. Tied securely with kitchen twine to keep in the stuffing, the meat rolls are simmered until tender in a pot of rich red gravy.

Landry, a resident of Metairie, prepares the dish several times a year for special occasions. She always serves it on the day it's made, presenting the sliced bruccioloni atop angel hair pasta reddened with the gravy. The remaining gravy gets passed at the table. Landry prefers to use veal, but you can use beef if you like. If you do, have your butcher tenderize it.

{MAKES 6 SERVINGS}

1 cup seasoned Italian bread crumbs

⅔ cup Parmesan cheese

7 cloves garlic, chopped

2 tablespoons chopped fresh parsley

⅔ cup olive oil

2 (1-pound pieces) veal top round or beef top round, ¼ inch thick and about 8 inches long

2 hard-boiled eggs, sliced

2 teaspoons salt, or to taste

½ teaspoon black pepper, or to taste

4 tablespoons butter

1 large onion, chopped

2 (6-ounce) cans tomato paste

¼ cup sugar

1 (14- to 16-ounce) can whole tomatoes, drained and chopped, and juice reserved

About 6 cups water

3 bay leaves

1 teaspoon Italian seasoning

3 sprigs fresh basil (optional)

2 beef bouillon cubes

Hot cooked pasta for serving, preferably angel hair

In a medium mixing bowl, combine the bread crumbs, ⅓ cup of the Parmesan, 2 cloves of the chopped garlic, the parsley, and ⅓ cup of the olive oil, blending well. Spread half the bread crumb mixture on each piece of veal, and distribute the egg slices over the stuffing.

Roll up each slice of veal snugly around the stuffing, tucking in the sides as you roll in order to keep in the stuffing, and tie securely with kitchen twine. Season the rolls with the salt and pepper.

In a large (about 7-quart) heavy saucepan, heat the remaining ⅓ cup of olive oil with the butter over medium heat until the butter melts. Add the bruccioloni and brown all over, about 8 minutes. Transfer the bruccioloni to a plate, and add the onions to the same saucepan. Cook over medium-low heat until limp and golden, about 5 minutes. Reduce the heat to low. Add the remaining 5 cloves chopped garlic and cook for 5 minutes. Stir in the tomato paste and sugar, raise the heat to medium-low, and cook for 5 minutes, stirring often. Add the chopped tomatoes, and cook for 5 minutes more.

Combine the reserved juice from the canned tomatoes with enough water to equal 6 cups. Add this liquid to the pan and bring to a boil. Stir in the bay leaves, Italian seasoning, basil (if using), bouillon cubes, and the remaining ⅓ cup Parmesan, and season with salt and pepper. Then add the bruccioloni. Cover and simmer until the meat is fork-tender, about 1 hour, thinning the sauce with water if necessary.

Transfer the bruccioloni to a cutting board. Cut off the kitchen twine, and slice each roll crosswise into three servings. Toss the pasta with some of the sauce and top with the bruccioloni. Pass the remaining sauce at the table. ❧

Calves Liver with Onions

CALVES LIVER COOKED with onions, and sometimes with bacon, was a longtime favorite at several local restaurants. Many people fondly recall the dish served at old Delmonico on St. Charles Avenue when Angie Brown and Rose Dietrich operated the restaurant. It was sometimes served as an open-faced sandwich, accompanied by French fries or the vegetable of the day.

This version, which is in Marcelle's book *Who's Your Mama, Are You Catholic, and Can You Make a Roux?* is from her family, who liked their liver served over a bed of creamy grits.

{MAKES 6 SERVINGS}

¼ cup cold bacon drippings

3 pounds calves liver, membrane removed

Salt

Cayenne pepper

2 large onions, thinly sliced

Hot cooked grits for serving

Spread the cold bacon drippings on the bottom of a large cast-iron skillet. Season the liver with salt and cayenne pepper to taste.

Add the liver to the cold drippings, then turn on the heat to medium-high. When the liver begins to brown, cook for a few more minutes, turning a couple of times, and add a few tablespoons of water and the sliced onions. Cook just until the onions wilt. (Do not overcook.) Slice the liver, and spoon the livers, onions, and gravy over the hot grits. Serve immediately. ❧

Creole Daube

In a 1997 *Times-Picayune* story about disappearing New Orleans dishes, Maureen Reed Detweiler, who has lived in Uptown most of her life, shared this family recipe for a classic home-cooked dish. Daube in New Orleans, as in France, is braised beef. The New Orleans version usually includes tomatoes, and is often served over spaghetti.

{MAKES 8 SERVINGS}

1 (4-pound) beef boneless rump or boneless chuck roast

4 cloves garlic, halved

Salt

Black pepper

6 tablespoons vegetable oil

¼ cup all-purpose flour

1½ cups chopped onions

1 cup chopped green bell peppers

2 cups chopped fresh or canned tomatoes

½ cup chopped fresh parsley

2 cups beef stock or water

Hot cooked rice or spaghetti for serving

Make 8 slits in the roast and insert half a garlic clove in each. Salt and pepper the roast.

Heat 2 tablespoons of the oil in a Dutch oven or another heavy pot with a lid and brown the roast well on both sides. Remove the meat and set aside.

Add the remaining ¼ cup of oil and the flour to the pot and stir over medium heat for 15 to 20 minutes to make a medium-dark roux. Add the onions and sauté until they begin to brown. Add the bell peppers, tomatoes, parsley, and stock, stir, then add the roast to the pot. Bring to a boil, cover, and simmer over low heat for 1½ hours. Check often and add more stock or water as needed. Slice the roast and serve with rice or spaghetti. ✒

Fair Grounds Corned Beef

AFTER A DEVASTATING fire at the New Orleans Fair Grounds in December 1994, *The Times-Picayune* featured an article about Pete deMarcay, then executive chef at the famed race track. After the fire, Chef deMarcay had to cook in a makeshift kitchen at the track. He shared his recipe for corned beef, a popular dish, especially on St. Patrick's Day. It was served in the clubhouse. People in New Orleans tend to have big St. Patrick's day parties, but the recipe is easy to cut in half if you wish.

{MAKES ABOUT 16 SERVINGS}

1 (10- to 12-pound) corned beef brisket

3 bay leaves

1 teaspoon ground ginger

1 teaspoon dill seed

10 whole cloves

1 tablespoon chopped red chiles, such as red jalapeños or cayennes

1 tablespoon whole black peppercorns

1 teaspoon ground mace

1 teaspoon ground cardamom

1 teaspoon mustard seeds

1 tablespoon ground coriander

½ teaspoon ground cinnamon

1 teaspoon ground allspice

¼ cup salt

Smothered cabbage for serving

Put the brisket in a heavy stockpot or soup pot and cover with water. Mix all the seasonings together except the salt. Put the seasonings in a cheesecloth bag, tie it closed, and add it to the water. Add the salt. Boil the brisket for 2½ to 3 hours. To test, stick a fork in the middle of the brisket; it should come out easily when done.

Let cool, then slice. Pour a little of the stock over the brisket for added flavor. Serve with your favorite smothered cabbage recipe. ❧

Kolb's Sauerbraten

A READER ASKED for a recipe from Kolb's, the German restaurant that operated from 1899 to 1994 on lower St. Charles Avenue. Another reader, J.C.J., found the recipe, and wrote that she always knew her mother's recipe-clipping habit would come in handy. J.C.J. said she was hoping to return to Metairie from her storm refuge in Covington.

"Mom loved to cook and always clipped recipes from the T-P through the years until she passed away in 2004," J.C.J. wrote. "The family home was drowned in Katrina but we were able to salvage more than we thought possible. We waited until things dried out more and about eight months after the storm we were able to retrieve many of the newspaper recipes that Mamma had so lovingly saved. Fortunately, she pasted them to index cards and put plastic sleeves over them, which helped protect them even more."

J.C.J. thought the Kolb's recipe looked so good that she fixed it for a New Year's party. "It came out great," she reported. "Very tasty and tender with a delicious gravy." It marinates for a week, so plan ahead.

{MAKES 8 TO 10 SERVINGS}

3 cups tarragon vinegar

4 cups water

½ cup sugar

¼ cup salt

4 bay leaves

12 whole cloves

½ teaspoon ground allspice

2 medium carrots, sliced

2 medium onions, sliced

1 green bell pepper, sliced

1 stalk celery, diced

¼ bunch parsley, chopped

1 (4-pound) beef bottom round roast

¼ cup vegetable oil

1 tablespoon all-purpose flour

1 tablespoon ground ginger

In a large mixing bowl, combine the vinegar, water, sugar, salt, bay leaves, cloves, allspice, carrots, onions, bell pepper, celery, and parsley. Whisk together to dissolve the sugar and salt. Put the beef in this marinade. Cover the bowl and refrigerate. Marinate the beef for a week, turning occasionally.

Remove the beef from the marinade (reserve the marinade) and wipe it dry with paper towels. Heat the oil in a heavy Dutch oven over medium-high heat, and sear the beef on all sides. Pour the marinade over the meat. Raise the heat, bring the mixture to a boil, then lower the heat and simmer, covered, until fork-tender, 2 to 3 hours.

Remove the meat from the pot and keep warm. Strain the cooking liquid and return it to the pot. Combine the flour and ginger and whisk into the liquid to thicken it. Cook, stirring, for a few minutes. Season with additional vinegar and/or sugar if needed to get the right sweet-sour taste to the gravy. Slice the meat and serve covered with the hot gravy. 🐎

Osso Bucco

Osso Bucco—WHICH literally means "bone for the mouth"—is an Italian dish made of veal shanks braised with olive oil, wine, stock, onions, and lots of other good things. Because of the large Sicilian population in New Orleans, this delectable dish often appears on many Italian restaurant menus in the city. It's usually brought to the table with cocktail forks for diners to dig out the marrow in the bones. Spectacular!

Traditionally, Osso Bucco is garnished with gremolata, a combination of minced parsley, lemon zest, and garlic. Risotto is the preferred accompaniment in Italy, but in New Orleans, pasta is often the side of choice.

{MAKES 4 TO 6 SERVINGS}

4 pounds veal shanks, cut into 2-inch pieces (have your butcher do this for you)

¼ cup all-purpose flour

Salt

Black pepper

Cayenne pepper

3 tablespoons butter

3 tablespoons olive oil

2 cups chopped onions

½ cup finely chopped celery

2 medium carrots, peeled and sliced into ¾-inch rounds

2 tablespoons minced garlic

1 cup dry white wine

¾ cup beef stock or broth

¾ cup chicken stock or broth

1½ cups canned crushed tomatoes with their juice

¼ cup chopped fresh basil, or 1 teaspoon dried (optional)

1 teaspoon dried rosemary leaves

GREMOLATA

2 tablespoons grated lemon zest

¼ cup minced fresh parsley

1 clove garlic, minced

Risotto or pasta for serving

Preheat the oven to 350 degrees F. Dredge the veal shanks in flour, shaking off the excess, and season them generously with the salt, black pepper, and cayenne.

In a large heavy skillet, melt the butter with the olive oil over medium-high heat. Brown the veal (you may have to do it in two batches), then transfer it to a large roasting pan. Add a little water to the skillet to deglaze, and then add the onions, celery, carrots, and garlic. Reduce the heat to medium and, stirring occasionally, cook for about 5 minutes, or until the vegetables are slightly soft.

Transfer the mixture to the roasting pan. Put the roasting pan over medium heat. Add the wine and cook for 1 minute. Add the beef and chicken stock, tomatoes, and herbs. Check the seasonings. You may want to add a little more salt, black pepper, and cayenne. Cover the roasting pan, and then bake for 1½ to 2 hours, or until the veal is very tender.

For the gremolata: Combine the lemon zest, parsley, and garlic.

When ready to serve, remove any fat that has risen to the surface of the gravy in the roasting pan. If you wish to thicken the gravy a bit more, cook it on top of the stove over high heat for 5 to 10 minutes, stirring occasionally. Serve the sauce over the veal, and garnish with the gremolata. Accompany with risotto or pasta. ❧

Pork Chops with Turnips

"MY NOMINEE FOR inclusion in the Post-K cookbook is from a [1996] column Marcelle Bienvenu did on smothered dishes. This one-dish meal is easy, the turnips are spicy, it's great with cornbread, and smells wonderful cooking on a cool evening. I would be grateful to have the recipe again," wrote Robin Wagner, who used to live in Lakeview, one of the areas most devastated by flooding.

{MAKES 8 SERVINGS}

8 pork chops, about ½ inch thick
    (about 3 pounds total)
Salt
Cayenne pepper
Black pepper
All-purpose flour for dusting
¼ cup vegetable oil
1 cup chopped onions
1 tablespoon minced garlic
6 medium turnips, peeled and coarsely chopped
About 1 cup water
Hot cooked rice for serving

Season the pork chops generously with salt, cayenne, and black pepper. Dust the chops lightly with flour.

Heat the oil in a large heavy pot over medium heat. Add the pork chops in batches and brown them evenly on both sides. Return the browned chops to the pan. Add the onions and garlic and cook until they are soft, about 5 minutes.

Add the turnips and cook, stirring often, until they are slightly soft, 3 to 4 minutes. Add the water, bring the mixture to a boil, then reduce the heat to medium-low. Cook until very tender, about 45 minutes, stirring occasionally, partially covered. If the mixture becomes dry, add more water. Adjust the seasonings and serve with rice.

Rabbit or Squirrel Sauce Piquant

COVINGTON RESIDENT COLLINS Christopher Dautreuil II shared this recipe with readers in 2000. He said he made it to feed crowds at hunting camps and for dinner parties at home. An avid sportsman, Dautreuil described the beauty of sunsets and sunrises from a duck blind in the marsh, which he compared to a religious experience.

{MAKES 4 SERVINGS}

1 cleaned wild rabbit, 1 domestic rabbit, or 1 chicken; or 4 cleaned squirrels, cut into serving pieces (see Note)

2 tablespoons light olive oil

1 tablespoon all-purpose flour

2 large onions, finely chopped

2 green bell peppers, finely chopped

4 stalks celery, finely chopped

2 cloves garlic, minced

2 bay leaves

Dash of ground sage

Cayenne pepper

1 (10-ounce) can Ro-Tel diced tomatoes and green chiles

2 tablespoons tomato paste

1 (4-ounce) can mushrooms, with their liquid

½ cup cooked sweet peas, drained and mashed

Salt

Small pinch of sugar

Hot cooked rice for serving

In a large dry Dutch oven over medium heat, sauté the rabbit until brown, 3 to 5 minutes per side. Remove from the pot and add the oil to the same pot, stirring thoroughly to loosen the browned bits. Add the flour and cook over medium heat until the roux turns medium brown, about 2 minutes, stirring frequently. Turn the heat to low and stir in the onions, bell peppers, celery, garlic, bay leaves, sage, and cayenne. Cover the pot and cook until the vegetables are soft and sticking to the pot a bit, about 30 minutes.

Add the tomatoes and tomato paste and cook for 10 minutes over medium heat, stirring frequently. Return the meat to the pot and simmer, covered, over low heat, until the meat is tender, about 1 hour, stirring occasionally. Add the mushrooms and their liquid and the peas. Season with salt and more cayenne to taste. Stir in the sugar and remove from the heat. Serve warm over rice.

NOTE: *If using wild game, soak it in whole milk overnight, refrigerated, turning once or twice.*

Rock's Grilled Baby Back Ribs

AFTER MARCELLE BIENVENU published her husband's recipe for baby back ribs in the newspaper, it became a favorite of our readers. Boiling the ribs in crab boil gives them a great flavor.

{MAKES ABOUT 4 SERVINGS}

1 bag Zatarain's Crawfish, Shrimp and Crab Boil seasoning mix

1 medium onion, quartered

2 lemons, halved

3 cloves garlic

2 racks baby back ribs (about 4 pounds total)

Olive oil for brushing ribs

1 tablespoon Creole seasoning

About 1 cup of your favorite barbecue sauce for brushing ribs

Put the Zatarain's bag, the onion, lemons, and garlic in a heavy pot, such as a Dutch oven, that is large enough to accommodate the ribs. Fill the pot two-thirds with water and bring to a boil. Add the ribs and cook at a boil for 20 minutes.

Prepare a medium-hot fire in a charcoal grill or preheat a gas grill. Transfer the ribs to a large platter to drain. Discard the crab boil bag and seasonings. Brush the ribs generously with olive oil and sprinkle with the Creole seasoning. Grill the ribs, turning twice, for 20 minutes. Remove from the grill and brush with barbecue sauce.

Lay the ribs on a cutting board, meat-side down, to cut into servings. Serve warm. ❧

Stuffed Pork Roast

MARCELLE ASSOCIATES A fond childhood Christmas memory with this recipe, which she shared in one of her columns. She wrote:

When we returned from the solemn and impressive Midnight Mass, we had our version of le réveillon, *an old New Orleans tradition of enjoying a meal together before going to bed to await the arrival of Papa Noël.*

Mama always had thinly sliced baked ham served with warm biscuits slathered with butter and dribbled with dark cane syrup. Tante Belle and Tante May poured their homemade cherry bounce in tiny pony glasses and everyone toasted the birth of Baby Jesus. Then it was off to bed.

But before Mama slipped under her pile of quilts, she shoved her huge roaster, with a large fresh pork roast, carefully stuffed with garlic, onions, and bell peppers, into the cavernous oven. It cooked while we slept.

I loved waking to the fragrance of that roast on Christmas morning! And no sooner than the first pot of coffee was made, there was always the appearance of Papa's best friend, Sheriff Charles Fuselier, Sr. A huge bear of a man, he arrived bearing gifts (a tin of pralines for Mama, a bottle of fine bourbon for Papa, and small gifts like coloring books, crayons, and tin soldiers for the children) and he embraced us in great hugs. The next best thing to the smell of the pork roast, as far as I was concerned, was Mr. Charlie's Old Spice aftershave! I knew then that the grand day of Christmas had indeed arrived!

{MAKES 12 TO 14 SERVINGS}

1 cup finely chopped onions
1 cup finely chopped green bell peppers
6 to 8 cloves garlic, thinly sliced

3 teaspoons salt
3 teaspoons cayenne pepper
1 teaspoon black pepper
1 (10- to 12-pound) fresh ham (pork) shank roast
Vegetable oil for rubbing roast
2 cups water
Hot cooked rice for serving

Preheat the oven to 450 degrees F.

Combine the onions, bell peppers, garlic, salt, cayenne pepper, and black pepper in a small bowl and mix well.

Set the roast on a large cutting board or platter. With a sharp boning knife, make 10 to 12 deep slits in the roast spaced several inches apart. Using your index finger, stuff the seasoning mixture into the slits, packing it in firmly. Season the outside of the roast generously with more salt and cayenne pepper. Rub the roast lightly with vegetable oil.

Place the roast in a heavy roasting pan and put it in the oven. When the bottom of the pan begins to sizzle, carefully add the water. Bake the roast until it browns evenly, 30 to 45 minutes. More water can be added if the pan becomes too dry. This will mix with the roast drippings and make a dark gravy, which you can use to baste the roast, and later pour over steamed rice.

When the meat is well browned, reduce the heat to 350 degrees F, cover with a lid or foil, and roast until the juices run clear and the meat is tender, or until an instant-read thermometer inserted into the roast registers 165 degrees F, 3 to 4 hours. Again, add more water if necessary to make gravy. Remove the roast from the oven and cool slightly before carving. Serve with rice.

Superior Rib Rack

"THIS RIB ROAST has always been my husband's favorite. We always have it for his birthday and a few other special occasions. But until I got these instructions from Marcelle's column, it was always hit or miss as to how it would turn out. This method works PERECTLY!" wrote Maureen Detweiler, who is known in New Orleans for her devotion to the local cuisine.

Marcelle featured this recipe in a column in 1993. She credited her friend Milou Roy for the roasting formula of 5 minutes per pound. It works if you want perfectly medium-rare ribs, but if you want them to be cooked to medium, use a meat thermometer. Although cookbooks differ on doneness temperatures, use these for this recipe: medium-rare, 125 degrees F; medium, 145 degrees, and well-done, 155 degrees.

{MAKES 10 TO 12 SERVINGS}

1 (10- to 15-pound) boned prime beef rib rack, trimmed
Vegetable or olive oil for rubbing roast
Salt
Cayenne pepper
Black pepper

Preheat the oven to 500 degrees F. Rub the rack with the oil and season generously with the salt, cayenne, and black pepper. Place the meat on a rack in a roasting pan and place it on the bottom shelf of the oven.

Roast for 5 minutes per pound. For example, if your rack weighs 10 pounds, leave it in for 50 minutes. Then turn off the oven and *do not open the door.* Let the rack remain in the oven for an additional 1 hour and 10 minutes. The total time in the oven should be 2 hours. So if the rack weighs 15 pounds, roast it for 1 hour and 15 minutes and leave in a turned-off oven for another 45 minutes. This will give you a perfect medium-rare roast. ❧

Nanny's Dill Pot Roast with Sour Cream Gravy

As word slowly filtered out to displaced citizens about *The Times-Picayune*'s recipe replacement project, e-mail arrived from all over the country. The request for this recipe came from a former New Orleanian who was living in Tennessee. She treasured the recipe, and so did the person who originally gave it to us, Susan Fortier Breedlove. Breedlove found this in the files of her late grandmother, Ann Bradoc Spring, whose heritage was Czech.

{MAKES 8 TO 10 SERVINGS}

1 tablespoon vegetable oil

1 (3- to 3½-pound) boneless chuck or rump roast

1 tablespoon salt

3 teaspoons dried dill weed

¼ teaspoon pepper

1 tablespoon distilled white vinegar

1 (14-ounce) can beef broth

3 tablespoons all-purpose flour dissolved in ¼ cup cool water

1 cup sour cream

Heat the oil in a Dutch oven, and brown the meat on all sides over medium-high heat. Sprinkle the meat with the salt, 2 teaspoons of the dill weed, and the pepper. Add ½ cup water and the vinegar to the bottom of the pan. Cover and cook over low heat until fork-tender, about 2 hours, adding the beef broth after 1 hour of cooking.

Transfer the roast to a serving platter and set aside. Raise the heat under the roasting pan to high, and gradually add the dissolved flour mixture to the pan drippings, stirring until smooth. Add the remaining 1 teaspoon of dill weed and simmer for 10 minutes, stirring frequently. Reduce the heat to low and gradually add the sour cream, gently stirring it in. Add more salt if needed. Spoon a little gravy over the roast, and pass the remaining gravy at the table. ❧

Natchitoches Meat Pies

In 2000, Ann Cloutier shared her recipe for a regional favorite, Natchitoches Meat Pies, given to her by her mother-in-law, Mary Cloutier, who made thousands of them. Mary Cloutier's perfected formula for these deep-fried meat pies was chosen to be the lead recipe in the *Cane River Cuisine* cookbook, published by the Service League of Natchitoches in 1974.

The only change Ann Cloutier made in her mother-in-law's recipe was to add garlic. Because the dough is quite sticky, she finds it's easier to roll out small portions at a time on a generously floured board. Cloutier normally triples the pie recipe to fill up the freezer. The pies can be served for dinner with a salad, and they are also popular as snacks, including at festivals. Although Cloutier usually makes 5-inch pies, you can also make smaller ones to serve as an appetizer.

{MAKES 26 TO 28 (5-TO 5½-INCH) PIES}

FILLING

1½ pounds ground beef

1½ pounds ground pork

1 cup chopped green onions (white and green parts)

2 or 3 cloves garlic, chopped

1 tablespoon salt

1 teaspoon coarsely ground black pepper

1 teaspoon red pepper flakes

½ teaspoon cayenne pepper

⅓ cup all-purpose flour

CRUST

About 2⅔ cups self-rising flour

⅓ heaping cup solid vegetable shortening, such as Crisco

1 large egg, beaten

¾ cup milk

Vegetable oil for deep-frying

For the filling: Combine the meats, green onions, garlic, salt, black pepper, red pepper flakes, and cayenne in a large Dutch oven. Cook over medium heat, stirring often, until the meat is no longer red and breaks up into tiny bits, about 15 minutes. Do not overcook.

Sift the flour over the meat mixture, and mix it in thoroughly. Remove from the heat. Put the meat in a large colander to drain off the liquid, and cool to room temperature.

For the crust: Sift the flour into a large bowl, and use a pastry cutter or two forks to cut the shortening into it until the bits of shortening are the size of peas. Mix in the egg and milk. Form dough into a ball (it will be very sticky).

Flour a board and a rolling pin heavily. Roll out about one-third of the dough at a time on the board to about ⅛-inch thickness, adding only enough flour to keep the dough from sticking. Cut the dough into 5- to 5½-inch circles, using the top of an old coffee pot or another round, sharp-edged dish or utensil of the correct size; or use a dumpling-maker form. (For cocktail-size pies, use a biscuit cutter.) Cut out all the dough circles before filling any, placing the circles on a cookie sheet. If it's necessary to stack them, place wax paper between them.

To assemble each pie, place a heaping tablespoon of filling on one side of a pastry round. (Fill cocktail-size pies with 1 teaspoon of filling.) Dampen the edge of the pastry with a fingertip dipped in water. Fold the pastry over the meat and crimp with the tines of a fork dipped in water, pressing the edges to seal. Prick each pie twice on the top with the tines of the fork. (At this point you can freeze the pies in zipper-top plastic bags. Do not thaw before frying.)

To serve, fry the pies in the vegetable oil in a deep-fat fryer on high until dark golden brown, about 2 minutes. Or heat the oil in a large pot to 350 degrees F before adding the pies. Drain on absorbent paper and keep warm in a low oven until ready to serve. ❧

Manuel's Hot Tamales

From her new home in Houston, K.W. wrote, "I too lost all my recipe books in Katrina. Fortunately, I typed all my clipped recipes and saved them on my computer at work. Several people have been looking for a recipe for Manuel's Hot Tamales.

"My mother found this recipe in the T-P in the 1970s and it has been a family favorite. I passed it along to a good friend who swears it's the easiest tamale recipe she has ever made, since it does not require making a corn meal paste but just rolling the meat in dry corn meal, which makes a perfectly even coating."

Manuel's was a popular local brand of Delta-style tamales. The family-owned company, located on Carrollton Avenue, was wiped out by the flooding after the levees failed, and never reopened.

{MAKES 85 TO 100 TAMALES}

SAUCE
1 (8-ounce) can tomato sauce
¼ teaspoon ground cumin
¼ cup chili powder
Salt
Black pepper

TAMALES
2 teaspoons garlic powder
2 teaspoons cayenne pepper
½ teaspoon black pepper
4 teaspoons salt
½ cup chili powder
1 (8-ounce) can tomato sauce
4 medium onions
½ cup water
¼ teaspoon ground cumin or cumin seed
3 pounds ground beef
1½ cups of yellow cornmeal
100 tamale papers

For the sauce: In a medium saucepan, combine the tomato sauce, cumin, chili powder, and the salt and pepper to taste. Bring to a boil, remove from the heat, and set aside.

For the tamales: Put all the tamale ingredients except the ground meat and cornmeal in a food processor and process until the onions are chopped very finely. Put the meat in a large baking pan and pour the tomato and spice mixture on top. By hand, mix very well.

Spread out the cornmeal in a saucer or shallow dish. Sink the tamale papers individually in a large bowl of water. Put one in, sink it, and add another until all are submerged. Set aside.

On a work surface, roll about 1 tablespoon of the tamale mixture at a time into an oblong shape, and then roll it in the cornmeal. Wrap each one in a tamale paper. Continue in this way until you've used up all of the tamale mixture.

Stack the tamales in a large roasting pan in layers, placing each layer perpendicular to the one below. Add enough water to cover the tamales. Pour the prepared sauce over the mixture, and cover.

Put the roasting pan across two burners on top of the stove. Simmer for 2 hours with the cover on. Check the contents occasionally. You may have to add more water to keep the tamales covered. ❧

Tamales with Green Salsa

J.C., ORIGINALLY FROM Chalmette, and now living in Thibodaux, wrote us, "A couple of years ago, I clipped a recipe for tamales with green salsa from *The Times-Picayune*. My whole family and friends enjoyed them very much. I would love to be able to replace that recipe. I left it on the kitchen counter when we did the Katrina road trip. I was planning to mix up a batch that weekend. My Chalmette home was destroyed that Monday/Tuesday. Please keep those recipes coming. It's my comfort connection to our old life."

The recipe published by *The Times-Picayune* originally came from B.D.B. of Harvey.

{MAKES 150 TO 180 TAMALES}

180 tamale papers

MEAT FILLING

3½ to 4 pounds ground beef

2 large onions, puréed

1 (3-ounce) container chili powder

½ teaspoon cumin

4 teaspoons salt

2 (8-ounce) cans Hunt's tomato sauce

1 cup water

⅔ cup cornmeal

2 teaspoons garlic powder

2 teaspoons black pepper

Cayenne pepper (optional)

CORNMEAL DOUGH

1 (1-pound) package Quaker yellow cornmeal

1 teaspoon salt, or to taste

5 tablespoons shortening, plus more if needed

¼ to ½ cup chili powder

2 (8-ounce) cans tomato sauce, such as Hunt's

Salsa Verde (Green Salsa) for serving (recipe follows)

Sink the tamale papers individually in a large bowl of water. Put one in, sink it, and add another until all are submerged. Set aside.

For the meat filling: In a large mixing bowl, combine all the ingredients thoroughly, adding cayenne to taste, if using. Roll the filling, 1 tablespoon at a time, into about 150 to 180 finger-sized logs. Set aside.

For the cornmeal dough: In a large mixing bowl, combine the cornmeal and salt with the shortening, blending well with your hands. The dough should be dark yellow and adhere easily to the outside of a meat log; if it doesn't, work in more shortening.

Enclose each meat log in about 1 teaspoon of the cornmeal dough by patting the dough around the log. Place on a paper and roll halfway up; then tuck in one side of the paper and finish rolling.

Cover the bottom of a large pot with chili powder. Add a layer of tamales and sprinkle the tops with more chili powder. Then add another layer, so that the tamales are perpendicular to the ones below and sprinkle the tops with chili powder. Continue in this fashion until all of the tamales are layered in the pot. Pour the tomato sauce on top, then add enough water so that all the tamales are covered. Wait a few minutes (because water will soak into the layers) and pour in additional water until the tamales are covered again.

Bring to a boil over high heat and cook for 5 minutes. Then reduce the heat and simmer for 45 minutes. Serve with the Salsa Verde. ❧

Salsa Verde (Green Salsa)

{MAKES ABOUT 2 CUPS}

4 cups water

12 tomatillos, husked

7 medium cloves garlic

4 to 8 serrano chiles

¼ cup plus 3 tablespoons coarsely chopped
　white onion

Salt

¾ cup cilantro leaves, with a bit of stem

¼ cup chopped fresh cilantro

Bring the water to a boil in a medium saucepan.
Add the tomatillos, 4 of the garlic cloves, the chiles,
and 3 tablespoons of the onions. Cook over medium
heat for 20 minutes. Drain, reserving the cooking
liquid, and cool.

Meanwhile, purée the remaining 3 garlic cloves in
a food processor, and add salt to taste. Add the
cilantro and blend. Add the tomatillo mixture,
with a little cooking water, and blend. The sauce
should have a slightly thick consistency.

To serve, pour the sauce into a serving bowl.
Garnish with the remaining ¼ cup chopped onions
and the chopped cilantro. ❧

PASTA
&
RICE

Marcelle is Creole and Cajun, but she also loves Italian food. Because this chapter has it all, it is her favorite. There are a couple of jambalaya recipes (pages 197 and 198) to satisfy the two schools of thought regarding this Louisiana dish. There are those who believe that jambalaya should not be reddened with the addition of tomatoes, and there are others who wouldn't have it any other way. Another regional recipe that we couldn't leave out is the popular New Orleans Monday bill of fare—Red Beans and Rice (page 205).

Get out your pasta pots because we have a wealth of Italian favorites—lasagna (page 199), Saucy Penne and Three-Cheese Bake (page 207), and two different versions of old school simmered sauces: Schwegmann's Spaghetti Sauce with Meatballs (page 208) and Meatballs and Spaghetti Sauce alla Turci (page 214). We can smell the sauces bubbling now!

PASTA & RICE

Angel Hair with Creole Tomatoes and Basil

WHEN CREOLE TOMATOES are in season, this is a delightful dish to serve on a warm evening. Garnished with fresh basil, and served chilled or at room temperature, you need only accompany the pasta with crusty Italian bread.

Use any flavorful local or heirloom tomato if you can't get your hands on a Creole one.

{MAKES 6 TO 8 SERVINGS}

1 pound dried angel hair pasta

½ cup extra-virgin olive oil

4 medium cloves garlic, minced

Salt

Red pepper flakes

1 pound Creole tomatoes, coarsely chopped, with their juice

1 cup shredded fresh basil leaves

Cook the angel hair pasta according to the package directions. Drain well and transfer to a large mixing bowl. Add the olive oil and garlic, and toss to coat evenly.

Add salt and red pepper flakes to taste. Add the tomatoes, including the juice that has accumulated, and toss with the mixture. Adjust the seasoning.

Pour the mixture onto a platter or into a shallow bowl and spread out evenly. Sprinkle with the basil and serve at room temperature or slightly chilled. ⚜

Chicken Lasagna

P. B. REQUESTED A recipe for Chicken Lasagna, which has a white, cheesy sauce. "If you can help me, I would appreciate it very much. Thanks to Katrina I have relocated to Lafayette, and hope to one day find all my great recipes," she wrote. The recipe came from Toni Marr of Belle Chasse; it had appeared in *The Times-Picayune* in 2002.

{MAKES 8 SERVINGS}

½ cup (1 stick) butter

½ cup all-purpose flour

4 cups milk

1 tablespoon garlic salt, plus 1 teaspoon

3 teaspoons parsley flakes

Salt

Black pepper

Pinch of red pepper flakes

1 tablespoon water

1½ pounds boneless, skinless chicken breasts, cut into ½-inch cubes

1 (4.5-ounce) can chopped green chiles with their liquid

3 tablespoons dried chopped onion

2 tablespoons minced fresh garlic

1 teaspoon onion powder

12 lasagna noodles

2 cups shredded Swiss cheese

2 cups shredded Monterey Jack–Cheddar cheese mix

Preheat the oven to 350 degrees F. In a 5-quart saucepan, melt the butter over medium heat. Add the flour and blend well. Slowly add the milk, stirring constantly, until all of it is added and the mixture is smooth. Add 1 tablespoon of the garlic salt, 2 teaspoons of the parsley flakes, salt and black pepper to taste, and the red pepper flakes. Simmer the sauce over low heat, stirring occasionally, while you cook the chicken.

To cook the chicken, pour the tablespoon of water into a large nonstick skillet. Add the chicken, green chiles, dried onion, fresh garlic, onion powder, the remaining 1 teaspoon of parsley flakes, the remaining 1 teaspoon of garlic salt, and more salt, black pepper, and red pepper flakes to taste. Cook over medium heat, stirring occasionally, until the chicken is white throughout, about 7 minutes. Add the cooked chicken to the pan of sauce, and cook over very low heat for about 15 minutes.

Meanwhile, cook the lasagna noodles according to the package instructions and drain well. Mix the cheeses together in a bowl.

Coat the bottom of a lasagna pan with a thin layer of sauce, so the lasagna doesn't stick to the bottom of the pan. Place a layer of 3 lasagna noodles in the pan, and top with about one-eighth of the cheese, then one-fourth of the sauce, and then another layer of cheese.

Continue layering in this fashion until all ingredients are used, ending with sauce, then cheese. Cover the pan with aluminum foil and bake for 1 hour or until piping hot. Remove from the oven, uncover the pan, and let the lasagna sit for about 15 minutes before serving. ❧

Irma Thomas's Macaroni and Cheese

THE BELOVED SOUL singer shared this recipe with Food section readers in a 1995 feature about the performers at Jazzfest. Eleven years later, after Thomas's home in Eastern New Orleans East was swamped by floodwater, *Times-Picayune* music writer Keith Spera wrote of the sixty-five-year-old soul queen:

> As the post-Katrina spotlight has shone on New Orleans music, no one has sparkled more brilliantly than Irma Thomas. Three weeks after the storm, she blew away a soldout Madison Square Garden in New York at the "From the Big Apple to the Big Easy" concert.
>
> Her rendition of the Bessie Smith standard "Backwater Blues" is a highlight of Our New Orleans, the benefit CD that has sold more than 130,000 copies nationwide. And on Feb. 8, she closed out the Grammy Awards alongside Allen Toussaint, Dr. John, Bruce Springsteen, Bonnie Raitt, Elvis Costello, Yolanda Adams, and Sam Moore.

Thomas's album *After the Rain*, recorded in 2006 and a best-seller at that year's Jazzfest music tent, won Thomas a Grammy in 2007, after nearly fifty years of work as a professional singer. Her mac and cheese is made with eggs, and is typical of the rich versions popular in the South.

{MAKES 8 TO 10 SERVINGS}

2 pounds macaroni

6 large eggs

¼ cup sugar

Salt

Black pepper

3 to 4 cups milk

1 pound total of several varieties of cheese, such as cheddar and American (or other leftovers from your cheese tray), cubed, plus additional grated cheese (optional) for the topping

Preheat oven to 350 degrees F. Coat one large or two medium baking dishes with nonstick spray.

Cook the macaroni according to the package directions (don't overcook), and drain.

In a large mixing bowl, beat the eggs with the sugar and the salt and pepper to taste. Add 3 to 4 cups milk, "depending on how soft you like the custard," Thomas says. "I like mine on the soggy side."

In the baking dish(es), toss the hot macaroni with the cheese cubes. Pour the custard mixture over all. Top with additional grated cheese (if using). Bake for 30 minutes.

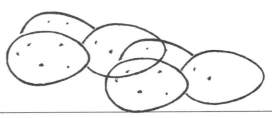

Chicken and Sausage Jambalaya

JAMBALAYA IS ONE of the great Louisiana stand-bys, which can be made with just about anything you have on hand. This recipe combines chicken (or turkey) and sausage. Although there is a bit of tomato paste, there are no tomatoes, which is why this is called a brown jambalaya. It's easy to put together, making it a good choice for weekday suppers as well as family gatherings, parties, fairs, and every festival.

{MAKES 4 TO 6 SERVINGS}

2 tablespoons vegetable oil

2 boneless, skinless chicken breast halves
(about 1 pound total), cut into 1-inch cubes

About 1½ teaspoons Creole or Cajun seasoning

½ pound smoked sausage, such as andouille
or kielbasa, sliced ¼ inch thick

1½ cups chopped yellow onions

1 cup chopped green bell peppers

3 cups water

1 tablespoon tomato paste

2 tablespoons chopped fresh parsley

2 tablespoon chopped green onions (green part only)

1½ cups long-grain rice

Heat the oil in a large heavy pot, such as a Dutch oven. Season the chicken pieces generously with the Creole or Cajun seasoning. Add the chicken to the pot and cook, stirring, over medium heat until evenly browned, about 5 minutes. Add the sausage and cook, stirring, for 2 minutes. Add the onions and peppers, and cook, stirring, until soft and golden, 5 to 6 minutes. Add the water, tomato paste, parsley, and green onions. Stir and bring to a boil.

Add the rice, cover the pot, and reduce the heat to medium-low. Cook until the rice is tender and has absorbed most of the liquid, 15 to 20 minutes. *Do not stir.* Fluff the mixture with a fork before serving. ❧

Jambalaya, My Way

JAMBALAYA IS SIMILAR to the Spanish paella. Both are rice-based and use an assortment of seafood, meats, and sausages. You can put almost anything you have on hand into either one, and no two cooks make them alike.

There is a constant argument in south Louisiana about whether jambalaya should be red (made with tomatoes) or brown (no tomatoes). New Orleanians lean to the red variety, which usually contains shrimp and ham. West of the Mississippi River, the brown version prevails, and is made with chicken and sausage (see page 197 for an example). Both are good. This is Marcelle Bienvenu's red jambalaya.

{MAKES 4 TO 6 SERVINGS}

6 tablespoons butter
½ cup chopped green onions (white and green parts)
½ cup chopped yellow onions
1 large green bell pepper, julienned
1 cup coarsely chopped celery
1 teaspoon minced garlic
½ pound medium shrimp, peeled and deveined
½ pound cubed boiled ham
½ pound smoked sausage, such as andouille or kielbasa, sliced ¼ inch thick (optional)
1 (16-ounce) can whole tomatoes, crushed, with their juices
1 cup chicken broth
Salt
Cayenne pepper
2 bay leaves
1 cup long-grain rice
Hot sauce for serving

Melt the butter in a large heavy pot over medium heat. Add the green onions, yellow onions, bell peppers, celery, and garlic. Cook, stirring, until they are soft and pale gold, 6 to 8 minutes. Add the shrimp and ham, and sausage (if using). Cook for 2 to 3 minutes, or until the shrimp turn pink. Stir in the tomatoes and the chicken broth. Season to taste with salt and cayenne. Add the bay leaves and the rice. Cover and reduce the heat to medium-low. Cook until the rice is tender and all the liquid is absorbed, about 25 minutes.

Remove the bay leaves and serve. Pass the hot sauce! ❧

Meatless Lasagna

For vegetarians and those watching their diets, this recipe was offered by West Jefferson Medical Center in 2002. It really is quite good.

{MAKES 6 TO 8 SERVINGS}

2 (15-ounce) containers low-fat or nonfat ricotta cheese

1 large egg

1½ teaspoons salt

¼ teaspoon dried oregano leaves

½ teaspoon black pepper

2 teaspoons crushed garlic (from a jar)

1 pound part-skim mozzarella cheese, grated

4¾ cups prepared pasta sauce, such as Classico, without cream or cheese

12 lasagna noodles, uncooked

3 medium zucchini, sliced ¼ inch thick

½ cup water

Preheat the oven to 350 degrees F. Coat a 9-by-13-inch baking pan with cooking spray.

In a large bowl, mix the ricotta, egg, salt, oregano, pepper, and garlic, and stir in about one-fourth of the mozzarella.

Spread one-third of the pasta sauce evenly over the bottom of the prepared baking dish. Layer with 4 noodles, half of the ricotta mixture, half of the zucchini, and one-third of the remaining mozzarella. Repeat the layers. Top with the last 4 noodles, the remaining sauce, and the remaining mozzarella. (The recipe may be prepared up to this point and refrigerated for several hours or overnight.)

When ready to bake, pour the water around the edges of the lasagna and cover the pan with foil. Bake for 1½ hours. ❧

Meaty Manicotti

JOAN GREGO OFFERED this recipe she clipped out of the newspaper about twenty years ago. We are glad she had it, as other readers had requested it.

{MAKES 6 SERVINGS}

2 slices white sandwich bread

1 pound ground beef

2 cloves garlic, minced

1 teaspoon salt

1 (32-ounce) jar good-quality marinara sauce

1 cup grated Romano cheese

1 pound mozzarella cheese, grated

2 large eggs, lightly beaten

1 pound manicotti pasta, cooked according to the package directions

Preheat the oven to 350 degrees F. Coat a 9-by-13-inch baking dish with nonstick spray. To make fresh bread crumbs, cut off the crusts and crumble the bread by rubbing pieces between your hands or whir in a food processor.

In a large skillet, over medium-high heat, cook the beef and garlic 10 to 15 minutes, until no pink can be seen in the meat. Pour off the excess fat. Stir in the salt, fresh bread crumbs, ½ cup of the spaghetti sauce, and ½ cup of the Romano cheese. Mix well. Add three-fourths of the mozzarella cheese and the eggs and mix well.

Carefully fill each manicotti tube with an equal portion of the mixture.

Spread 2 cups of the spaghetti sauce in the bottom of the prepared pan. Arrange the manicotti in the dish. Pour the remaining sauce over the center third of the manicotti. Cover with foil and bake for 30 minutes. Remove the foil and sprinkle with the remaining ½ cup of Romano cheese and the remaining mozzarella. Bake, uncovered, until the cheese is bubbly and brown, about 20 minutes longer. ❧

Mexican Lasagna

THIS FAVORITE, PUBLISHED in 1997, was developed by Harvey native Cynthia Shields Viator. It's great to prepare for a group!

{MAKES 15 TO 20 SERVINGS}

2 tablespoons vegetable oil

1 small yellow onion, finely chopped

1 small green bell pepper, finely chopped

2 large cloves garlic, minced

2 pounds lean ground beef

1 (10-ounce) can Ro-Tel diced tomatoes and green chiles

1 (1¼-ounce) package taco seasoning

2 (8-ounce) cans tomato sauce

2 tablespoons sugar

1 (8 ounce) package lasagna noodles

1 (8-ounce) container sour cream

1 (8-ounce) package cream cheese, softened

¼ cup finely chopped green onion (green part only)

1 pound pepper Jack cheese

1 pound American cheese

¼ cup sliced black olives

In a 4-quart saucepan, heat the oil over high heat. Add the onion, bell pepper, and garlic. Sauté until the onion is translucent, about 2 minutes, stirring occasionally. Add the beef and tomatoes and cook for 15 minutes, breaking up the meat chunks and stirring occasionally. Remove from the heat and skim off any fat. Stir in the taco seasoning and cook, stirring, over low heat for 5 minutes. Add the tomato sauce and sugar, and simmer for 15 minutes

Meanwhile, preheat the oven to 325 degrees F. Coat a 9-by-13-inch baking dish with cooking spray.

Cook the lasagna noodles in a pot of boiling water until al dente, or firm to the bite. In a medium bowl, blend the sour cream and cream cheese, and then stir in the green onions. Set aside. Shred the cheeses and mix them together.

Spread half of the noodles in the bottom of the prepared dish. Cover with half of the meat mixture, then half of the sour cream mixture, and half of the shredded cheeses. Repeat the layers and sprinkle the olives evenly over the top.

Cover with aluminum foil and bake for 1 hour, or until bubbly. Cool slightly before serving. ❧

Mr. B's Crawfish Risotto

MR. B'S BISTRO was shut down by Katrina, but after a complete renovation, the popular French Quarter restaurant is back in business. This risotto is a favorite during the crawfish season.

{MAKES ABOUT 6 SERVINGS}

5 cups chicken stock
2½ tablespoons olive oil
3 medium onions, finely diced
1 pound arborio rice
2 red bell peppers, finely diced
2 green bell peppers, finely diced
1 jalapeño pepper, minced
1 tablespoon minced garlic
¼ cup julienned sun-dried tomatoes
¼ cup grated Parmesan cheese
4 tablespoons butter
1 pound peeled crawfish tails
Salt
Black pepper

Pour the stock into a saucepan with a lid over high heat. When the stock comes to a gentle boil, reduce the heat to low.

Heat the oil in a large heavy pot, such as a Dutch oven, over medium heat. Add one third of the onions and cook, stirring, until golden, about 3 minutes. Add the rice and stir with a wooden spoon until the rice is evenly coated with the oil, 1 to 2 minutes. Increase the heat to medium-high and add 1 cup of the hot stock, stirring constantly. When the rice has absorbed most of the liquid, add another cup of broth and continue stirring. Continue cooking off the stock in this way and adding more. After about 10 minutes, add the bell and jalapeño peppers, the remaining onions, the garlic, and sun-dried tomatoes. Continue adding the stock and stirring until the rice is al dente, or firm to the bite, about 8 minutes longer.

Remove the risotto from the heat and stir in the Parmesan, butter, and crawfish tails. Taste and add salt and pepper, if needed. Serve immediately. ❧

Pasta with Shrimp Sauce

PUBLISHED IN 2002 to accompany a *Times-Picayune* column about St. Joseph's altars, this recipe exemplifies the typical savory offering. Because St. Joseph's Day is on March 19, during Lent, the offerings are meatless. And because it's an Italian celebration, pasta often appears on the altars, in dried form, set in vases like bouquets, as well as in cooked dishes.

{MAKES 6 TO 8 SERVINGS}

⅓ cup olive oil

¼ cup chopped garlic

1 cup chopped green bell peppers

1 cup chopped onions

3 cups chopped tomatoes

1 tablespoon dried basil leaves

1 tablespoon dried oregano leaves

Salt

Red pepper flakes,

Black pepper

½ cup (1 stick) butter

1 pound medium shrimp, peeled and deveined

½ cup chopped fresh parsley

1 pound spaghetti

Grated Parmesan cheese for serving

Heat the oil in a large heavy pot over medium heat. Add the garlic, bell peppers, and onions, and cook, stirring, until soft and pale gold, about 5 minutes. Add the tomatoes, basil, oregano, and salt, red pepper flakes, and black pepper to taste.

Cover and cook over medium-low heat, stirring occasionally, until the mixture thickens, 30 to 40 minutes. Add the butter, shrimp, and parsley, and cook until the shrimp turn pink, about 5 minutes.

Cook the spaghetti according to the package directions and drain. Mix the sauce with the spaghetti and serve hot. Pass the Parmesan cheese at the table. ✤

Semolina's Muffuletta Pasta

THE STYLE BOOK of *The Times-Picayune* spells the famed sandwich "muffuletta," but it's spelled "muffaletta" on many menus all over south Louisiana. It really doesn't matter how it's spelled; New Orleanians claim it as their own. Supposedly, the sandwich was introduced in 1906 at Central Grocery on Decatur Street in the French Quarter.

This incredible sandwich is made with a round loaf of crusty Italian bread, which is split in half, then layered with provolone cheese, Genoa salami, and lots of olive salad. Olive salad is sold all over the metro area, though some folks prefer to make their own. It usually contains a mixture of two kinds of chopped or sliced olives, pimientos, celery, garlic, pickled onions, capers, oregano, parsley, olive oil, red wine vinegar, and salt and pepper.

The Semolina restaurants have taken the sandwich as inspiration for this muffuletta pasta. The recipe appeared in the newspaper in 2003.

{MAKES 2 SERVINGS}

2 tablespoons extra-virgin olive oil
2 ounces ham, cut into matchsticks
2 ounces salami, cut into matchsticks
½ cup Semolina's Olive Salad (recipe follows)
2 cups cooked penne pasta
1 tablespoon grated Parmesan cheese for garnish
½ cup grated provolone cheese for garnish
Toasted sesame seeds for garnish
Chopped fresh parsley for garnish

Heat the olive oil in a large skillet over medium heat, and sauté the ham and salami just until they start to brown slightly. Add the olive salad and cooked pasta, and sauté until the penne is hot. Transfer to a serving platter and garnish with Parmesan, provolone, sesame seeds, and parsley.

Semolina's Olive Salad

{MAKES ABOUT 2 CUPS}

1 cup chopped green olives
½ cup sliced or chopped black olives
½ cup chopped tomatoes
1 tablespoon minced garlic
1 teaspoon chopped fresh basil
1 teaspoon cracked black pepper

Combine all ingredients in a medium bowl. Allow the mixture to marinate for at least 2 hours before use. Leftovers will keep for several weeks in an airtight container in the refrigerator.

Red Beans and Rice

The humble dish of red beans and rice, eaten for Monday lunch or dinner in most New Orleans homes and restaurants, became the "I miss it most" dish craved by Louisiana evacuees after Hurricane Katrina. The first nomination for our cookbook project came from B.C.R. of New Orleans, who offered his version of red beans and rice, which he adapted from the one on the back of the package of Camellia red beans, the preferred local brand. "If there is one single important New Orleans dish, this is it. This is a dish everyone enjoys, rich and poor, black and white," B.C.R. wrote. He quoted the old jump-rope jingle from John Churchill Chase's iconic *Frenchmen, Desire, Good Children, and Other Streets of New Orleans*:

> *Red Beans and Rice*
> *Quartée red beans, quartée rice,*
> *Little piece of salt meat to make it taste nice,*
> *Lend me the paper and tell me the time,*
> *When papa passes by he'll pay you the dime.*

B.C.R. signed his note the way Louis Armstrong liked to sign his letters, "Red Beans and Ricely Yours." Even if you can make this dish in your sleep, here is B.C.R.'s version.

{MAKES 8 TO 12 SERVINGS}

1 pound dried red kidney beans
½ pound fatty ham or another seasoning meat, such as salt meat, pickle meat, or smoked ham hock
1 medium yellow onion, chopped
1 or 2 stalks celery, chopped
1 green bell pepper, chopped
1 clove garlic, minced
1 large bay leaf
1 to 2 teaspoons Creole seasoning
Salt
Black pepper to taste
2 tablespoons chopped fresh parsley, or more to taste
¼ cup chopped green onions (green part only)
Hot cooked rice for serving
Hot sauce for serving

Pick over the beans to remove any stones or broken beans. Soak overnight in a large bowl with about 3 inches of water to cover. Drain the water, rinse the beans, drain again, and set aside.

Render the ham or seasoning meat in a Dutch oven over medium heat to obtain the fat, then remove the meat and set aside. Sauté the onion, celery, bell pepper, and garlic in the rendered fat, adding a little oil if needed, until softened. Add the beans, return the meat to the pan, and pour in 8 to 10 cups water, or enough to cover everything by at least a couple of inches. Bring to a boil. Add the bay leaf and Creole seasoning to the beans, then reduce to a simmer and gently cook, uncovered, for about 1½ hours, until the beans are tender. Add more water while cooking, if necessary.

Toward the end of the cooking time, mash some beans with a spoon against the side of the pot to make the mixture creamier, if desired, and add the salt and pepper to taste, the parsley, and the green onions. Or, if you prefer, use the parsley and green onions as a garnish. Discard the bay leaf and serve in bowls over white rice. Pass the hot sauce. ❧

Rice Pilaf

THIS IS ONE of those great side dishes that goes with just about everything, from baked chicken and grilled meats to Beef Kabobs (page 168) and Chicken with Apricots (page 152).

{MAKES 6 SERVINGS}

2 cups short-grain rice

4 tablespoons butter

2 cups coarsely chopped onions

1 cup sliced almonds, toasted

1 cup raisins

2 tablespoons chopped pimientos

4 cups chicken broth

Salt

White pepper

Preheat the oven to 350 degrees F. Wash the rice and drain it. Set aside.

Melt the butter in an ovenproof saucepan with a lid over medium heat. Add the onions and cook, stirring, until soft and golden, about 10 minutes. Add the rice, almonds, raisins, and pimientos. Pour in the broth and season to taste with the salt and pepper. Cover the pan with a lid and bake until the liquid is absorbed and the rice is tender, 20 to 30 minutes. Serve warm.

Saucy Penne and Three-Cheese Bake

D.M. WAS SEEKING a recipe that she believed she clipped from one of the newspaper's coupon magazines at least ten years ago. "I have been looking for a recipe I had before the hurricane called cheesy rotini. It had ground beef, ricotta cheese, and other ingredients which I can't remember. It had rotini noodles, and I think at least two other cheeses and maybe bell pepper and onion. I have tried finding it on Web sites, in books, and I have had no luck. . . . Do you have any suggestions on where I can find this recipe? It was really great!"

Another reader located a recipe in her files that is similar to the one that D.M. requested. "I found it many years ago in the coupon flyer of a T-P Sunday newspaper. It is a layered dish and calls for Luxury penne rigate pasta rather than rotini," she wrote. "My family really enjoys this dish, and I thought your readers might like to give it a try." Penne rigate is simply penne with ridges to catch the sauce.

{MAKES ABOUT 6 SERVINGS }

½ pound lean ground beef

1 (25-ounce) jar spicy tomato and pesto pasta sauce

1 (15-ounce) container ricotta cheese

½ pound mozzarella cheese, shredded

¼ cup grated Parmesan cheese

1 large egg, lightly beaten

½ pound penne rigate or penne, such as Luxury brand, cooked according to the package directions and drained

Preheat the oven to 350 degre[...] a 2½-quart baking dish.

Cook the ground beef in a saucepan o[...] heat until browned. Pour off the fat and [...] pasta sauce.

In a medium mixing bowl, combine the ricotta, 1 cup of the mozzarella, the Parmesan, and the egg.

In the prepared baking dish, layer the penne, sauce and beef mixture, and cheese mixture. Repeat the layers. Sprinkle with the remaining mozzarella and bake for 35 to 40 minutes, until hot and bubbly and lightly browned on top.

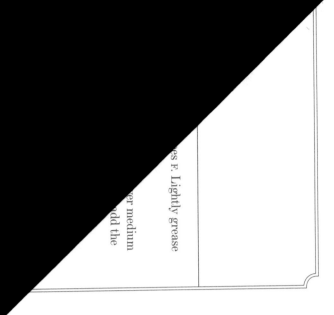

es F. Lightly grease

er medium

dd the

Sauce with Meatballs

{MAKES 8 TO 10 SERVINGS}

SAUCE

½ cup (1 stick) butter

1 cup chopped green onions

2 jumbo yellow onions, chopped

1 cup chopped celery

2 cups chopped green bell peppers

½ cup chopped fresh parsley

5 cloves garlic, minced

2 tablespoons Italian seasoning

5 fresh bay leaves

1 (28-ounce) can whole Italian tomatoes

3 (6-ounce) cans tomato paste

3 (8-ounce) cans tomato sauce

Salt

Black pepper

1 teaspoon sugar

MEATBALLS

2 pounds ground beef, preferably coarsely ground

1 cup chopped green onions (green part only)

1 jumbo yellow onion, chopped

2 cups chopped celery

½ cup chopped fresh parsley

1 cup chopped green bell peppers

5 cloves garlic, chopped

6 large eggs, lightly beaten

1 cup seasoned Italian bread crumbs

Salt

Black pepper

1 cup olive oil, or as needed

Hot cooked spaghetti, preferably al dente
(firm to the bite), for serving

Grated Romano cheese for serving

buy goldfish, eyeglasses, a po-boy, fresh shrimp, a McKenzie's pound cake, a drink at the full bar, and a window air-conditioning unit all in one place. But in the 1990s, economic conditions and new competing markets caused the stores to close.

However, many New Orleanians have fond memories of the supermarkets as well as the meatballs and spaghetti recipe from John Schwegmann, which appeared in the grocer's ads in the newspaper. Readers have asked for this recipe several times, both before and after Katrina. Fans will tell you the long-simmered sauce is the best they have ever made. For a complete meal, you need to add only a green salad, some crisp French bread, and your choice of a good red wine.

For the sauce: Melt the butter in a large heavy pot, such as cast-iron. Add the green onions, yellow onions, celery, bell peppers, parsley, garlic, and Italian seasoning and sauté over medium heat for about 15 minutes, until the vegetables are very tender. Add the bay leaves and whole tomatoes and mash the tomatoes against the side of the pot. Lower the heat and simmer for 1 hour. Then add the tomato paste and sauce and salt and pepper to taste. Cover and simmer for 2 hours. Add the sugar and simmer, covered, for another 2½ hours, stirring occasionally. If the sauce looks too thick, add a little water.

For the meatballs: About ½ hour before the end of the cooking time for the sauce, prepare the meatballs. Mix all the ingredients except the olive oil together in a large bowl. Roll into 1½- to 2-inch balls. Heat a few tablespoons of the olive oil in a large skillet, and sauté the meatballs in batches, adding more oil as needed, until nicely browned and cooked through.

Add the meatballs to the sauce and continue simmering for another 30 to 45 minutes. Remove the bay leaves. Serve over spaghetti and top with freshly grated Romano. 🐘

Semolina's Crawfish Roban

THANKS TO F.B. of Slidell, G.M. of Jefferson, and others, here is the recipe for crawfish roban, which was requested by D.R. of Mandeville. The dish is a favorite entrée at the Semolina restaurants. It can also be made with shrimp.

{MAKES ABOUT 8 SERVINGS}

2 cups Roban Sauce (recipe follows)

1 pound cooked peeled crawfish tails or shrimp

1½ pounds cooked pasta, such as angel hair
  or linguine

¼ cup chopped green onion (green part only)
  for garnish

Heat the sauce just to a simmer in a large sauté pan. Add the crawfish and cooked pasta, and toss to coat in the sauce. Cook only long enough to heat the pasta. Garnish with chopped green onion and serve.

Roban Sauce

{MAKES ABOUT 2 CUPS}

4 tablespoons butter

2 tablespoons chopped garlic

1 cup chopped green onions (green part only)

1 quart heavy cream

1 tablespoon blackened redfish seasoning
or Creole seasoning, such as Tony Chachere's.

Melt the butter in a saucepan over medium heat, add the garlic and green onions, and cook just until the garlic releases its flavor. Add the heavy cream and cook until reduced by nearly half. When reduced, the sauce should heavily coat the back of the spoon. Add the blackened red fish seasoning, taste, and add more if desired.

Variation: To make 1 or 2 servings, heat 1 tablespoon of vegetable oil in a large skillet over medium heat. Add 2 ounces of fresh fish such as redfish or trout, cubed; 2 ounces of scallops; and 2 ounces of shrimp. Sauté until the seafood is cooked. Add 1 cup of Roban Sauce and bring to a boil. Pour the sauce and seafood over 2 cups of cooked pasta shells and garnish with 2 tablespoons of chopped green onions, 1 tablespoon of chopped fresh parsley, and red pepper flakes to taste.

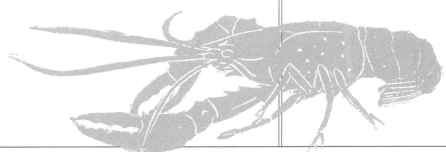

Shrimp and Tasso Sauté

In March 2000, Marcelle Bienvenu published this fairly easy recipe in her column. It packs together a lot of different flavors, the ingredients are usually readily at hand, and it's great when you need to whip something up at the last minute.

{MAKES 4 SERVINGS}

2 tablespoons vegetable oil
½ cup chopped yellow onions
¼ cup chopped red bell pepper
¼ cup finely chopped celery
½ teaspoon salt
⅛ teaspoon cayenne
1 teaspoon Tabasco sauce
1 cup chopped tasso or smoked ham
1½ cups sliced mushrooms
1 tablespoon chopped garlic
1 pound medium shrimp, peeled and deveined
½ cup shrimp stock or chicken broth
⅓ cup dry white wine
¼ cup chopped green onions (green part only)
¼ cup chopped fresh parsley
Hot cooked rice or pasta for serving

Heat the oil in a large skillet over medium heat. Add the onions, bell pepper, celery, salt, cayenne, Tabasco, and tasso and sauté over high heat for about 5 minutes, or until the vegetables are wilted and slightly brown. Add the mushrooms, garlic, shrimp, stock, and white wine and cook, stirring often, for 5 minutes. Add the green onions and parsley and adjust the seasonings. Serve over rice or your favorite pasta. ❧

Pasta with Smoked Mussels and Capers

THE BEGINNING OF hurricane season in 2006 prompted a review of evacuation planning tips in the Food pages. Stephanie Bialobok of Metairie sent a thoughtful list of tips, as well as her favorite evacuation recipe. Her note provided a glimpse of how one family coped.

"I have been planning for hurricane evacuation since Hurricane Georges came much too close for comfort in 1998," she wrote. In 2005, in the aftermath of Katrina, her family was evacuated to Lafayette. When they realized they would be away from home for a while, Bialobok explained, "We bought a small charcoal grill and charcoal and cooked simple things like burgers, chicken breasts, or fish fillets. . . . Out-of-town friends sent us a care package in late September, containing several cans of smoked mussels and smoked oysters. I had no idea of what to do with these items, and then I found the following recipe. This meal became a wonderful diversion for us and was so easy to prepare. Would that I knew at the time that five months later I would be evacuated still!"

{MAKES 4 SERVINGS}

½ pound elbow macaroni

3 to 4 ounces canned smoked mussels
   or oysters, drained

1 (2½-ounce) can smoked sardines packed in oil

1 tablespoon capers

Large handful fresh parsley

2 tablespoons fresh lemon juice

2 tablespoons olive oil

½ teaspoon salt

½ teaspoon red pepper flakes

¼ cup sliced green onions (green part only)

Cook the macaroni according to the package directions. Meanwhile, coarsely chop the mussels, sardines, capers, and parsley and combine them in a large mixing bowl. Add the lemon juice and olive oil and season with the salt and red pepper flakes.

When the pasta is done, drain and shake dry and add to the bowl. Toss with the green onions, reserving some for garnish. Serve warm. Refresh any leftovers with vinaigrette. ⁊

Spaghetti Sauce with Olives

JOHN SCHLUTER WROTE US, "As the cook for the New Orleans Fraternal Order of Police, I have used many of the published recipes from the paper. The one I used most, and a hit with the men and women of the Department, was Marcelle Bienvenu's meat sauce in red gravy. As with most others, I lost this. Would love to see a copy of it. Thanks."

When they were small, Marcelle Bienvenu's great-nieces and great-nephews loved this dish.

{MAKES 6 TO 8 SERVINGS}

3 (8-ounce) cans tomato sauce

1 (6-ounce) can Italian-style tomato paste

1 tablespoon fresh lemon juice

1 tablespoon dark brown sugar

⅓ cup red wine vinegar

½ teaspoon dried oregano leaves

½ teaspoon dried basil leaves

3 tablespoons grated Romano cheese

½ cup sliced black olives

2 tablespoons olive oil

1 pound lean ground beef

¾ cup chopped onions

½ cup chopped celery

1 tablespoon chopped garlic

1 cup sliced white button mushrooms

Salt

Red pepper flakes

Hot cooked pasta of your choice for serving

Combine the tomato sauce, tomato paste, lemon juice, sugar, vinegar, oregano, basil, cheese, and olives in a large saucepan. Bring the mixture to a boil, then reduce the heat to medium-low and simmer, stirring occasionally, for 20 minutes.

Heat the oil in a large skillet over medium-high heat. Add the beef and cook, stirring, until it is evenly browned, about 5 minutes. Add the onions, celery, and garlic and cook until they are soft, 4 to 5 minutes. Add the mushrooms and cook, stirring, until they are slightly soft, 2 to 3 minutes more. Add this mixture to the tomato mixture. Season to taste with salt and red pepper flakes. Serve over the cooked pasta.

Meatballs and Spaghetti Sauce alla Turci

In 1997, THE TIMES-PICAYUNE received this request from a reader: "I hope you can help me find a recipe that I've coveted for years! Many New Orleanians fondly remember Turci's Restaurant on Poydras Street. Unfortunately, it closed down many years ago and I still miss their delicious Italian cooking.

"Ever since then I've been looking for the recipe for the wonderful house specialty, which was called Spaghetti alla Turci. It was a classic, dark red (almost maroon) sauce, the kind which has been slow-cooked all day. It was the perfect blend of flavors—slightly tart and slightly sweet. The sauce also had chunks of chicken breast and anise-flavored sausage in it."

There seem to have been several versions of Turci's pasta sauce recipe floating around, but this is the one from Theresa Turci's great-grandson, Neil A. Peyroux. He passed along the recipe to the food columnist Myriam Guidroz, noting that he could not provide exact measurements because Turci was an instinctive cook who did not measure ingredients. Guidroz then filled in the quantities.

The recipe is slightly different from the version in *Gourmet Cooking*, by Earl Peyroux, Neil's uncle. Fans should note that the book also features several other Turci family recipes.

{MAKES ABOUT 8 SERVINGS}

¼ pound ground veal

¼ pound ground pork

½ pound raw chicken gizzards, ground in a food processor

5 tablespoons olive oil

½ cup finely diced onions

½ cup finely diced celery

1 to 2 cloves garlic

½ cup chopped green bell pepper (optional)

2 ounces fatty ham, diced

3 (8-ounce) cans tomato paste

About 4 cups chicken broth

Salt

Black pepper

1 teaspoon sugar

1 bay leaf

¼ teaspoon dried thyme leaves, or to taste

¼ teaspoon dried basil leaves, or to taste

¼ teaspoon dried oregano leaves, or to taste

MEATBALLS

1 large egg, beaten

½ cup seasoned Italian bread crumbs

½ pound ground veal

½ pound ground pork

Salt

Black pepper

1 tablespoon olive oil

½ pound boneless, skinless chicken breasts, cut into bite-sized pieces

½ pound white button mushrooms, trimmed

Hot cooked spaghetti for serving

In a large skillet, brown the veal, pork, and the ground chicken gizzards in 1 tablespoon of the olive oil over medium heat. Drain off any extra fat and reserve the meat.

In a large heavy pot, heat the remaining ¼ cup of olive oil and cook the onions, celery, garlic, and bell peppers (if using) until soft and the onions are translucent, but not browned. Add the diced ham and the browned meat. Stir in the tomato paste, and keep stirring until it loses its bright red color. Add the chicken broth. Season to taste with the salt and pepper and add the sugar, bay leaf, thyme, basil, and oregano.

Bring to a simmer, cover, and cook over very low heat for at least 1 hour, and preferably 2. If the gravy becomes too thick or sticks to the pot, add a little more chicken broth. The sauce improves in flavor if made in advance, so if possible, cook the sauce to this point a day early and refrigerate; then reheat to a simmer before proceeding.

For the meatballs: Mix together the beaten egg, the bread crumbs (dampened with a little water), and the veal and pork. Season with the salt and pepper and shape into small meatballs. Heat the olive oil in a large skillet over medium heat and brown the meatballs. Take care to brown just the outside to form a thin crust. Add the meatballs to the simmering sauce along with the chicken and mushrooms. Simmer for at least 1 hour, stirring occasionally. Add water or more chicken broth if the sauce gets too thick. Taste and correct the seasoning as needed. Serve over spaghetti. ❧

CASSEROLES

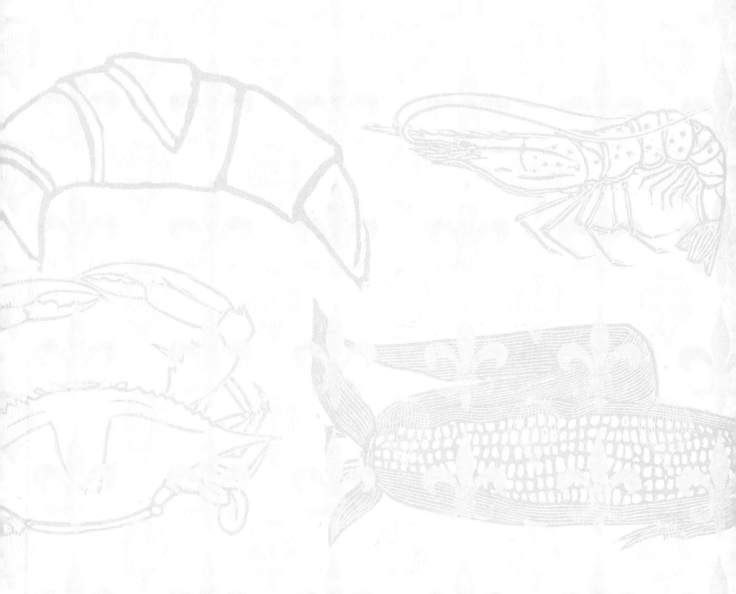

While some people seem to think casseroles are passé, we happen to think they are lifesavers, especially when you have to serve a gang. Most need only a salad and crusty French bread as accompaniments to make a delightful meal.

The Chicken Tamale Casserole (page 222) is great for any kind of family gathering, and the Crabmeat Casserole (page 223) makes a fine main course for an elegant luncheon.

The Mirliton Casserole with Crabmeat, Crawfish, and Shrimp (page 225) is definitely for seafood lovers, as is the casserole of oysters and artichokes (page 226).

Because most of the casseroles can be made ahead of time, you'll have more time to enjoy your guests when they arrive. We like that! And these are ideal potluck bring-alongs as well.

CASSEROLES

Brenda Huchingson's Holiday Casserole

ABOUT THIRTY YEARS AGO, when Brenda Huchingson's children, Michael and Julia, were very young, she got plenty of practice adapting dishes to suit their tastes. For example, after serving her offspring traditional roast turkey with stuffing one holiday season, she discovered that they liked chicken much better than turkey and could more easily deal with meat when it was served off the bone. She also learned that the stuffing was their favorite part of the meal. So Huchingson invented a holiday casserole for them, and her creation is still a family favorite.

"After they were older, I tried to change to a more grown-up main dish for Thanksgiving and Christmas meals, but everyone was adamant that I serve 'the casserole,'" the Kenner resident said. This attractive dish is great for potlucks and family gatherings any time of the year. It can be assembled a day ahead and baked at the last minute.

{MAKES 10 TO 12 SERVINGS}

1 (24-ounce) loaf whole-grain bread of choice, such as Pepperidge Farm's whole-wheat, or 9-grain

1 (3- to 4-pound) chicken, cut into serving pieces; or 4 to 6 whole chicken breasts

⅓ cup cream sherry, plus 2 tablespoons

3 tablespoons Italian seasoning

1 pound fresh hot sausage

2 large onions, chopped

2 large carrots, peeled and coarsely grated

1 large apple (any kind), peeled and chopped

½ cup dried cranberries

1 cup coarsely chopped pecans

½ cup (1 stick) butter, melted, plus 6 tablespoons, cut into pats

Salt

Black pepper

Paprika for sprinkling

Preheat the oven to 350 degrees F. Spread out the bread slices on cookie sheets and bake for 5 minutes. Leave in the oven overnight to dry. Crumble the bread with your hands into a large mixing bowl.

Put the chicken in a pot and cover with water. Add the ⅓ cup sherry and 1 tablespoon of the Italian seasoning. Bring the water to a boil, lower the heat to medium, and cook the chicken until very tender. Take the chicken out of the pot and set aside until cool enough to handle, reserving the broth. Remove the skin and bones, leaving the meat in large pieces.

While the chicken is cooling, preheat the oven again to 350 degrees F. Grease a 9-by-13-inch baking pan.

Sprinkle the remaining 2 tablespoons of Italian seasoning over the bread crumbs in the large bowl.

In a large skillet over medium heat, cook the sausage until done, breaking up the meat into small bits. Use a slotted spoon to transfer to the bowl with the bread crumbs. Cook the onions in the fat remaining in the skillet (add vegetable oil if needed), over medium-high heat until tender, about 5 minutes. Add the carrots, and cook for 2 minutes. Stir in the apples, and continue cooking until barely tender, about 5 minutes more. Add this mixture, along with the cranberries and pecans, to the bowl of bread and sausage. Mix well. Moisten the mixture with about 4 cups of the reserved chicken broth, the remaining 2 tablespoons of sherry, and the melted butter. Season to taste with salt and pepper.

Spread half the stuffing in the bottom of the prepared baking pan. Top with the chicken, then with remaining stuffing. Dot the top of the casserole with the pats of butter, and sprinkle with paprika. Bake, uncovered, until the top is bubbly and browned, about 40 minutes. Serve warm. 🐾

Cabbage Casserole

QUICK AND EASY, this casserole can accompany beef, chicken, or pork. It's a good dish to serve on New Year's Day, when cabbage traditionally is eaten in the South, so you will have something green—money—in your pocket during the coming year.

{MAKES ABOUT 4 SERVINGS}

1 pound lean ground beef
2 teaspoons sugar
1 teaspoon ground allspice
1 small head cabbage, cored and coarsely chopped
Salt
Cayenne pepper
Black pepper
Bread crumbs for sprinkling

Preheat the oven to 350 degrees F. Coat an 8-by-10-inch casserole dish with nonstick cooking spray.

In a large heavy pot, brown the ground beef over medium heat. Add the sugar, allspice, and cabbage. Season to taste with the salt, cayenne, and black pepper and stir to mix. Cook, stirring occasionally, until the cabbage is tender, about 15 minutes.

Pour the mixture into the casserole dish, and sprinkle the bread crumbs on the top. Bake for 20 minutes, or just until bubbly around the edges. Serve warm. 🌿

Chicken Tamale Casserole

MAURY MCCURDY RENDEIRO of New Orleans got this recipe for her Southwestern-style casserole a while ago from her mother, Susie Seal. "She knew we were getting ready to take a group deep-sea fishing and that I was trying to find something I could make ahead and bring down to the houseboat to just heat up. It was perfect and everyone loved it. Now I make it all of the time," Rendeiro wrote us. She often doubles the easy recipe, cooking it in an aluminum foil turkey-roasting pan.

{MAKES 12 TO 16 SERVINGS}

2 (15-ounce) cans tamales

2 large onions, finely chopped

¼ cup sliced pickled jalapeño peppers

¼ cup sliced pickled banana peppers (optional)

2 (4.5-ounce) cans chopped green chiles with their juice

3 cups grated cheddar cheese

1 (10.5-ounce) bag corn chips

2 (15-ounce) cans hot chili with beans

4 chicken breast halves (about 1½ pounds total), poached and cut into bite-size pieces (see Note)

1 (10-ounce) can enchilada sauce

Preheat the oven to 350 degrees F. Coat a 9-by-13-inch baking pan with nonstick cooking spray. Remove the papers from the tamales, reserving all the juices from the papers and cans. Cut the tamales into bite-size pieces and arrange them evenly in the bottom of the pan. In layers, add half of the following: onions, jalapeños, banana peppers (if using), chopped green chiles, cheese, and corn chips. Top with the contents of 1 can of chili with beans and the reserved tamale juices.

Next, layer with the chicken and the remaining onions, jalapeños, banana peppers (if using), chopped green chiles, cheese, and corn chips, and the second can of chili with beans. Poke a few holes in the top of the casserole with your finger or a knife, and pour the enchilada sauce over the top and around the sides.

Cover with aluminum foil and bake for 1 hour. Uncover and continue baking until brown on top, about 15 minutes more, checking often so the top doesn't burn. Serve warm. ❧

NOTE: *To poach the chicken breasts, cook, covered, in a large skillet in boiling salted water for 10 minutes, or until cooked through.*

Crabmeat Casserole

WHEN FRESH CRABMEAT is readily available, this is a good casserole to serve for a casual gathering. It's a favorite dish when Marcelle Bienvenu's large family gathers at their camp at Catahoula Lake near the Atchafalaya Basin. Accompany it with a green salad tossed with a tart vinaigrette and crusty French bread. If you don't want to use the claw meat, feel free to use all lump crabmeat.

{MAKES ABOUT 4 SERVINGS}

4 tablespoons butter

½ cup chopped green onions (white and green parts)

½ cup chopped celery

½ cup chopped green bell peppers

2 tablespoons all-purpose flour

1 cup milk

2 tablespoons fresh lemon juice

Salt

Cayenne pepper

½ pound lump crabmeat, picked over for shells and cartilage

½ pound claw crabmeat, picked over for shells and cartilage

¼ cup fine dry bread crumbs

¼ cup grated Parmesan cheese

Preheat the oven to 350 degrees F. Lightly grease a 9-inch square baking dish. Melt the butter in a heavy saucepan over medium heat. Add the green onions, celery, and bell peppers and cook, stirring, until they are soft and lightly browned, 5 to 6 minutes. Whisk in the flour. Slowly add the milk, stirring constantly until the mixture is thick and creamy. Add the lemon juice and season with the salt and cayenne pepper to taste. Gently fold in the crabmeat. Spoon the mixture into the prepared dish and top with the bread crumbs and cheese. Bake for 20 minutes, or until bubbly and lightly browned on top. ❧

Eggplant Casserole

J.S. OF BATON ROUGE asked if readers could help him find a recipe for an eggplant casserole like the one served at the long-gone A & G Cafeteria. "From what I remember," wrote J.S., "it seemed to be very simple, mostly eggplant and perhaps cracker crumbs, and onions, with a coating of bread crumbs. It had to be baked. It was moist but not runny. Most of the recipes you find for eggplant casserole have tomatoes in it. This recipe did not."

M.G. came to the rescue with a recipe and a note: "In 1981, [columnist] Angus Lind published such a recipe sent by a friend. This could be put in a casserole, sprinkled with bread crumbs, and baked briefly. It contains only eggplant, seasonings, and egg to bind it."

{MAKES 4 SERVINGS}

1 medium eggplant, peeled and cut into ½-inch cubes

1 small onion, finely chopped

½ cup Sauternes wine

4 tablespoons butter

2 large eggs, beaten

½ cup seasoned Italian bread crumbs

½ teaspoon salt

½ teaspoon black pepper

In a medium saucepan, combine the eggplant, onion, and Sauternes wine. Cover and cook over medium heat until the eggplant is tender, 15 to 20 minutes.

Stir and mash the eggplant with a fork or potato masher. Add the butter and stir until melted. Add the beaten eggs. Cover for 5 minutes to cook the eggs. Stir in the seasoned bread crumbs, salt, and pepper. Let set for 10 to 15 minutes, then eat and enjoy. 🦐

Mirliton Casserole
with Crabmeat, Crawfish, and Shrimp

"THANK YOU SO MUCH for this project! There have been many recipes over the years I have liked," wrote one reader who had lived in a suburb of New Orleans devastated by Katrina. "The one I really need is the mirliton casserole. It tasted like my Grandma's. I had tried to duplicate it over the years but never quite could. I made the recipe for Thanksgiving after it was in the paper and my mother wondered where I got the old family recipe!" The reader called it "the best mirliton recipe ever" and noted that her family missed it on the Thanksgiving after Katrina.

Seafood casseroles made with mirlitons (called "chayotes" elsewhere) are a Thanksgiving favorite in our area. This is the recipe the reader was looking for. It was created by native New Orleanian Carole Katz. The recipe halves easily.

{MAKES 24 TO 30 SIDE-DISH SERVINGS}

12 medium to large mirlitons, scrubbed

Butter for greasing, plus 1 cup (2 sticks), plus 2 tablespoons

4 cups finely chopped onions

6 large cloves garlic, minced

6 medium bay leaves

¼ cup minced fresh parsley

1 medium yellow bell pepper, finely chopped

1 medium red bell pepper, finely chopped

1 pound lump crabmeat, picked over for shells and cartilage

1 pound peeled crawfish tails, coarsely chopped

1 pound peeled boiled shrimp, coarsely chopped

1 teaspoon salt

¾ teaspoon black pepper, or to taste

¾ teaspoon Tabasco sauce, or to taste

3 tablespoons Worcestershire sauce

About 2½ cups seasoned Italian bread crumbs

TOPPING

¾ cup seasoned Italian bread crumbs

½ cup (1 stick) butter, cut into thin pats

In a large pot, boil the mirlitons whole until they are fork-tender, 45 minutes to 1 hour. Let cool, then peel. Remove and discard the seeds and any stringy pulp. Chop the pulp into small pieces and put in a colander to drain. Set aside or, if preparing ahead, cover and refrigerate; drain well before using.

Preheat the oven to 375 degrees F. Butter two 9-by-13-inch baking pans or large casserole dishes

In a 7-quart saucepan or a Dutch oven, melt the butter over high heat. Add the onions and garlic, and cook until the onions are clear, about 7 minutes, being careful not to burn the garlic. Stir in the drained mirlitons, bay leaves, and parsley. Reduce the heat and simmer for 20 minutes, stirring occasionally to keep the mixture from sticking to the bottom of the pan. Stir in the bell peppers, then add the crabmeat, crawfish, and shrimp, being careful to keep lumps of crabmeat intact as much as possible. Mix in the salt, pepper, Tabasco, and Worcestershire.

Gradually add enough bread crumbs, about 2½ cups, to absorb all the liquid. Once done, the mixture should be moist but not too wet. Continue cooking for 5 minutes more, stirring and scraping the bottom of the pan almost constantly. Remove the bay leaves from the mixture and transfer the mixture to the prepared pans.

For the topping: Sprinkle the top of the casseroles evenly with the ¾ cup bread crumbs and dot with the pats of butter. (If making ahead, refrigerate or freeze; thaw before baking.) Bake, uncovered, until the casserole is heated through and bubbly, and the top starts to brown, about 35 minutes. ❧

Oyster and Artichoke Casserole

MARCELLE BIENVENU'S MOTHER loved this version of oyster and artichoke casserole. This recipe may also be spooned into small pastry shells, heated, and served as hors d'ouevres.

{MAKES 4 TO 6 ENTRÉE OR 12 APPETIZER
   SERVINGS}

6 whole artichokes

½ cup (1 stick) butter or margarine

3 tablespoons all-purpose flour

⅔ cup finely chopped green onions (white and green parts)

1 teaspoon minced garlic

2 cups oyster liquor

Pinch of dried powdered thyme

Pinch of dried powdered oregano

Pinch of dried powdered marjoram

½ cup finely chopped fresh parsley

Salt

Black pepper

6 dozen oysters, drained and cut into smaller pieces if large

Thin slices of lemon for garnish (optional)

Paprika for garnish (optional)

In a large soup pot, cover the artichokes with water and bring to a boil. Lower the heat slightly and boil the artichokes until tender. Drain and let cool. When cool enough to handle, scrape the tender pulp from the leaves into a medium bowl. Clean the hearts and mash them together with the pulp.

Melt the butter in a large skillet over medium heat and stir in the flour slowly and constantly until smooth and well blended. Add the green onions and garlic and cook until the green onions are slightly wilted. Add the oyster liquor, thyme, oregano, marjoram, parsley, and the salt and pepper to taste. Simmer for 15 minutes.

Add the oysters and cook slowly until the edges curl. Add the mashed artichokes and blend into the mixture. Spoon the mixture into individual 4-ounce casserole cups. Garnish with the lemon slices, sprinkled with paprika, if desired.

Variation: The casserole can also be served in 3- to 4-inch pastry shells. Put the pastry shells on a baking sheet and bake at 375 degrees F until browned, about 15 minutes. Spoon the oyster-artichoke mixture into the shells and serve immediately. 🍃

Shrimp and Crawfish Fettuccini

THIS INCREDIBLY RICH dish is ideal to serve to a crowd. It originally appeared in Marcelle's column, and we received many requests to include it in this cookbook.

{MAKES ABOUT 12 SERVINGS}

1½ cups (3 sticks) butter

3 cups chopped onions

2 cups chopped green bell peppers

1 cup chopped celery

½ cup all-purpose flour

½ cup chopped fresh parsley

1½ pounds medium shrimp, peeled and deveined

1½ pounds peeled crawfish tails

2 cups half-and-half

1 pound Velveeta or American cheese, cubed

2 tablespoons chopped pickled jalapeño peppers

2 teaspoons chopped garlic

Salt

Cayenne Pepper

1 pound fettuccine, cooked according to the package directions and drained

1 cup grated Parmesan cheese

Preheat the oven to 350 degrees F.

Melt the butter in a large heavy Dutch oven over medium heat. Add the onions, bell peppers, and celery and cook, stirring often, for 10 minutes, or until they are wilted and pale gold. Add the flour and cook, stirring often, for 2 minutes. Add the parsley, shrimp, and crawfish. Cook, stirring often, for about 5 minutes, or until the shrimp turn pink. Add the half-and-half, cheese, jalapeños, and garlic. Stir until the cheese is completely melted and the mixture thickens, about 5 minutes. Season to taste with the salt and cayenne.

Arrange the fettuccine in a 3-quart casserole and pour the seafood mixture over it evenly. Sprinkle the top of the casserole with the Parmesan cheese. Bake for about 10 minutes, or until the mixture bubbles. ✥

The Only Casserole Recipe You'll Ever Need

In 1997, THE RECIPE exchange column of *The Times-Picayune* reprinted D.D.'s request for easy casseroles for the new mothers whom D.D. counseled. G.B., a reader from Violet, replied, "I'm always surprised when I see someone looking for casserole recipes, because when I was in Boy Scouts, I learned an easy way to create a nearly infinite variety of casseroles." Below is G.B.'s template.

{MAKES ABOUT 6 SERVINGS}

1 to 3 cups of casserole base (noodles, rice, or potatoes)

1 (10.75-ounce) can sauce (such as cheese soup, cream of mushroom soup, brown gravy)

1 cup cut-up fish or meat (such as canned tuna, cooked chicken, sausage)

About 1 (1-pound) can vegetables (such as peas, green beans, mixed vegetables)

Grated cheese, bread crumbs, or prepared french fried onions, such as French's

Preheat the oven to 350 degrees F. Coat a medium casserole dish with nonstick cooking spray.

Select a casserole base. This can be noodles or rice prepared according to the package directions, or boiled and sliced potatoes. Put the base in a large mixing bowl.

To the cooked base add a sauce. This can be canned soup or gravy or a prepared sauce made from the mixes that come in foil envelopes. Stir in cut-up fish or meat and add canned or cooked vegetables. Transfer the mixture to the prepared casserole dish. For a finishing touch, top with grated cheese, bread crumbs, or french fried onions. Bake in the oven for 20 minutes, or until browned and bubbly, and serve. ❧

Variations:

"The combinations are endless," G.B. wrote. "You'll never need a casserole recipe again." He recommended the following combinations:

— Rotini noodles, cheddar cheese soup, tuna, green peas

— Noodles, brown gravy, sour cream, slices of leftover steak, mushrooms

— Spaghetti, canned spaghetti sauce, Italian sausage, chopped tomatoes

— Rice, cream of chicken soup, chicken, carrots

— Scalloped potato mix (from a box) and corned beef

VEGETABLES

everal of the recipes included here are holiday favorites. The Glorified Cabbage (page 237) is a popular one for New Year's Day, while the Ruth's Chris Special Sweet Potato Casserole (page 243) and Sweet Potato Pudding (page 249) can go to the table for Thanksgiving, Christmas, or New Year's.

There are two recipes for stuffed bell peppers (pages 234 and 247) because they are a year-round choice. It seems that everyone loves the Piccadilly-Style Carrot Soufflé (page 242). It makes a great side dish to any meal and could almost be a dessert because it's both rich and sweet.

Although we found several versions of stuffed eggplant, we chose the one on page 248 because we had many requests for it. Ah, and the Eggplant Josephine (page 236)—well, it took us four months to find. We thank Nancy Burris, our head librarian, for tracking it down, and we are glad to include it here.

Vegetables

Café Degas' Stuffed Red Peppers

In 2003, when the New Orleans Museum of Art featured "Jefferson's America and Napoleon's France," twenty restaurants created special appetizers to serve on commemorative souvenir plates. Café Degas developed this dish for the promotion. To make it, use the canned small, cone-shaped, fire-roasted red peppers, which are available in Italian markets, or you can roast your own (see Note).

{MAKES 4 SIDE DISH OR 10 APPETIZER
 SERVINGS}

4 tablespoons butter

1 cup sliced white button mushrooms

½ cup diced onions

1 tablespoon minced garlic

½ bunch kale, chopped

½ pound fresh spinach, chopped

2 tablespoons bread crumbs

½ cup walnuts, toasted and roughly chopped

6 ounces cream cheese

6 ounces goat cheese

2 large eggs

Salt

Black pepper

10 fire-roasted red peppers (see Note)

Olive oil for brushing

Lemon-Butter Sauce (optional, recipe follows)

Preheat the oven to 350 degrees F.

Melt 1 tablespoon of the butter in a skillet over medium heat. Add the mushrooms and cook, stirring, for 3 to 5 minutes, until tender. Set aside.

Melt 1 tablespoon of the butter in the skillet over medium heat. Sauté the onions and garlic until very soft. Add the kale and spinach and cook until no raw taste remains. Add the cooked mushrooms.

In a small saucepan, melt the remaining 2 tablespoons of butter over medium heat and toast the bread crumbs in it. In a large bowl, combine the crumbs with the walnuts and cheeses. Add the eggs, one at a time, mixing well after each addition. Season with the salt and pepper.

Add the walnut and cheese mixture to the spinach mixture. Toss the ingredients together and spoon the mixture into the peppers, packing them lightly.

Line up the peppers in a baking pan and brush them with olive oil. Bake for 30 minutes. Remove from the oven and brush again with olive oil. Serve immediately, drizzled with the Lemon-Butter Sauce (if using). ❧

NOTE: *To roast your own peppers, hold a small red bell pepper over a gas burner until it's blackened all over. Transfer to a paper bag to cool the pepper. Then peel off the blackened skin. Alternately, roast the peppers under a broiler, turning often with a pair of tongs and watching them closely, until the skins are completely blackened. Cool and peel.*

Lemon-Butter Sauce

{MAKES ABOUT 1½ CUPS}

2 shallots, chopped

½ cup fresh lemon juice

1 cup heavy cream

4 tablespoons butter, cut into chunks

In a small saucepan, cook the shallots in the lemon juice over medium heat until the liquid reduces by half. Add the heavy cream and cook, reducing the cream slightly. Stir in the butter and serve. ❧

Creole Okra

In 2001, Monique Y. Wells's French cookbook *La Cuisine Noire Americaine* was published in English under the title *Food for the Soul*. Wells, a native Texan with Louisiana Creole roots, and a veterinary pathologist, had followed her dream and moved to Paris. There was one problem, however. She found herself scouring the Parisian markets for sweet potatoes and okra. This recipe from the cookbook, which accompanied an article by Dale Curry in *The Times-Picayune*, was one of her mother's favorites.

{MAKES 4 TO 6 SERVINGS}

1 pound okra

2 tablespoons vegetable oil

1 medium onion, chopped

1 to 2 cloves garlic, minced

1 (8-ounce) can tomato sauce

1 chicken bouillon cube

1 cup water

1 teaspoon salt

½ to 1 teaspoon black pepper

½ to 1 teaspoon dried basil leaves

¼ to ½ teaspoon garlic powder (optional)

Trim off the stems and cut the okra crosswise into ¾-inch pieces. Heat the oil in a large saucepan or a Dutch oven. Sauté the okra, stirring frequently, so that it browns on all sides. Add the onion and garlic, and sauté until softened. Stir in the tomato sauce.

Dissolve the bouillon cube in the water, and add to the pan. Add the salt, pepper, basil, and garlic powder (if using). Reduce the heat and simmer, stirring occasionally, for 30 to 45 minutes, until all slime has disappeared. Taste occasionally and correct the seasoning.

Variation: Add cooked spicy sausage or cooked shrimp 5 to 10 minutes before the end of the cooking time. ⊱

Eggplant Josephine

LEONA CERNY, from Slidell, wrote us "There was a beautiful restaurant on the Gulf Coast called the White Pillars, and one of my favorite dishes was called Eggplant Josephine. It [had] a delicious sauce served over fried eggplant. This sauce was dark reddish brown and slightly sweet. If possible please try to find this recipe as I have spent hours looking through all my cookbooks!"

We started looking, and finally found this recipe. It appeared in *The Commercial Appeal* in Memphis during the 2004 holiday season. The combination of the meat sauce, crabmeat, and hollandaise makes this a rich, special occasion dish.

{MAKES 4 TO 6 SERVINGS}

1 large eggplant

2 tablespoons all-purpose flour

3 tablespoons olive oil

4 tablespoons butter

½ cup Sauternes wine

1 pound lump crabmeat, picked over for shells and cartilage

1 (26-ounce) jar Italian spaghetti sauce with meat

1 (8-ounce) package mozzarella cheese, shredded

HOLLANDAISE SAUCE

2 large egg yolks

2 cups mayonnaise

1½ teaspoons Worcestershire sauce

2 tablespoons dry mustard

Salt

White pepper

Preheat the oven to 450 degrees F. Coat a shallow baking pan with nonstick cooking spray.

Peel the eggplant and slice ¾ to 1 inch thick. Sprinkle the slices with the flour. Heat the oil in a large skillet and sauté the eggplant until lightly browned. Set aside.

Melt the butter in a medium saucepan and add the wine. Add the crabmeat and simmer for 6 minutes. Set aside.

To assemble the dish, lay the eggplant slices in the bottom of the prepared pan. In layers add the crabmeat mixture, meat sauce, and shredded cheese. Bake until the cheese is melted, bubbly, and begins to brown, about 20 minutes.

Make the hollandaise sauce: In a medium bowl, beat the egg yolks until frothy. Stir in the mayonnaise and then the Worcestershire. Add the dry mustard and the salt and pepper to taste.

Serve the eggplant with some warm hollandaise on each slice. ❧

Glorified Cabbage

Several versions of this dish have appeared in the newspaper over the years, but this one, from Marcelle Bienvenu's column, really does glorify the lowly cabbage. Because local tradition dictates that eating cabbage on New Year's Day will ensure good fortune, by all means offer this to those who think they don't like cabbage. Then watch them gobble it up!

{MAKES 6 TO 8 SERVINGS}

4 slices white bread
½ cup milk
1 large cabbage, cored and chopped
2 tablespoons vegetable oil
1½ cups chopped onions
½ cup chopped green bell peppers
½ cup chopped celery
1 tablespoon chopped garlic
1 cup heavy cream
½ cup (1 stick) butter
Salt
Cayenne pepper
1 tablespoon chopped fresh parsley
½ pound mild cheddar cheese, grated
¼ cup fine dry bread crumbs

Preheat the oven to 350 degrees F. Coat a casserole dish with nonstick cooking spray.

Toast the bread, soak in the milk in a shallow dish, and squeeze dry. Set aside.

Boil the cabbage in a pot full of water until just tender. Drain and set aside.

In a large saucepan, heat the oil over medium heat. Add the onions, bell peppers, celery, and garlic. Cook, stirring, until soft and pale gold, 6 to 8 minutes. Add the cabbage and reduce the heat to medium-low. Cook, covered, until very tender, about 10 minutes.

Tear the soaked bread slices into bits and add to the pot. Add the cream and butter and cook, stirring, until the butter is melted, about 5 minutes. Season to taste with the salt and cayenne. Add the parsley and stir to mix well.

Transfer the mixture to the prepared casserole dish and sprinkle evenly with the cheese and bread crumbs. Bake until bubbly and hot, 20 to 30 minutes. ❧

Let-Um Have It Eggplant

WHEN JOHN UNGER JR. was injured in an industrial accident in 1976, he took up cooking as a hobby. A tall, strapping, tattooed man from the Irish Channel neighborhood of New Orleans, Unger was the subject of a *Times-Picayune* article in 1993. This dish is one of his favorites.

{MAKES ABOUT 6 SERVINGS}

2 medium or large eggplants

About 3 tablespoons fresh lemon juice

2 tablespoons salt

2 cups ice cubes

3 large eggs

1 cup whole milk

1 tablespoon granulated garlic

2 cups seasoned Italian bread crumbs

Peanut oil for frying

1 cup grated Parmesan cheese

1 cup (2 sticks) butter

½ teaspoon liquid crab boil

½ pound lump crabmeat, picked over for shells and cartilage

1 pound small shrimp, peeled and deveined

1 large yellow onion, finely chopped

1 bunch green onions, finely chopped

1 medium green bell pepper, finely chopped

2 stalks celery, chopped

1 tablespoon minced garlic

¼ pound mushrooms, thinly sliced

2 tablespoons all-purpose flour

1 (8-ounce) package cream cheese

1 pint half-and-half

3 or 4 drops Tabasco sauce

1 teaspoon fresh lemon juice

Dash of white pepper

Dash of cayenne pepper

Dash of black pepper

½ teaspoon paprika

1 tablespoon Worcestershire sauce

To make the eggplant more crisp when fried, peel it and slice ¼ inch thick. Add enough water to a large bowl to fill it about two-thirds full, and add the lemon juice and salt. Submerge the eggplant in the water and put the ice cubes on top. Refrigerate for 1 hour.

Combine the eggs, milk, and granulated garlic in a shallow bowl and whisk to blend. Put the bread crumbs in another shallow bowl. Drain the eggplant and pat dry. Dip the eggplant first in the milk mixture, then dredge in the bread crumbs.

In a large skillet over medium heat, warm the oil and fry the eggplant slices in batches until golden on both sides. Drain on paper towels and sprinkle with Parmesan cheese while the eggplant is still hot.

Melt 4 tablespoons of the butter over medium heat in a large saucepan. Add ¼ teaspoon of the liquid crab boil and the crabmeat and cook for 2 minutes. Add another 4 tablespoons of butter, another ¼ teaspoon of liquid crab boil, and the shrimp. Cook until the shrimp turn pink. Remove from the heat and pour off the liquid in the pan.

To make the sauce, melt the remaining stick of butter in a large heavy pot, such as a Dutch oven, over medium heat. Add the yellow onion, green onions, bell pepper, and celery. Cook, stirring, until soft, about 3 minutes. Add the garlic and mushrooms and cook, stirring, for 2 minutes. Add the flour and mix well. Break the cream cheese into small pieces and add to the pot, stirring until the cream cheese is melted and the mixture is smooth. Add the half-and-half, Tabasco, lemon juice, white pepper, cayenne, black pepper, paprika and Worcestershire.

Mix well and continue cooking over medium heat until the sauce is thick and smooth. Add the drained crabmeat and shrimp and stir gently. Remove from the heat and serve with the fried eggplant. ✺

Maquechou

ON THE FIRST anniversary of Hurricane Katrina, physician Justin Lundgren offered his plan for "the lost tribe of New Orleans" to commemorate the event in a respectful, positive, and moving way: a ritual Katrina dinner. He established a Web site urging "the entire New Orleans diaspora" to "sit down simultaneously, fork in hand, to tell the world that this was a special place, a special community, one worth fighting to restore." With symbolic foods, readings, a candle blessing, and more, Lundgren based his ritual on the Passover seder—with a little voodoo thrown in. New Orleans food experts chimed in with their suggestions. Professor Jessica Harris had excellent ideas, such as including king cake to symbolize our joy in life.

The anniversary was commemorated in other culinary ways, too. At the Crescent City Farmers Market, a Community Thanksgiving Picnic was held. Tables were decorated with "a river of red beans to remember" and orchids. "Don't Leave Home Without Them: Essential Recipes for Evacuation" were handed out, too.

This is Harris' recipe from *Beyond Gumbo*, one of her many cookbooks. Spelled various ways (such as macque choux) and prounounced "mock shoe," this is a Cajun-country favorite.

{MAKES 4 TO 6 SERVINGS}

2 tablespoons butter

4 cups fresh corn kernels (about 6 to 8 ears)

2 large onions, finely chopped

1 pint light cream

2 tablespoons minced pimientos

Dash of Tabasco sauce

Salt

Freshly ground black pepper

Melt the butter over medium heat in a 3-quart saucepan, and sauté the corn for 2 to 3 minutes, or until tender. Add the onions and cook for 5 minutes, stirring occasionally. Heat the cream in a small saucepan or in a glass measuring cup in the microwave and gradually add it to the corn and onion mixture, stirring occasionally. Cover, lower the heat, and simmer for 10 minutes. Add the pimientos, Tabasco, and the salt and pepper to taste. Cook for an additional 2 to 3 minutes. Adjust the seasoning, and serve hot. ❧

Marinated Green Beans

Amy Cyrex Sins lived in Lakeview, ten houses from the breach of the 17th Street Canal. When her beloved recipes and cookbooks were lost, along with all her other possessions, she couldn't ask her relatives for copies, because they lived in the area and also lost everything.

Sins poured her heart and soul into a new self-published cookbook, which she could take with her the next time she evacuated. She called it *Ruby Slippers Cookbook: Life, Culture, Family and Food After Katrina,* and she illustrated it with lots of photos, creating a moving snapshot of life the first six months after the flood. She tested recipes in the tiny kitchen of an apartment in the French Quarter where she and her husband lived while they rebuilt their home. This recipe became one of Sins' new favorites.

{MAKES 6 SERVINGS}

1½ cups white wine vinegar

½ cup olive oil

1½ cups water

1 tablespoon whole black peppercorns

½ teaspoon liquid crab boil

1 jalapeño, diced

2 teaspoons kosher salt

2 tablespoons mustard seeds

1 tablespoon Creole seasoning

¼ cup olive juice from a jar of green olives

4 cloves garlic, sliced

1 pound green beans, stem ends trimmed

1 red bell pepper, cut into strips

1 yellow bell pepper, cut into strips

Put all the ingredients except the green beans and peppers in a medium saucepan and bring to a boil. Reduce the heat and simmer for 15 minutes.

Put the green beans and bell peppers in a shallow dish and pour the simmering marinade over them. Cover with plastic wrap. Let cool, then transfer to a plastic freezer bag and refrigerate for several hours, or until ready to serve, turning the bag occasionally. Serve chilled. ❧

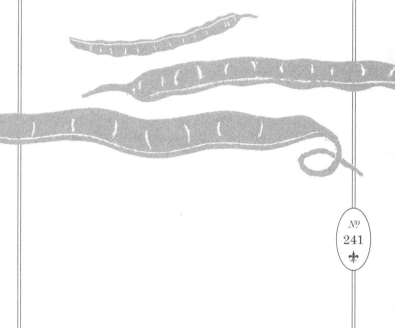

Piccadilly-Style Carrot Soufflé

In November 2005, Judy Walker, the food editor of *The Times-Picayune*, received this note from a faithful reader, B.B. of Baton Rouge: "Welcome back to circulation. I missed *The Times-Picayune*, and am so glad to see you back. I like the idea of Rebuilding Recipes and remember how you helped my daughter-in-law . . . after [Hurricane] Ivan." (She had asked for a favorite recipe her daughter-in-law lost on the Gulf Coast in 2004.)

B.B. describes herself as a Gentilly girl (a neighborhood in New Orleans). She shared this recipe, one of her favorite Thanksgiving dishes, which she adapted from *Southern Living* magazine. Carrot soufflé has been a much-requested recipe over the years, especially around the holidays. It is popular because many in the South have enjoyed it at Piccadilly Cafeterias, and it is easily made at the last minute.

{MAKES 12 SERVINGS}

3 pounds carrots, peeled and sliced

1½ cups (3 sticks) butter or margarine

6 large eggs

½ cup all-purpose flour

1 tablespoon baking powder

3 cups sugar

1 tablespoon vanilla extract

Preheat the oven to 350 degrees F. Lightly grease two 1½-quart soufflé or baking dishes.

Cover the carrots with water in a large saucepan and bring to a boil. Continue boiling for 15 minutes, or until tender, and drain.

In a food processor, combine the carrots with the remaining ingredients. Process until smooth, stopping once to scrape down the sides. Spoon into the two prepared baking dishes. Bake until the mixture sets and is lightly browned, about 1 hour. Serve immediately. ❧

Ruth's Chris
Special Sweet Potato Casserole

EVER SINCE RUTH'S CHRIS first shared the recipe for its popular sweet potato casserole with *The Times-Picayune* in 2004, it has been a holiday favorite of many readers. The Ruth's Chris Steak House chain of restaurants was founded in New Orleans by the late Ruth Fertel, who loved this dish, which was developed by executive chef Jim Cannon.

{MAKES 6 TO 8 SERVINGS}

CRUST

1 cup light brown sugar

⅓ cup all-purpose flour

1 cup chopped nuts, preferably pecans

⅓ stick butter, melted

Butter for greasing

FILLING

3 cups mashed cooked sweet potatoes (about 3 pounds, see Note)

1 cup sugar

½ teaspoon salt

1 teaspoon vanilla extract

2 large eggs, well beaten

½ cup (1stick) butter, melted

For the crust: Combine the ingredients in a small bowl and set aside.

Preheat the oven to 350 degrees F, and butter a baking dish.

For the filling: Combine the sweet potatoes, sugar, salt, vanilla, eggs, and butter in a mixing bowl and stir to blend well.

Pour the mixture into the prepared dish. Sprinkle the surface evenly with the crust mixture and bake for 30 minutes. Allow to set for at least 30 minutes before serving. ❧

NOTE: *To cook the sweet potatoes, put the whole potatoes (do not peel) on a baking sheet and cook at 400 degrees F for 30 minutes. Reduce the heat to 375 degrees F and bake until tender, about 45 minutes. Let cool, and then peel and mash with a potato masher.*

Seafood-Stuffed Bell Peppers

Paulette Rittenberg's "Home Cooking" column in *The Times-Picayune* offered this recipe in April 2000. It came from Metairie resident Nicole Boyd, who learned how to make stuffed bell peppers just like those prepared by her mother, Celeste Boyd. "Since the bread absorbs a lot of the seasoning as the peppers cook, you have to overseason them so they come out right," said Nicole, who sometimes adds cayenne pepper, too.

{MAKES 12 SIDE-DISH SERVINGS}

8 medium green bell peppers
1½ tablespoons vegetable oil
1 large onion, chopped
½ cup chopped fresh parsley
3 cloves garlic, minced
1½ pounds ground beef
1 pound shrimp, peeled, deveined, and chopped
1 (8-ounce) can crabmeat with the liquid
1 teaspoon Tony Chachere's Creole seasoning
1 (18-ounce) loaf stale white sandwich bread
2 tablespoons butter, softened or melted
Cayenne pepper (optional)
About ⅓ cup fine dry bread crumbs for sprinkling

Cut the bell peppers in half lengthwise, and remove the seeds and membranes. Fill a large pot with water and boil the peppers for 10 minutes. Drain well.

Meanwhile, heat the oil in a large skillet over high heat. Add the onion, parsley, and garlic, and cook, stirring, until the onions are browned, about 5 minutes. Transfer to a bowl.

In the same skillet, cook the beef over medium heat until it is no longer pink, about 6 minutes, breaking it into small bits. Add the shrimp, crabmeat, and onion mixture, folding all the ingredients together. Continue cooking for 10 minutes more. Season heavily with the Creole and remove from the heat.

Preheat the oven to 350 degrees F. Chop 4 of the parboiled bell pepper halves and mix into the meat mixture. Transfer the mixture to a large mixing bowl.

Sprinkle the bread slices, including the heels, with water. (They should be slightly damp, not soaking wet.) Add the bread to the bowl and stir until the bread disappears into the mixture. Add the butter and taste for seasoning. The stuffing should be very generously seasoned. Add more Creole seasoning and the cayenne (if using).

Stuff the mixture into the remaining bell pepper halves and arrange them on a baking sheet. Sprinkle with bread crumbs. Bake, uncovered, until the bread crumbs are nice and toasty, 20 to 30 minutes. Serve immediately. (You can also let cool, wrap well, and freeze for later.)

Spinach Madeleine

MANY SOUTH LOUISIANA residents will not sit down to Thanksgiving dinner unless there's a large casserole of Spinach Madeleine on the buffet table. This is the most famous recipe from arguably the most famous community cookbook on the planet, *River Road Recipes,* first published in 1959 by the Junior League of Baton Rouge. More than 1.3 million copies of *River Road Recipes* are in print.

When Kraft Foods quit making an essential ingredient, jalapeño cheese rolls, south Louisiana cooks panicked. Velveeta Mexican Mild cheese has become the substitute of choice.

{MAKES ABOUT 8 SERVINGS}

2 (10-ounce) packages frozen chopped spinach

4 tablespoons butter

2 tablespoons all-purpose flour

2 tablespoons chopped onions

½ cup evaporated milk

½ teaspoon black pepper

¾ teaspoon celery salt

¾ teaspoon garlic salt

1 teaspoon Worcestershire sauce

Salt

Cayenne pepper

6 ounces pasteurized processed Mexican-style cheese, such as Velveeta Mexican Mild, cut into small pieces

Buttered bread crumbs (optional, see Note)

Preheat the oven to 350 degrees F. Coat a 9-inch square casserole dish with nonstick cooking spray.

Cook the spinach according to the package directions. Drain and reserve ½ cup of the liquid from the pot.

Melt the butter in a saucepan over low heat. Add the flour, stirring until blended and smooth, but not brown. Add the onions and cook until soft but not browned. Add the milk and reserved liquid from the spinach, stirring constantly to avoid any lumps. Cook, stirring, until smooth and thick. Add the pepper, celery salt, garlic salt, Worcestershire, and the salt and cayenne to taste. Add the cheese and stir until it is completely melted.

Pour into the prepared casserole and top with buttered bread crumbs (if using). Bake until bubbly, about 30 minutes. Serve warm. ✿

NOTE: *To make buttered bread crumbs, cut off the crusts of 2 slices of bread and crumble in a food processor or by rubbing between your hands. Melt 2 tablespoons of butter in a saucepan over medium heat and sauté the crumbs for 1 minute.*

Submitted by River Road Recipes/Junior League of Baton Rouge, Inc. From River Road Recipes: The Textbook of Louisiana Cuisine. *www.juniorleaguebr.org*

Squash and Pepper Kabobs

During the summer, when squash and bell peppers are at their peak, this is a delightful, easy recipe to slap on the grill. Serve the kabobs with rice pilaf or roasted new potatoes.

{MAKES 4 SERVINGS}

⅓ cup olive oil

2 tablespoons red wine vinegar

1 clove garlic, minced

2 teaspoons minced fresh thyme, or ½ teaspoon dried

½ teaspoon salt

¼ teaspoon freshly ground black pepper

1½ pounds yellow squash or zucchini, cut into 1-inch pieces

1 medium red bell pepper, cut into 1-inch pieces

1 medium green bell pepper, cut into 1-inch pieces

10 to 12 large white button mushrooms, stemmed

Whisk together the oil, vinegar, garlic, thyme, salt, and pepper in a large mixing bowl. Add the vegetables and toss to coat evenly. Let stand for about 30 minutes.

Prepare a medium fire in a charcoal grill or preheat a gas grill.

Remove the vegetables from the marinade and reserve the marinade. Thread the bell peppers, squash pieces, and mushrooms alternately onto skewers. Arrange the skewers on the grill rack. Grill, turning occasionally and brushing with the reserved marinade, until lightly browned, 8 to 10 minutes. Serve warm. 🎕

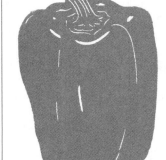

Stuffed Bell Peppers

JUST ABOUT EVERYONE in south Louisiana has a favorite stuffed bell pepper recipe. This one came from Marcelle Bienvenu's mother. The combination of the eggplant and ground beef or turkey is a great pairing.

{MAKES 12 SIDE-DISH SERVINGS}

6½ large green bell peppers
2 tablespoons vegetable oil
1 large onion, finely chopped
2 stalks celery, finely chopped
1½ pounds lean ground beef or ground turkey
2 medium eggplants, peeled and cubed
Salt
Cayenne pepper
1½ cups fine dry bread crumbs
½ cup grated Romano cheese

Preheat the oven to 375 degrees F. Cut 6 of the bell peppers in half lengthwise and remove the seeds and membrane. Finely chop the remaining ½ bell pepper.

Drop the 12 bell pepper halves in a pot of boiling water for a minute or so. Remove from the pot, drain, and let cool.

Heat the vegetable oil over medium heat in a large saucepan. Add the onions, chopped bell pepper, and celery. Cook, stirring, until they are soft, 3 to 4 minutes. Add the ground beef and brown well, breaking it up into bits. Add the eggplant, cover, and cook, stirring often, until it's tender and soft. Season to taste with the salt and cayenne.

Add just enough enough bread crumbs to bind the mixture, about 1 cup. Stuff the mixture into the bell pepper halves, and sprinkle with the remaining bread crumbs and the Romano cheese. Bake until the bread crumbs and cheese are lightly browned, about 20 minutes. (These peppers freeze well. Wrap well before storing in the freezer.)

Variation: Instead of the bread crumbs, use cooked rice to thicken the stuffing. 🌶

Stuffed Eggplant

As you may imagine, there are many versions of this dish, a popular one in the New Orleans area. This recipe came from P.S. of Marrero.

{MAKES 8 SERVINGS}

½ cup olive oil

2 cups finely chopped onions

3 cloves garlic, minced

½ cup finely chopped celery

½ cup chopped green bell peppers

1 pound small to medium shrimp, peeled, deveined, and chopped

4 medium eggplants, boiled until tender, and drained

⅓ cup grated Parmesan cheese

¼ teaspoon dried oregano leaves

¼ teaspoon dried thyme leaves

¼ teaspoon cayenne pepper

1 bay leaf

⅓ cup chopped fresh parsley

½ cup fine dry bread crumbs, plus extra for sprinkling

Salt (optional)

Preheat oven to 350 degrees F.

In a large saucepan heat the oil over medium-low heat. Add the onions, garlic, celery, bell peppers, and shrimp, and cook, stirring, until the vegetables are soft and golden, about 10 minutes.

Cut the cooked eggplant in half lengthwise. Scoop out most of the flesh, leaving a sturdy shell. Set aside the shells and add the flesh to the shrimp mixture. Stir in the cheese, oregano, thyme, cayenne, bay leaf, parsley, and bread crumbs. Mix well and simmer, stirring occasionally, for 30 minutes. Season with salt (if using). Remove the bay leaf.

Fill the eggplant shells with the stuffing, and sprinkle with extra bread crumbs. Place in a large baking dish and bake until browned. ✖

VARIATIONS:

— Instead of stuffing the eggplant shells, put the filling in a buttered casserole dish and bake.

— The filling mixture can also be used to stuff bell peppers or squash.

— Substitute ground beef, ham, or bacon for the shrimp.

Sweet Potato Pudding

SWEET POTATOES ARE a staple on holiday menus, and this is one of those classic recipes that the locals love. One of the region's most popular sweet potatoes is the Beauregard variety, developed in Louisiana.

{MAKES 6 TO 8 SERVINGS}

Butter for greasing, plus 4 tablespoons, at room temperature

3 cups mashed cooked sweet potatoes (see Note on page 243), or 1 (29-ounce) can sweet potatoes, drained and mashed

1 cup sugar

2 large eggs, lightly beaten

1 cup grated coconut

½ cup milk

1 teaspoon vanilla extract

TOPPING

1 cup firmly packed light brown sugar

1 cup chopped pecans

½ cup all-purpose flour

½ cup (1 stick) margarine or butter, melted

Pinch of salt

Preheat the oven to 350 degrees F. Butter an 8-inch square baking dish.

In a large mixing bowl, beat together the sweet potatoes, sugar, 4 tablespoons butter, eggs, coconut, milk, and vanilla. Pour into the prepared baking dish.

For the topping: In a small bowl, combine the ingredients and stir until well mixed. Spoon the mixture over the sweet potatoes. Bake for 1 hour, until bubbly. ❧

CAKES & PIES

The recipes in this chapter are especially interesting. We were over-whelmed by the many duplicate requests for these tasty treats. More than ten readers "just had to have the recipe for the Gooey Butter Cake" (page 267). And you can't imagine how many people wanted a recipe for a dump cake. We found several and decided to go with Pineapple Dump Cake (page 259).

We had never heard of a Russian Cake (page 281), which is made with leftover pieces of cake and is also known as Creole trifle, until we began researching the cake for this book. Leave it to New Orleanians to figure out how to use leftovers to make an incredible work of art and flavor!

The Baptist Hospital's American Cheese Pie (page 255) is a tasty, pudding-like treat that brought back lots of sweet memories for many of our readers. And even if you don't have a sweet tooth, you *must* make Maylie's Whiskied Prune Pie (page 272)—it's delicious!

Although king cakes (pages 264 and 270) are available at just about every bakery, grocery store, and supermarket all over the New Orleans area during the Carnival season, you should make your very own one year just to say you did so.

Judy Walker, our food editor, says the Blueberry Gâteau (page 257) "rocks," so you might want to give it a try. Marcelle Bienvenu's personal favorite is the mile-high pie (page 273) from the Pontchartrain Hotel.

We trust you'll find a favorite or two in these offerings.

CAKES & PIES

Bananas Foster Pie

BANANAS COOKED IN butter, brown sugar, and rum and served over ice cream is a New Orleans favorite. This is one of many excellent variations on the theme.

{MAKES 12 SERVINGS}

2 quarts vanilla, almond praline, or butter pecan ice cream, softened

1 (9-inch) graham cracker crust

4 tablespoons unsalted butter

½ cup packed light brown sugar

¼ teaspoon ground cinnamon

¼ cup dark rum

6 medium bananas, peeled and cut into ¼-inch slices.

Spread the softened ice cream evenly over the crust. Freeze until firm, 3 to 4 hours.

Just before serving, melt the butter in a large skillet over medium heat in a large skillet. Stir in the brown sugar, cinnamon, and rum. Add the bananas and heat through.

To serve, cut the pie into wedges and spoon equal amounts of the banana mixture over each serving.

Baptist Hospital's American Cheese Pie

WE RECEIVED SEVERAL requests for recipes from the cafeteria at Baptist Hospital in New Orleans. B.B. from Baton Rouge sent in this recipe for a most unusual pie, which was served at the cafeteria for many years. Although some versions of the pie do specify American cheese (hence the name), this one calls for cheddar.

{MAKES 6 TO 8 SERVINGS}

½ cup (1 stick) unsalted butter, at room temperature
¾ cup plus 2 tablespoons sugar
1 teaspoon all-purpose flour
2 large eggs
½ cup grated cheddar cheese
⅓ cup milk
1 teaspoon vanilla extract
1 unbaked 9-inch pie shell

Preheat the oven to 350 degrees F.

In a medium mixing bowl, beat together the butter, sugar, and flour with an electric mixer until creamy. Add the eggs, beating well, then add the grated cheese, milk, and vanilla.

Pour the mixture into the unbaked pie shell and bake until the custard sets, 40 to 50 minutes. 🐎

Berry Nutty Pie

THE TIMES-PICAYUNE received a request from a reader who had long been searching for the recipe for her husband's favorite strawberry pie. The problem was that the person who used to bake this pie for her husband was his ex. "At every occasion that calls for a special dessert, that pie is ALL he talks about!!!" she wrote. Her own dessert efforts always fell "a distant second to a memory."

L.H. of Folsom discovered the recipe in her files, exactly as described, an unusual combination of meringue, chocolate, nuts, and buttery cracker crumbs, baked and topped with sliced strawberries. In a national recipe contest, it had won $100,000 for Bobbie C. Meyer, a teacher from Chauvin.

{MAKES 8 SERVINGS}

3 large egg whites, at room temperature

¾ cup sugar

½ teaspoon baking powder

¾ cup semisweet chocolate morsels

½ cup pecan pieces

1 cup crumbs of buttery-flavored crackers, such as Ritz Crackers (see Note)

1 teaspoon almond extract

1 cup whipping cream

2 tablespoons confectioners' sugar

½ teaspoon vanilla extract

1 pint strawberries, hulled and cut into ¼-inch slices

Preheat the oven to 350 degrees F. Grease a 9-inch pie plate, or coat it with nonstick cooking spray.

In a small deep bowl, beat the egg whites with an electric mixer until soft peaks form.

Combine the sugar and baking powder and gradually add the mixture to the egg whites, beating until stiff peaks form.

Set aside 2 tablespoons of the chocolate morsels and coarsely chop the rest.

Set aside 1 tablespoon of the pecan pieces and process the rest in a food processor until ground. In a small bowl, combine the cracker crumbs, chopped chocolate, and ground pecans. Fold into the egg whites along with the almond extract. Spread the mixture in the prepared pie plate. Bake for 25 minutes. Let cool completely.

In small deep bowl, beat the cream, confectioners' sugar, and vanilla with an electric mixer until stiff peaks form.

Set aside ¾ cup of the strawberry slices to use for garnish, and fold the remaining berries into the whipped cream. Spread over the baked layer. Garnish with the reserved strawberries, pecans, and chocolate morsels. 🌿

NOTE: *You can crush the crackers in a food processor, or put them in a zip-top bag, shut it securely, and smash them with a rolling pin.*

Blueberry Gâteau

WHEN FRESH BLUEBERRIES are in season, this is the way to go! The cake is moist and absolutely delicious.

{MAKES 6 SERVINGS}

1 cup all-purpose flour, plus 1 teaspoon

1 teaspoon baking powder

½ teaspoon kosher salt

½ cup (1 stick) unsalted butter, at room temperature

1 cup sugar

¼ teaspoon vanilla extract

2 large eggs

1 pint blueberries

1 teaspoon fresh lemon juice

Confectioners' sugar for dusting

Preheat the oven to 350 degrees F. Lightly grease a 9-inch springform pan and dust with flour, or line the bottom of a 9-inch round cake pan with parchment paper, and grease and flour the pan.

In a small bowl, whisk together the 1 cup flour with the baking powder and salt and set aside.

In a medium bowl, use an electric mixer on high speed to beat the butter, sugar, and vanilla until fluffy, about 3 minutes. Add the eggs, one at a time, and beat until well blended. Reduce the speed to low and gradually add the flour mixture. Beat until smooth.

Pour the batter into the prepared pan. In a medium bowl, combine the blueberries with the remaining 1 teaspoon of flour and the lemon juice. Spoon the blueberry mixture over the batter.

Bake for 1 hour, or until a cake tester inserted in the center comes out clean. Remove from the oven and let the cake cool in the pan for 10 minutes. If using a springform pan, slide a thin knife around the sides of the cake to release it before removing the side of the pan. Dust with confectioners' sugar before serving. ❧

Classic Bacardi Rum Cake

New Orleanians have a long history with rum, which was the base of many early drinks, so it's not surprising that this cake is a favorite of our readers. We received many requests for it and had several recipes in our archives. Here is one that Y.G. of Kenner sent in 1997.

{MAKES ABOUT 10 SERVINGS}

CAKE

1 cup chopped pecans or walnuts
1 (18.25-ounce) box yellow cake mix
1 (3.25-ounce) package vanilla instant pudding
4 large eggs, lightly beaten
½ cup cold water
½ cup vegetable oil
½ cup dark rum (80 proof), such as Bacardi

GLAZE

½ cup (1 stick) unsalted butter
¼ cup water
1 cup sugar
½ cup dark rum (80 proof), such as Bacardi

For the cake: Preheat the oven to 325 degrees F. Grease and flour a 10-inch tube pan or a 12-cup Bundt pan. Sprinkle the nuts over the bottom of the pan. In a large mixing bowl, mix all the remaining ingredients together, then and pour over the nuts. Bake for 1 hour, or until a cake tester inserted near the center comes out clean and the cake pulls away from the sides of the pan. Let cool in the pan for 10 minutes before turning it out onto a rack to cool completely.

For the glaze: While the cake is cooling, melt the butter in a small saucepan. Stir in the water and sugar. Boil for 5 minutes, stirring constantly. Remove from the heat and stir in the rum.

When the cake has cooled, prick the top all over with the tines of a fork. Drizzle the glaze over the top and sides of the cake. ❧

Pineapple Dump Cake

C.H. ASKED FOR a simple cake recipe that she described this way: "You first covered the bottom of a baking dish with crushed pineapple. The other ingredients, I think, were coconut and nuts and a package of dry cake mix." It was a favorite in her house. "I clipped it, made it for every occasion and people loved it," she wrote. "My home in Bay St. Louis, Miss., was completely destroyed and all contents lost. If anyone can furnish this recipe, it would be greatly appreciated. I have people asking me to make it but can't remember how. Thanks."

We published this recipe in 2000. It is one variation of a formula that has been around forever, which takes its inelegant name from the lack of mixing required. Although no coconut is included, you (or C.H.) can add a cup, along with the pecans.

{MAKES 12 TO 16 SERVINGS}

1 (20-ounce) can crushed pineapple
1 (18.25-ounce) box yellow cake mix
1 cup chopped pecans
1 cup (2 sticks) unsalted butter

Preheat the oven to 350 degrees F.

Spread out the pineapple evenly in a 9-by-13-inch baking pan. Sprinkle the cake mix over the pineapple, then sprinkle the pecans over the cake mix. Cut the butter evenly into pats and arrange over the top. Bake for 50 to 55 minutes, until the cake springs back when lightly touched. Cool in the pan before cutting. ❧

Ebinger's All-Chocolate Blackout Cake

THIS RECIPE APPEARED in the first recipe exchange column by *The Times-Picayune*'s Food editor, Judy Walker, after Hurricane Katrina. She had written the column on the Saturday before the disaster. She rewrote it three months later, when the newspaper was back in operation. The column is reprinted here:

Way back in a time that seems so far away— about three months ago—reader R. McC. of New Orleans wrote that she wanted a recipe for Blackout Cake. She wanted to surprise a friend, whose favorite cake is the blackout one.

I don't know if R. McC. still needs this recipe. But I do know that many of us may want to start the re-creation of recipe collections, so here is the recipe I found for her.

It seems appropriate that we start with something rich, chocolate, and complicated enough to take our minds off everything else for a few hours. This recipe is in the 1992 New York Cookbook: From Pelham Bay to Park Avenue, Firehouses to Four Star Restaurants, *by Molly O'Neill.*

She painstakingly re-created a longed-for cake from a Brooklyn, N.Y., bakery, Ebinger's, that closed in 1972. And there, at the end of the long recipe, was the New Orleans note.

"Please note that these ingredients make a very runny filling that pleased the 12 devout Ebingerists who taste-tested different versions of this cake. Those who desire a less syrupy consistency may stir in an additional one to two tablespoons of cornstarch.

The now-defunct McKenzie's bakery of New Orleans baked a dearly beloved version of the Blackout Cake. We understand from local aficionados that the filling in the McKenzie version was firmer, more like pudding, therefore requiring four tablespoons of cornstarch."

What can I say? Molly O'Neill rocks.

{MAKES 10 TO 12 SERVINGS}

CAKE LAYERS

Unsalted butter for greasing, plus 1 cup (2 sticks), softened slightly

½ cup unsweetened Dutch-process cocoa powder (see Note)

2 tablespoons boiling water

2 (1-ounce) squares unsweetened chocolate, chopped

¾ cup milk

2 cups sugar

4 large eggs, separated

2 teaspoons vanilla extract

2 cups all-purpose flour

1 teaspoon baking powder

1 teaspoon baking soda

1 teaspoon salt

FILLING

1 tablespoon plus 1¾ teaspoons unsweetened Dutch-process cocoa powder

2 cups boiling water

¾ cup plus ½ teaspoon sugar

1 ounce bittersweet chocolate, chopped

¼ cup cornstarch dissolved in 1 tablespoon cold water (use 2 tablespoons cornstarch for a runnier filling)

¼ teaspoon salt

1 teaspoon vanilla extract

2 tablespoons unsalted butter

FROSTING

1 (12-ounce) package semisweet chocolate, chopped

¾ cup (1½ sticks) unsalted butter

½ cup hot water

1 tablespoon light corn syrup

1 tablespoon vanilla extract

For the cake layers: Preheat the oven to 375 degrees F. Butter and lightly flour two 8-inch round cake pans. Put the cocoa in a small mixing bowl and whisk in the boiling water to form a paste.

In a medium saucepan over medium heat, combine the chopped chocolate and milk. Stir frequently until the chocolate melts, about 3 minutes. Remove from the heat. Whisk a small amount of the hot chocolate milk into the cocoa paste to warm it. Whisk the cocoa mixture into the milk mixture. Return the pan to medium heat and stir for 1 minute. Remove and set aside to cool until tepid.

With an electric mixer, beat the butter and sugar together in a large mixing bowl until light and fluffy. Beat in the egg yolks, one at a time, and the vanilla. Slowly stir in the chocolate mixture. In a medium mixing bowl, stir together the flour, baking powder, baking soda, and salt. Using a spatula or a wooden spoon, slowly add the flour mixture to the chocolate mixture. Fold in until just mixed.

In another bowl, whisk the egg whites until soft peaks form. Using a spatula, gently fold the egg whites into the batter. Divide the batter between the prepared pans. Bake until a cake tester inserted in the center comes out clean, 45 minutes. Cool the cakes in the pans on racks for 15 minutes. Gently remove the cakes from the pans and continue to cool.

For the filling: While the cakes are baking, combine the cocoa and boiling water in a small saucepan over low heat. Stir in the sugar and chocolate. Add the dissolved cornstarch paste and salt to the pan and bring to a boil, stirring constantly. Boil for 1 minute. Remove from the heat and whisk in the vanilla and butter. Transfer the mixture to a bowl. Cover and refrigerate until cool.

For the frosting: While the cakes are cooling, melt the chocolate in a double boiler over hot, but not simmering, water (or in a bowl set over a saucepan of hot water), stirring until smooth. Remove the top of the double boiler from the heat and whisk in the butter, one tablespoon at a time. Return the top to the heat, if necessary, to melt the butter.

Whisk in the hot water all at once and continue whisking until smooth. Whisk in the corn syrup and vanilla. Cover and refrigerate for up to 15 minutes before using.

Use a sharp serrated knife to slice each cake layer horizontally in half to form 4 layers. Set one layer aside. Place one layer on a cake round or plate. Generously swath the layer with one-half of the filling. Add the second layer and repeat. Set the third layer on top. Quickly apply a layer of frosting to the top and sides of the cake. Refrigerate for 10 minutes.

Meanwhile, crumble the remaining cake layer. Apply the remaining frosting to the cake. Sprinkle it liberally with the cake crumbs. Store the cake in a cool place and serve within 24 hours. ❧

NOTE: *The most commonly available cocoa is unsweetened, not Dutch-process. Hershey makes both types, so check the label.*

N⁰ 261 ⚜

Fig Cake

FIGS ARE A cherished fruit, grown in backyards all across south Louisiana. This cake recipe was given to Marcelle Bienvenu by a coworker, Vickie Cortez, when they worked together at Oak Alley Plantation on the River Road, between New Orleans and Baton Rouge. Vickie said it was a favorite recipe of her family during the Christmas season.

{MAKES 8 TO 10 SERVINGS}

2 cups sugar

3 large eggs

1 cup vegetable oil

1 cup whole milk

2 cups all-purpose flour

2 teaspoons ground cinnamon

1 teaspoon salt

1 teaspoon baking soda

2 cups fig preserves, homemade (page 347), or store-bought, mashed

1 cup pecan pieces

Preheat the oven to 350 degrees F. Coat a 12-cup Bundt pan with nonstick cooking spray.

In a large mixing bowl, beat the sugar and eggs together with an electric mixer until fluffy. Add the vegetable oil and stir well to blend. Add the milk and mix well.

In a separate bowl, stir together the flour, cinnamon, salt, and baking soda. Add to the sugar and egg mixture, stirring to blend. Add the fig preserves and pecans. Stir again to blend. Pour into the Bundt pan and bake until the cake sets and a cake tester inserted in the center comes out clean, about 1 hour.

Cool the cake in the pan for 10 minutes, then turn out onto a wire rack to cool completely. ❧

Galette des Rois
(French King Cake)

EVERY YEAR WHEN Carnival season starts, readers ask for king cake recipes. The New Orleans king cake custom grew from the gâteau des rois served on Epiphany or Twelfth Night in France. The traditional New Orleans version is usually similar to a brioche type of yeast dough, and is topped with the purple, green, and gold Carnival colors. The baker hides a plastic baby inside the cake, and whoever gets the the baby brings a king cake to the celebration the next year. (Originally, the baker hid a bean in the cake but over the years, the practice evolved from a bean to the small figurine.)

T.L. of Metairie asked for a recipe he lost in the storm, which had been published in *The Times-Picayune* about fifteen years earlier. The cake is made with puff pastry instead of the usual brioche-style dough, and has a filling flavored with praline liqueur. It is the French version of king cake, and is quite popular in New Orleans. The recipe originally was shared by Myriam Guidroz, who wrote the recipe exchange column for many years.

{MAKES 8 TO 10 SERVINGS}

1 (17.75-ounce) package frozen puff pastry

FILLING

3 tablespoons all-purpose flour

½ cup sugar

3 large eggs

1 teaspoon vanilla extract

¼ cup praline liqueur

1½ cups milk

1 cup marshmallow creme

1 small plastic baby figurine or bean

TOPPING

½ cup chopped pecans

1 cup light brown sugar

2 tablespoons praline liqueur

About 2 tablespoons milk (optional)

OPTIONAL FROSTING

2 cups confectioners' sugar

Purple, green, and gold food coloring

Thaw the pastry just until pliable, but still cold to the touch. Lightly flour a pastry board and rolling pin. Preheat the oven to 400 degrees F. Lightly grease a 12- to 14-inch pizza pan or large cookie sheet. If using a pizza pan, you will make a round cake; if using a cookie sheet, you will make an oval cake.

Unfold one sheet of pastry onto the floured board and place a second sheet on top of it. To make a round cake, flatten the pastry with the rolling pin into a square with 12½-inch sides. For an oval cake, flatten the pastry into a 9-by-13-inch rectangle.

Cut a large circle or oval out of the pastry, and then cut out the center, leaving a pastry ring about 3½ inches wide. (Freeze the cutout and trimmings for future use.) Place the pastry ring on the prepared pan and bake for about 25 minutes, or until well puffed and golden. Cool slightly and separate the two layers with a sharp knife, preferably a serrated one.

For the filling: In a large mixing bowl, beat together thoroughly the flour, sugar, and eggs with a wooden spoon. Add the vanilla and liqueur.

In a medium saucepan, bring the milk just to a boil and then pour it into the egg mixture, stirring vigorously. Pour through a strainer back into the saucepan in case there are any tiny bits of egg. Cook over medium heat until the custard thickens and boils. (It may look curdled but will smooth out as it cooks.) Cool, covered with plastic wrap, so that no skin forms, and refrigerate. Just before using, fold in the marshmallow creme to lighten the custard. Spread the filling over the bottom layer of the cake and bury the bean or baby in the filling.

For the topping: Combine the pecans, brown sugar, and praline liqueur in a small bowl. Add the milk, if needed, a little at a time to give the mixture a spreadable consistency.

Preheat the oven to 375 degrees F. Place the top layer of the king cake on a well-greased cookie sheet or pizza pan. Spread the topping evenly on the top. Bake for about 5 minutes, or until the topping melts and bubbles. Remove from the pan with a spatula (the topping is very hot) and place on top of the filled bottom layer.

For the optional frosting: If you would like to add the traditional purple, green, and gold topping, mix the confectioners' sugar with just enough water to make a slightly runny paste. Divide into 3 portions and color each batch with a few drops of food coloring. Drizzle each color from the tip of a spoon over the cooled cake. ❧

Gâteau de Sirop

MADE WITH CANE syrup, this confection, which translates literally from the French as "cake of syrup," is very popular in Acadiana, and has been for a long time. Since most people have all the ingredients at hand, the cake can be whipped up quickly, and the aroma while it bakes is fabulous. This is Marcelle Bienvenu's version.

{MAKES ABOUT 8 SERVINGS}

⅓ cup shortening

⅓ cup sugar

⅓ cup pure cane syrup, such as Steen's

⅓ cup boiling water

1 large egg

½ teaspoon baking powder

1 teaspoon ground cinnamon

1 teaspoon salt

1 teaspoon ground nutmeg

½ teaspoon baking soda

1½ cups sifted all-purpose flour

Whipped cream or vanilla ice cream for serving (optional)

Preheat the oven to 350 degrees F. Coat a 5-by-8-inch loaf pan with nonstick cooking spray.

Combine the shortening, sugar, syrup, and boiling water in a large bowl and stir to blend. In a small bowl, lightly beat the egg. Add it to the shortening mixture.

Sift together the baking powder, cinnamon, salt, nutmeg, baking soda, and flour. Add a little at a time to the shortening mixture. Beat with a wooden spoon until smooth.

Pour the batter into the prepared pan and bake for 35 to 45 minutes, or until a cake tester inserted near the center comes out clean. Let cool for 10 minutes in the pan, then turn out onto a rack. Slice and serve warm with ice cream or whipped cream if desired. 🍂

Gooey Butter Cake

In 1993, *The Times-Picayune* food columnist Myriam Guidroz wrote, "Two well-organized readers sent in the authentic recipe from scratch for Gooey Butter Cake as requested by J.C.K. They are identical clippings from the *St. Louis Globe-Democrat* of June 11, 1970." This highly unusual cake has a base made with yeast, which is topped by a thick, rich, and gooey filling.

{MAKES 2 CAKES, EACH SERVING 6 TO 8}

CAKE

¼ cup milk

¼ cup water

4 tablespoons unsalted butter or margarine, at room temperature

1 package active dry yeast

2¼ to 2½ cups all-purpose flour

¼ cup sugar

½ teaspoon salt

1 large egg

GOOEY BUTTER FILLING

1 cup (2 sticks) unsalted butter, softened

½ cup shortening

¾ cup sweetened condensed milk (not evaporated milk, see Note)

¾ cup white corn syrup

2 large eggs

¾ cup all-purpose flour

1½ teaspoons vanilla extract

Pinch of salt

For the cake: In a small saucepan, heat the milk and water with the butter over low heat until warm. The butter doesn't have to melt.

In a large mixing bowl, thoroughly mix the yeast with ¾ cup of the flour, the sugar, and the salt. Add the liquids to the dry ingredients. Beat with an electric mixer for 2 minutes at medium speed scraping the bowl occasionally. Add about ¼ cup more flour, or enough to make a thick batter. Add the egg. Beat on high speed for 2 minutes, scraping the bowl occasionally. Stir in enough additional flour so that the dough holds together and can be turned out onto a floured board, but is still sticky. After the dough is turned out, work in just enough flour to handle easily, then knead for about 5 minutes, or until the dough is smooth and elastic.

Grease and flour two 8-inch square baking pans, 2 inches deep. Divide the dough between the pans and shape so it fills the pans completely, pressing it up against the sides. It will rise a little in the pans as you prepare the filling. Preheat the oven to 350 degrees F.

For the Gooey Butter Filling: With an electric mixer, beat the butter and shortening in a large mixing bowl until fluffy. Add ½ cup of the condensed milk and beat until light. Add the syrup and mix thoroughly. Add the eggs, one at a time, mixing in thoroughly, and continue beating until the batter is light and fluffy. Beat in the flour and the remaining ¼ cup of condensed milk alternately, a little at a time. Add the vanilla and salt and mix well.

Pour this filling over the yeast dough in the pans and bake for 30 minutes, or until lightly browned at the edges. When removed from the oven, the filling will have an unbaked appearance because of the high sugar content, but it will set some after cooling. 🍃

NOTE: *If you don't have sweetened condensed milk, you can stir together ½ cup of milk and 1 cup of sugar and use that instead.*

Heavenly Hash Cake

HEAVENLY HASH CANDY, a combination of chocolate, marshmallows, and pecans, has been a popular treat in New Orleans for years. It is made locally by the Elmer Candy Corporation, established in the city in 1855, and still in operation in Ponchatoula. This cake is indeed heavenly and is made with the components of the original candy. There are several recipes for the cake; this one was given to the newspaper by A.L. of New Orleans.

{MAKES 12 TO 16 SERVINGS}

CAKE
4 large eggs, lightly beaten
2 cups sugar
1 cup (2 sticks) unsalted butter or margarine, melted
2 teaspoons vanilla extract
1½ cups self-rising flour
¼ cup unsweetened cocoa powder
1½ cups chopped pecans
2½ to 3 cups miniature marshmallows

FROSTING
¼ cup unsweetened cocoa powder
1 (1-pound) box confectioners' sugar
4 tablespoons unsalted butter or margarine, melted
1 cup milk

For the cake: Preheat the oven to 350 degrees F. Grease a 9-by-13-inch baking pan and set aside.

In a large mixing bowl, combine the eggs, sugar, butter, and vanilla and stir to blend. Gradually add the flour and cocoa, stirring to mix well. Stir in the pecans.

Pour the mixture into the prepared pan and bake for 30 to 35 minutes, or until a cake tester inserted near the center comes out clean. Put the marshmallows on top of the cake as soon as it is removed from the oven. Set aside to cool in the pan.

For the frosting: Combine the cocoa, confectioners' sugar, and butter in a mixing bowl. Add the milk a little at a time, stirring to blend. Pour the frosting over the cake and allow it to set for about 15 minutes before cutting the cake into squares to serve. ❦

Hummingbird Cake

MANY RECIPES EXIST for this very simple but delicious Southern cake. Some suggest you use layer pans; others recommend a Bundt pan. The ingredients—pineapple, bananas, and pecans—are more or less the same. This recipe suggests you pour the cake batter into a Bundt pan. It was sent by Mrs. Jim Schultz, who noted that it is from a community cookbook, *Lone Star Legacy II*, published by the Austin Junior Forum in 1985.

{MAKES 10 TO 12 SERVINGS}

3 cups all-purpose flour
1 teaspoon baking soda
1 teaspoon salt
1 teaspoon ground cinnamon
2 cups sugar
1½ cups oil
1 teaspoon butter flavoring
3 large eggs
1 (8-ounce) can crushed pineapple with the juice
2 medium bananas, chopped
1 cup chopped pecans

Preheat the oven to 350 degrees F. Grease and flour a large Bundt pan.

In a large mixing bowl, combine all ingredients by hand, stirring well before each new ingredient is added. Pour the batter into the Bundt pan. Bake for 60 to 70 minutes, or until a cake tester inserted near the center comes out clean.

Remove from the oven and cool slightly before turning the cake out onto a wire rack to let cool completely. ❧

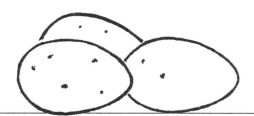

Used with permission of the Austin Junior Forum, The Caswell House, Austin, Texas.

King Cake

WHILE KING CAKES are easy to come by in New Orleans bakeries during the Carnival season, there are those who choose to make their own. Every year during the holiday, *The Times-Picayune* receives requests for king cake recipes. This one is a classic and appeared in the newspaper in 2003. The recipe, unlike the French king cake on page 264, is made with a yeast dough.

{MAKES 12 SERVINGS}

DOUGH

¼ cup warm water (105 to 115 degrees F)

1 envelope active dry yeast

¼ cup warm milk (105 to 115 degrees F)

½ cup (1 stick) unsalted butter or margarine, softened

2 tablespoons sugar

½ teaspoon ground nutmeg

½ teaspoon salt

3 to 3½ cups all-purpose flour

2 large eggs

CINNAMON FILLING

4 tablespoons unsalted butter, melted

⅔ cup packed light brown sugar

1½ teaspoons ground cinnamon

1 red bean, pecan half, or small plastic baby figurine

FROSTING

1 cup confectioners' sugar, sifted

¼ teaspoon almond extract

1 to 2 tablespoons milk

Purple, green, and yellow paste food coloring

For the dough: Pour the warm water into a large warmed bowl. Sprinkle in the yeast and stir until it dissolves. Stir in the warm milk, butter, sugar, nutmeg, and salt. Add 1 cup of the flour and blend well. Stir in the eggs and enough of the remaining flour to make a soft dough.

Lightly flour a flat work surface, and turn out the dough. Knead until smooth and elastic, about 5 minutes, adding more flour if the dough sticks. Put in a large greased bowl, and turn to grease the top of the dough. Cover with a kitchen towel and let rise in a warm, draft-free place until doubled in size, about 1 hour.

For the filling: Punch the dough down. Transfer to the lightly floured work surface and use a rolling pin to roll into a 30-by-9-inch rectangle. Brush with the melted butter. Combine the brown sugar and cinnamon in a small bowl. Sprinkle the brown sugar mixture over the dough to within ½ inch of the edges. Beginning at the long end, roll up tightly, as for a jelly roll. Pinch the seam to seal. With a sharp knife, cut the roll in half lengthwise, and carefully turn the halves so that the cut sides face up. Join the ends, pinching them to form one ring, keeping the cut sides up. Transfer the ring to a large greased baking sheet.

If using a red bean or pecan half, push it into the underside of the dough to hide it. (A baby charm will go in after baking.) Cover and let rise in a warm, draft-free place until doubled in size, 20 to 40 minutes. Preheat the oven to 350 degrees F.

Bake for 30 minutes, or until lightly browned. Remove the cake from the baking sheet and let cool on a wire rack. (If using a plastic baby figurine, push it into the underside of the cake.)

For the frosting: In a small bowl mix together the sugar, almond extract, and milk until smooth. Divide among three smaller bowls. Tint one mixture purple, the second one green, and the third one yellow, mixing each one well. Drizzle each color over the top of the cake.

Mandarin Orange Cake

In July 2005, P.C. asked "Exchange Alley," *The Times-Picayune*'s recipe exchange column, for a recipe for this cake. B.D. of Meraux and C.C. of River Ridge sent in nearly identical recipes, and both noted that the recipe had produced unfailingly delicious results for many years. One recipe called for ¼ teaspoon baking powder, however, and one called for ¼ teaspoon baking soda. This recipe has been around absolutely forever and almost every other version omits this small amount of leavening.

{MAKES 10 TO 12 SERVINGS}

CAKE

1 (18.25-ounce) box yellow cake mix

¼ teaspoon baking powder or baking soda (optional)

1 cup oil

4 large eggs, lightly beaten

1 (11-ounce) can mandarin orange sections with their juice

FROSTING

1 (20-ounce) can crushed pineapple with juice

1 (3¼- or 5⅝-ounce) package instant vanilla pudding mix

1 (8- or 9-ounce) container nondairy whipped topping

For the cake: Preheat the oven to 350 degrees F. Grease and flour three 8-inch cake pans.

Mix the cake mix, baking powder (if using), oil, and eggs with an electric mixer in a large mixing bowl. Add the mandarin oranges, juice and all, and mix by hand to prevent mashing the orange sections. Pour into the prepared cake pans. Bake for 15 to 20 minutes, or until the cakes pull away from the sides. Let cool completely in the pans.

For the frosting: Mix all the ingredients in a large bowl. Place a cake layer on a plate and frost the top. Cover with the second layer and frost the top and sides of the cake. Refrigerate the cake until ready to serve. ❧

Maylie's Whiskied Prune Pie

AFTER A READER wrote in wanting to help an eighty-year-old New Orleans native taste a prune pie again, *Times-Picayune's* food editor, Judy Walker, was deluged with recipes from kind people. Lake Douglas, of New Orleans, sent the recipe for the Whiskied Prune Pie served at Maylie's on Poydras Street, which closed in 1986. The restaurant's recipes were preserved in *Maylie's Table d'Hôte Recipes.*

"I recall the pie being very dense, crunchy from pecans and the crust. It was delicious at Maylie's, and something I always ordered there," Douglas wrote. "Maylie's was a French Creole restaurant [dating from the 1870s], long before it was trendy to be Creole. Going there was always like stepping back in time and/or going to an unpretentious cafe in an out-of-the-way neighborhood in a small French city.

"I used to make this a lot, but haven't for years," he added. "I made a standard pie crust and always used pecans."

For clarification of the original recipe, Walker thanked Mary Len Costa, a family friend of the Maylie family. It was Costa's mother-in-law who originally encouraged the Maylies to do the cookbook. Costa has made this pie for thirty years—without pecans. She makes sure to use good whiskey, has sometimes substituted brandy, and has on occasion added a bit of orange zest. She thinks it was served with whipped cream at the restaurant.

{MAKES 6 TO 8 SERVINGS}

1 pound extra-large pitted prunes

Juice of ½ lemon

1 cup sugar, or more to taste

2 to 4 tablespoons whiskey

½ cup chopped pecans (optional)

1 unbaked 8-inch pie shell, plus strips of dough for a lattice top crust (see Note)

1 tablespoon unsalted butter

Confectioners' sugar for sprinkling

Preheat the oven to 350 degrees F.

Combine the prunes, lemon juice, and the sugar in a saucepan. Cook gently over low heat, stirring occasionally, until the mixture has a syrupy consistency. Watch closely so the sugar doesn't burn. Let cool and stir in the whiskey. (If the mixture looks too runny, dissolve a little cornstarch in the whiskey. To make the filling thinner, add a little water if needed.)

Add the pecans (if using) to the filling. Fill the pie shell and place strips of dough in a crisscross pattern to make a lattice across the top. Dot with the butter.

Bake for about 45 minutes, or until the crust is brown and the filling is set. Let cool and sprinkle with confectioners' sugar. ?&

NOTE: *Use your favorite pastry dough recipe or refrigerated pie crust to make the pie shell and lattice strips.*

The Pontchartrain Hotel's Mile High Pie

PROBABLY ONE OF the most popular and well-known New Orleans desserts of the twentieth century was this Mile High Pie, created more than fifty years ago and served in the Caribbean Room at the Pontchartrain Hotel on St. Charles Avenue.

{MAKES 8 TO 12 SERVINGS}

CRUST
1½ cups sifted all-purpose flour
½ teaspoon salt
½ cup shortening
4 to 5 tablespoons cold water

FILLING
1½ pints vanilla ice cream, slightly softened
1½ pints chocolate ice cream, slightly softened
½ pint strawberry ice cream, slightly softened
½ pint peppermint ice cream, slightly softened

MERINGUE
8 large egg whites
½ teaspoon vanilla extract
¼ teaspoon cream of tartar
½ cup sugar

Chocolate Sauce (recipe follows)

For the crust: Preheat the oven to 450 degrees F. Sift together the flour and salt. Cut in the shortening with a pastry cutter or two knives until the pieces are the size of small peas. Sprinkle 1 tablespoon of cold water over the flour mixture and gently toss with a fork. Repeat until all the flour is slightly moistened. Form into a ball and roll out to ⅛-inch thickness on a lightly floured work surface. Fit loosely into a 9-inch pie pan. Prick the crust with a fork to prevent bubbling. Bake for 10 to 12 minutes, until lightly browned. Let cool.

For the filling: Layer the vanilla ice cream on the bottom of the cooled pie shell, and in layers add the remaining flavors. Place the pie in the freezer while you make the meringue.

If necessary, remove the racks inside your oven in order to put the pie under the broiler, because the pie will be very tall. Preheat the broiler.

For the meringue: In a large mixing bowl, use an electric mixer to beat the egg whites with the vanilla and cream of tartar in a large mixing bowl until soft peaks form. Gradually add the sugar, beating until the egg whites are stiff and glossy and the sugar is dissolved. Spread meringue over the ice cream, sealing it to the edges of the pastry.

Broil for 30 seconds to 1 minute to brown the meringue. Freeze the pie for several hours or overnight. Cut into wedges and drizzle some of the Chocolate Sauce over each serving. ♣

Chocolate Sauce

{MAKES ABOUT 1 CUP}

2 (1-ounce) squares German sweet chocolate
2 (1-ounce) squares unsweetened chocolate
½ cup sugar
½ cup heavy cream

In the top of a double boiler (or a bowl set over a saucepan of simmering water), melt the chocolate with the sugar and ¼ cup of the cream, stirring until well blended and thick. Add as much of the remaining cream as necessary to achieve a pourable consistency. ❧

Moist Microwave Chocolate Cake

PLENTY OF FEMA-SUPPLIED travel trailers still dotted the Katrina-damaged region when a mother from Metairie sent in this recipe in June 2006. "This recipe is for those living in trailers like my daughter, who is afraid to light the oven or doesn't want to use up the propane gas too quickly," she wrote.

Even after residents were able to start sleeping in their damaged homes, many continued to cook in FEMA trailers while their kitchens were being restored. Others, who were rebuilding their flooded houses, were living on the second floor, where they cooked for months in improvised kitchens located in bathrooms, spare bedrooms, and laundry rooms. A microwave oven was invaluable.

{MAKES 6 TO 8 SERVINGS}

CAKE

4 tablespoons unsalted butter, at room temperature

½ cup sugar

2 large eggs

1 cup chocolate syrup

½ cup all-purpose flour

½ teaspoon baking powder

½ teaspoon vanilla extract

FROSTING

1 cup miniature marshmallows

2 tablespoons unsalted butter

½ cup sugar

2 tablespoons evaporated milk

¼ cup semisweet chocolate chips

½ teaspoon vanilla extract

For the cake: In a medium mixing bowl, beat the butter and sugar with an electric mixer until creamy. Add the eggs and beat until fluffy. Add the syrup, flour, baking powder, and vanilla and beat until blended. Pour into an 8-inch glass square baking dish. Bake on high in a microwave oven, uncovered, for 7 minutes and 30 seconds.

For the frosting: While the cake is hot, sprinkle the miniature marshmallows evenly over the top. In the microwave, melt the butter on high for 1 minute in a medium microwave-safe bowl. Stir in the sugar and evaporated milk. Cook, uncovered, on high for 1 minute. Quickly mix in the chocolate chips and vanilla. Pour the mixture over the warm cake and the melting marshmallows. Use a heat-proof spatula to swirl the frosting with the marshmallows until blended. 🐝

Mojito Sorbet

When Creole Creamery opened in the spring of 2004, Uptown New Orleans flocked there for a taste of sorbet made with fresh herbs or a riveting, unusual flavor of ice cream, such as cotton candy or strawberry margarita. This sorbet, shared by Chef Bryan Gilmore, is particularly refreshing on a steamy summer day.

{MAKES 4 SERVINGS}

15 sprigs fresh mint
¾ cup sugar
2 cups water
¼ cup fresh lime juice
¼ cup white rum
1 tablespoon lime zest
4 thin lime wheels for garnish (optional)

Tear or roughly chop 9 mint sprigs. Finely chop 2 sprigs (but not 4 small sprigs for garnish). In a medium saucepan over medium heat, combine the sugar and water and bring to a boil. As soon as the sugar has dissolved, lower the heat and add the torn mint sprigs. Simmer for 2 minutes. Remove from the heat and let cool.

Strain the mixture through a fine sieve. Discard the mint, and transfer the mixture to a large non-reactive bowl. Add the lime juice, rum, finely chopped mint, and lime zest. Stir well, or mix briefly in a blender. Transfer to an ice-cream machine and process according to the manufacturer's instructions.

Garnish each serving with a reserved small sprig of mint. Or, for a more dramatic presentation, serve in a martini glass garnished with a wheel of lime. ❧

New York-Style Cheesecake

WHEN DALE CURRY wrote about Christmas office parties for *The Times-Picayune* in 1998, she reported that this cheesecake was a favorite at Walk, Haydel and Associates, an engineering design firm. The New York–style cheesecake was made by Dorothea Scaglione, who is originally from Brooklyn and got her recipe from her mother.

"Everybody who tastes it tells me they've stopped eating other cheesecakes," said Scaglione.

Several readers remembered this recipe and asked for it to be included here. This cheesecake is best made a couple of days before serving.

{MAKES ABOUT 20 SERVINGS}

Butter for greasing

2¼ pounds (4½ large packages) cream cheese, at room temperature

1½ cups sugar

3 cups sour cream

1 tablespoon vanilla extract

9 large eggs

Preheat the oven to 350 degrees F. Position the oven rack in the middle of the oven. Butter the inside of a large springform pan and cover the outside with aluminum foil.

In the large bowl of an electric mixer, or in the bowl of a food processor, thoroughly beat together the cream cheese and sugar. Gradually mix in the sour cream and vanilla. Add the eggs one at a time, beating after each addition, and continue beating until you have a smooth mixture with no lumps. The smoother the consistency, the creamier the cheesecake will be. (Scaglione uses a food processor for this step, creaming the ingredients in 3 batches.)

Pour the mixture into the springform pan and place the pan inside a larger pan. Pour hot water into the outer pan to a depth of about ½ inch. Place the pans in the center of the oven rack.

Bake for 1 hour. Turn the oven off and leave the oven door closed for 1 additional hour. This is extremely important so the cheesecake will have the correct consistency. Remove the cheesecake from the oven. Remove the springform pan from the water bath, remove the foil from the pan, and let the cake cool to room temperature in the pan. Cover the cheesecake tightly, still in the pan, and refrigerate. (Or wrap well in 2 sheets of aluminum foil and store in the freezer for up to 3 months.)

When ready to serve, run a sharp knife around the inside of the springform pan before releasing the clasp. ❧

Piña Colada Cake

M.L.B., WHO WAS displaced to Oklahoma after Katrina raged through Arabi, requested a recipe for this cake. We searched our files, but nothing came up. Then we received a batch of recipes mailed by A.W. in Terrytown, and in the package was this recipe. It was meant to be.

{MAKES 12 SERVINGS}

1 (18.25-ounce) box yellow cake mix, such as Duncan Hines Butter Recipe Golden cake mix

1 (14-ounce) can sweetened condensed milk

1 (14-ounce) can cream of coconut

1 cup chopped pecans

1 cup coconut flakes

1 (8-ounce) container nondairy whipped topping

Make the cake according to the package directions and bake in a 9-by-13-inch baking pan.

While the cake is baking, combine the sweetened condensed milk and the cream of coconut. When the cake is done, make holes with the tines of a fork all over the top of the cake.

Pour the milk mixture evenly over the cake while it's still warm. Allow the cake to cool, then refrigerate.

When the cake is well chilled, combine the pecans and coconut flakes and sprinkle over the top of the cake. Spread with whipped topping and serve. 🍃

Praline Cheesecake

A READER WHO lost almost everything in the Katrina floods was able to retrieve a few recipes from a shoe box in her attic. She sent us this recipe, which she had clipped from *The Times-Picayune* in 2001, so that others might enjoy it. This cheesecake is incredibly rich and ideal for just about any occasion.

{MAKES 10 TO 12 SERVINGS}

1½ cups graham cracker crumbs

3 tablespoons sugar

3 tablespoons unsalted butter, melted

3 (8-ounce) packages cream cheese, at room temperature

¾ cup firmly packed light brown sugar

2 tablespoons all-purpose flour

3 large eggs

1 teaspoon vanilla extract

½ cup finely chopped pecans

2 cups sweetened whipped cream

½ cup pecan halves, toasted

Preheat the oven to 350 degrees F. Cover the outside of an ungreased 9-inch springform pan with aluminum foil.

In a small bowl, combine the graham cracker crumbs, sugar, and butter and mix well. Press this mixture into the prepared pan. Bake for 10 minutes and remove from the oven.

In the large bowl of an electric mixer, beat the cream cheese until smooth. Gradually add the brown sugar and flour, mixing well. Add the eggs, one at a time, beating well after each addition. Beat in the vanilla, and stir in the chopped pecans by hand.

Pour this mixture over the crust. Bake for 40 to 45 minutes, or until the mixture sets. Remove from the oven and let cool to room temperature in the pan on a wire rack.

Refrigerate for at least 8 hours, still in the pan. Before serving, remove the sides of the spring-form pan, running a sharp knife around the inside before releasing the clasp. Top the cake with whipped cream and pecan halves. ❧

Pumpkin Cheesecake

IF YOU'RE LOOKING for a holiday dessert recipe, consider this one, which makes a very large cheesecake. Although the recipe calls for a 9-inch springform pan, you can use a 10-inch if you have it. If you like, substitute ground nuts for all or part of the graham cracker crumbs in the crust.

{MAKES 16 SERVINGS}

CRUST
1½ cups graham cracker crumbs
⅓ cup unsalted butter or margarine, melted
¼ cup sugar

CHEESECAKE
3 (8-ounce) packages cream cheese, softened
1 cup granulated sugar
¼ cup packed light brown sugar
2 large eggs
1 (15-ounce) can pure pumpkin (not pie filling)
⅔ cup evaporated milk
2 tablespoons cornstarch
1¼ teaspoons ground cinnamon
½ teaspoon ground nutmeg

TOPPING
1 pint sour cream, at room temperature
⅓ cup sugar
1 teaspoon vanilla extract

Preheat the oven to 350 degrees F. Cover the outside of an ungreased 9-inch springform pan with aluminum foil.

For the crust: Combine the graham cracker crumbs, butter, and sugar in a medium mixing bowl. Press onto the bottom and 1 inch up the sides of the prepared pan. Bake for 6 to 8 minutes. Do not let the crust brown. Let cool on a wire rack for 10 minutes.

For the cheesecake: In the large bowl of an electric stand mixer, beat the cream cheese, granulated sugar, and brown sugar until fluffy. Beat in the eggs, pumpkin, and evaporated milk. Add the cornstarch, cinnamon, and nutmeg and beat well. Pour into the prepared crust. Bake for 55 to 60 minutes, or until the edges are set but the center still jiggles slightly.

For the topping: While the cheesecake is baking, combine the sour cream, sugar, and vanilla extract in a small bowl and mix well. When the cheesecake has finished baking, spread over the surface of the warm cheesecake. Bake for 5 minutes more. Let cool in the pan on a wire rack.

Refrigerate for several hours or overnight. Run a sharp knife around the inside of the pan, release the clasp, and remove the sides of the springform pan before serving. ❧

Rosie's Sweet Potato Pies

M.B., A DISPLACED New Orleanian in Houston, asked us for this recipe. She wrote, "I tried to hold on to that recipe for the longest, until Katrina came along. It was the best sweet potato pie ever."

Many locals prefer sweet potato pie over pumpkin pie for the holidays. The recipe, first published in *The Times-Picayune* in 1997, came from Linda Barry Sevalia, who got it from her mother, Rosie Barry of Detroit. The family made these pies for all their festive get-togethers, including Thanksgiving and Christmas. Sevalia usually made the pie filling a day or two ahead, refrigerated it, and baked the dessert on the day she wanted to serve it.

{MAKES 24 TO 32 SERVINGS (FOUR 9-INCH PIES)}

3 pounds sweet potatoes (about 2 large ones)

½ cup (1 stick) unsalted butter, at room temperature

1 (12-ounce) can evaporated milk

2 cups sugar

2 tablespoons ground nutmeg

1 tablespoon vanilla extract

6 large eggs

4 unbaked 9-inch pie shells

Ice cream or sweetened whipped cream for serving (optional)

Scrub the potatoes but do not peel. In a large saucepan, cover them with water, bring to a boil, and boil them until very tender, about 1 hour. Drain.

Preheat the oven to 375 degrees F.

When cool enough to handle, peel the potatoes and put them in the large bowl of an electric stand mixer. Add the butter, evaporated milk, sugar, nutmeg, vanilla, and eggs. Beat until the mixture is smooth. (If making the filling ahead of time, cover and refrigerate until ready to bake the pies.)

Pour the filling into the pie shells and bake until the crusts are golden brown and the filling is set, 30 to 35 minutes. Serve warm or at room temperature, topped with ice cream or sweetened whipped cream, if desired. ❧

Russian Cake

RUSSIAN CAKE, ALSO known as Creole trifle, is a favorite of our readers, who have requested the recipe for it numerous times. The late *Times-Picayune* columnist Myriam Guidroz's famous recipe for Russian cake called for building a special mold and packing fifteen pounds of leftover cake in it. This more manageable version requires no carpentry skills. It was sent to the newspaper's recipe exchange column a few years ago by C.D. of Metairie.

{MAKES 9 TO 12 SERVINGS}

5 to 6 cups assorted broken pieces of cake, such
  as pound cake, or yellow or chocolate cake

1 cup sweet juice, such as pineapple
  or fruit cocktail syrup

¾ cup red wine

Ice cream or sweetened whipped cream
  for serving (optional)

In large mixing bowl, mix the cake pieces together with a wooden spoon. Transfer to a deep 8-inch square cake pan or a round baking dish. Pack down very tightly with the back of the spoon.

Pour the sweet juice evenly over the top of the cake and let it soak in for about 4 minutes; then pour the red wine evenly over the cake. Pack it down firmly again. Cover the pan or dish with plastic wrap. Refrigerate for at least 4 hours.

To serve, cut the cake into rectangles or wedges and carefully lift each serving onto a plate with a spatula or pie server. Top with a scoop of vanilla ice cream or whipped cream, if desired. Store the leftovers, tightly covered, in the refrigerator. ❧

Solari's Cheesecake

A.W. OF TERRYTOWN has been collecting recipes from the Food section of *The Times-Picayune* for forty years. She came through with this recipe for E.B. of Baton Rouge, who wanted to re-create the ultralight cheesecake sold at the now-defunct Solari's. The cheesecake was made for them for years by Chef Warren Leruth. "When I was a little girl, my Aunt Elena worked for Solari's," A.W. wrote.

This version of the cheesecake was originally published in the newspaper's recipe exchange column by Myriam Guidroz, who cut down Chef Leruth's restaurant-size proportions.

{MAKES 16 SERVINGS}

Butter for greasing, plus 2 tablespoons unsalted butter, at room temperature

1 package (about 12) very dry ladyfingers

1 pound ricotta cheese

½ cup milk

2 large eggs, plus 3 large egg whites, at room temperature

2 tablespoons cornstarch

2 teaspoons vanilla extract, or 3 or 4 drops lemon extract

Pinch of salt

Pinch of cream of tartar

¾ cup sugar

Fruit for garnish, such as blueberries or sliced strawberries (optional)

Grease a 9-inch springform pan generously with butter and cover the outside with aluminum foil. Preheat the oven to 350 degrees F.

Crumble the ladyfingers into small pieces with your fingers. Use half of the pieces to line the bottom of the springform pan. Reserve the rest.

Combine the ricotta, milk, 2 whole eggs, cornstarch, vanilla, and 2 tablespoons butter in the bowl of a food processor. Process until well mixed and smooth. (If you don't have a food processor, mix the cornstarch into a smooth paste with a little of the cold milk before adding it to the other ingredients; then beat until smooth with a wooden spoon.)

In a large mixing bowl, combine the salt and cream of tartar with the egg whites and beat with an electric mixer at high speed until soft peaks form. Beat in the sugar, about 2 tablespoons at a time. Continue beating until you cannot taste or feel a single grain of sugar.

With a rubber spatula, fold in the ricotta mixture gently but thoroughly. Pour into the prepared springform pan. Sprinkle the top of the cheesecake with the reserved crumbled ladyfingers. Place the pan in a larger baking dish and add about ½ inch of hot water to the larger dish. Bake for approximately 45 minutes, or until the cake is set. (If the ladyfinger crumbs brown too quickly, cover loosely with a piece of aluminum foil.)

Cool the cake in the pan until lukewarm. Run a sharp knife around the inside of the pan, loosen the clasp to release the side of the pan, and transfer the cake to a serving dish. Chill thoroughly.

If desired, garnish the top with fruit just before serving. ❧

Tartes à la Bouillie
(Sweet Dough Pies)

BOUILLIE IS THE French word for "boiled," and refers to the boiled custard filling for these old-fashioned pies, which are very popular in south Louisiana. Marcelle Bienvenu has written about the ladies in the small fishing village of Catahoula, near St. Martinville. They make hundreds of these pies to sell at their local church fair, and often include them on the menu for their Good Friday meal. They fill the sweet pie crusts with custard, blackberry, or coconut fillings.

The Catahoula ladies do not usually put tops on the pies, but any extra dough can be used to make a lattice top if you like. If you're making pies on a hot and humid day, it is wise to refrigerate the dough for an hour or two so that it will be easier to work with. You can also use the dough to make turnovers or sugar cookies. (See the variations.)

{MAKES 24 TO 32 SERVINGS (FOUR 9-INCH PIES)}

SWEET DOUGH
¾ cup vegetable shortening
1 cup sugar
½ cup milk
2 large eggs
1 teaspoon vanilla extract
4 cups all-purpose flour
4 teaspoons baking powder

Blackberry, Custard, or Coconut Filling (facing page)

Preheat the oven to 350 degrees F.

In a large mixing bowl, beat the shortening and sugar with an electric mixer until creamy. Combine the milk, eggs, and vanilla in a medium mixing bowl. Stir this mixture into the shortening and sugar and blend well.

Combine the flour and baking powder in a mixing bowl. Alternate blending the liquid mixture with the dry ingredients. Continue to alternate adding the mixtures until the dough comes away from the sides of the bowl.

Divide the dough into 4 equal parts. Roll out the first piece of dough on a lightly floured work surface to make a 12-inch circle. Place in a 9-inch pie pan and crimp the edges. Repeat with the remaining 3 pieces of dough.

Fill each pie with the filling of your choice. Bake until the crust is golden brown and the filling is set, about 30 minutes. Cool on a rack.

VARIATIONS:

Turnovers—You can also use the dough to make small turnovers. Roll the dough into smaller circles, about 5 inches in diameter, add about 3 tablespoons of filling to each one, fold over the crust, and bake until golden brown, about 15 minutes.

Sugar Cookies—Skip the filling and use the dough to make cookies. Roll out the dough a bit thicker than you would for pie crust, and cut out shapes with cookie cutters. Place on cookie sheets and bake at 350 degrees F until golden brown, 8 to 10 minutes.

Blackberry Filling

{MAKES ENOUGH FOR FOUR 9-INCH PIES}

1 quart blackberries
1½ to 2 cups sugar
¼ cup water

Wash the berries and drain well. Pick them over and remove any stems. Adjust the amount of sugar according to how sweet you want the filling to be. Combine the sugar and water in a large pot and bring to a boil. Add the berries and cook, stirring often, until the mixture thickens, 20 to 30 minutes. Cool before adding to the crust. ❧

Custard Filling

{MAKES ENOUGH FOR FOUR 9-INCH PIES}

1 (12-ounce) can evaporated milk
½ cup of cornstarch dissolved in ¾ cup water
1 cup sugar, or more to taste
2 large eggs
1 teaspoon vanilla extract

Combine all the ingredients in a large saucepan. Slowly bring the mixture to a gentle boil and cook, stirring, over medium heat until the custard thickens. Cool and spoon into the pie crusts. ❧

Coconut Filling

{MAKES ENOUGH FOR FOUR 9-INCH PIES}

1 (12-ounce) can evaporated milk
½ cup of cornstarch dissolved in ¾ cup water
1 cup sugar, or more to taste
2 large eggs
1 teaspoon vanilla extract
1 cup shredded coconut

Combine all the ingredients except the coconut in a large saucepan. Slowly bring the mixture to a gentle boil and cook, stirring, over medium heat until the custard thickens. Cool, add the coconut, and spoon into the pie crusts. ❧

COOKIES & CANDIES

he cookies prepared by the Italian community for the St. Joseph's Day altars start off this chapter. There were many requests for anise cookies (page 290), and Italian Seed Cookies (page 302), which we were happy to provide.

Being an avid herb grower, Marcelle Bienvenu was pleased to locate the recipe for Rosemary Cookies (page 310), which are very tasty. She has made several batches and can attest to the fact that they don't last long in the cookie jar. For those of you who are fans of Steen's 100% Pure Cane Syrup, by all means add Aunt Winnie's Syrup Cookies (page 292) to your cookie repertoire.

For holiday gift-giving, we have Fig Cakes (page 296), Gold Brick Fudge (page 298), and Praline Cookies (page 309). And for those of you who want to walk down memory lane, we have the brownie recipe from McMain Girls High School (page 304) dating to the 1940s.

Cookies & Candies

Ursuline Academy Anise Cookies

St. Joseph's Day, celebrated on March 19, is an important holiday for Roman Catholics, especially those of Sicilian descent. The tradition of staging a St. Joseph's Day altar was brought to New Orleans by Sicilian immigrants. Here in Louisiana, their descendants continue the custom, building elaborate altars in church halls, private homes, and restaurants. Anise cookies are a mainstay on the altars, and there are many recipes for these toothsome delights.

J.M. of Metairie sent us this one, and wrote, "I make an icing of confectioners' sugar and milk (adding green and red food coloring to look pretty at Christmas). This is a good recipe, taken from *Recipes and Reminiscences of New Orleans* by the Ursuline Academy Parents Club, a book that's also known as the 'Ursuline Cookbook.'"

{MAKES 2 TO 3 DOZEN COOKIES}

2 teaspoons anise seeds
½ cup (1 stick) unsalted butter, at room temperature
¾ cup sugar
2 large eggs
2 cups all-purpose flour
½ teaspoon baking powder
¼ teaspoon salt

Preheat the oven to 350 degrees F. Lightly grease two cookie sheets.

Crush the anise seed coarsely with a mortar and pestle or food processor, and mix with the butter in a large mixing bowl. With an electric mixer, gradually blend in the sugar. Beat the eggs into the mixture.

Sift the flour with the baking powder and salt. Gradually stir the flour mixture by hand into the butter and sugar mixture. Mix the dough until all the ingredients are well blended and smooth.

Shape the dough into 1-inch balls and place them 2 inches apart on the cookie sheets.

Bake for 10 minutes, or until lightly browned. Cool the cookies on racks and store in airtight containers. ❧

Used with permission from Ursuline Academy, 2635 State St., New Orleans.

Anise Drops

STACY DEMORAN ALLBRITTON sent us this recipe for Anise Drops, which she treasures. The formula produces a thin, white, chewy cookie, lightly flavored with anise. At first glance the confection appears to have icing on top, but the "icing" is actually a delicate shell that forms as the cookie bakes.

Allbritton's fascination with Anise Drops began when she was small and her River Ridge family visited her late grandmother, Kathryn Demoran, in Bay St. Louis, Mississippi. "We loved going there," the Slidell resident says. "Grandma would always take my sister, Paige, and me for walks by a bakery, and she would let us each pick out a cookie. We both always picked out the same kind. It was perfectly white and perfectly round, and it had little colors [nonpareils] on top. They were so pretty and different."

After Allbritton grew up and got married, she and her husband lived in Virginia for three years. She and Grace VanDerveer, a coworker at the Red Cross in Norfolk, attended a cookie swap with several colleagues just before Christmas one year. Once home, Allbritton tasted a cookie from her stash. "I didn't know what it was until I bit into it, and then a flood of memories came back from childhood," she said. She later found out VanDerveer was the baker and begged her for the recipe.

Allbritton said it's essential to beat the batter for a full 20 minutes as directed in the recipe so the distinctive shell forms on top of the cookie. The only change she made in VanDerveer's recipe was to sprinkle nonpareils on top to make them look just like the ones she remembered from Bay St. Louis. The cookies are refrigerated overnight, right on the cookie sheet, before baking.

{MAKES ABOUT 20 COOKIES}

All-purpose Flour for dusting, plus 1¾ cups
½ teaspoon salt
½ teaspoon baking powder
3 large eggs, at room temperature
1 cup plus 2 tablespoons sugar
1 tablespoon anise seeds, or 1 teaspoon anise extract
About 1 tablespoon nonpareils

Grease and flour two cookie sheets. Sift the 1¾ cups flour with the salt and baking powder and set aside. In the large bowl of an electric mixer beat the eggs on medium speed until very foamy, about 2 minutes. Gradually beat in the sugar and continue beating for at least 20 minutes more. Reduce the mixer speed and beat in the flour mixture. Beat for 3 minutes more, then add the anise.

Drop the batter by heaping teaspoons, about 1½ inches apart, onto the prepared cookie sheets, swirling the dough with the back of a spoon to form perfectly round cookies. Sprinkle the nonpareils on top and refrigerate overnight.

Preheat the oven to 325 degrees F.

Bake the cookies until light gold (not brown) on the undersides, about 10 minutes. Let cool on the cookie sheets briefly before transferring to wire racks to cool completely. Store in an airtight container. ❧

Aunt Winnie's Syrup Cookies

CANE SYRUP IS a favorite ingredient in south Louisiana. It is drizzled on biscuits, toast, and pancakes and appears in many recipes. C.S. Steen's Syrup Mill has been making pure cane syrup in Abbeville for more than eighty-five years. The company's recipe for these "little dry cakes" has long been a favorite of Cajun children. They were traditionally offered as an after-school snack with café au lait.

{MAKES 6 TO 8 DOZEN COOKIES}

2 cups Steen's 100% Pure Cane Syrup

1 teaspoon baking soda

1½ cups sugar

1 cup (2 sticks) unsalted butter, at room temperature

5 large eggs

5½ cups all-purpose flour

1½ teaspoons ground allspice

1 teaspoon ground cloves

1 cup milk

1¾ cups raisins

1 cup chopped pecans

Preheat the oven to 375 degrees F.

Combine the syrup and baking soda in a medium mixing bowl. Beat with a wooden spoon until golden.

In a large mixing bowl, combine the sugar and butter and beat until fluffy with an electric mixer. Add the eggs, one at a time, beating well between each addition. In another medium bowl, combine the flour with the allspice and cloves. Add this mixture alternately with the milk to the butter and egg mixture, beating well after each addition. Add the syrup mixture and mix well. Stir in the raisins and nuts with a wooden spoon.

Drop the dough by tablespoons, about 1 inch apart, on an ungreased cookie sheet. Bake until golden brown, 10 to 12 minutes. ❧

Brownies to Die For

FROM PEARL RIVER, L.D. wrote to us, "I am hoping that you can help me. I lost every recipe and cookbook I owned in the hurricane. While I wish I could retrieve each and every one, I would really like to have a recipe you posted several months ago. It was called Brownies to Die For."

This recipe was an instant hit the minute it was shared by local mystery writer Barbara Colley, who writes the Charlotte LaRue series, about a wise, crime-solving housekeeper in the Garden District.

{MAKES 16 BROWNIES}

BROWNIES

½ cup shortening

6 tablespoons unsweetened cocoa powder

2 tablespoons unsalted butter or stick margarine

2 medium eggs

1 cup sugar

1 teaspoon vanilla extract

¾ cup sifted all-purpose flour

½ teaspoon baking powder

½ teaspoon salt

1 cup broken pecans

FROSTING

4 tablespoons unsalted butter or stick margarine

3 tablespoons milk

2 tablespoons unsweetened cocoa powder

2 cups confectioners' sugar

½ teaspoon vanilla extract

Preheat the oven to 350 degrees F. Lightly coat an 8-inch square baking pan, 2 inches deep, with non-stick cooking spray.

For the brownies: In a medium microwave-safe bowl, microwave the shortening, cocoa, and butter on high for 1 minute, or until the butter and shortening are completely melted. Stir well and set aside to cool.

In a large mixing bowl, beat the eggs with an electric mixer until they are fluffy. Beat in the sugar, then add the cooled chocolate mixture and the vanilla.

Sift together the flour, baking powder, and salt. Add the sifted ingredients to the chocolate mixture and beat well. Fold in the pecans. Pour the batter into the prepared pan.

Bake for 30 to 35 minutes. Ten minutes before the brownies are done, prepare the frosting.

For the frosting: Microwave the butter, milk, and cocoa in a microwave-safe bowl on high for 20 seconds, or until the butter has melted and is bubbly. Stir well and add the confectioners' sugar. Return to the microwave for 10 seconds on high, then add vanilla. Beat well.

While the brownies are still hot from the oven, spread the frosting on the top. Let cool in the pan on a rack. Then cut into 16 squares.

Carol Klein's Turtle Cookies

THE RECIPE WAS requested by S.G. and J.G., formerly of the flood-devastated Lakeview neighborhood in New Orleans, and now living in Walker, near Baton Rouge. "We have been displaced and would like to introduce our newest neighbors to some of the old New Orleans sweet things," they wrote *The Times-Picayune*. "We would appreciate any help you can give us on this endeavor."

K.S. sent this recipe, which belonged to her late friend, Carol Klein. "I don't know where she got the recipe from, but it's great!" K.S. said. "These cookies taste just like the original McKenzie's bakery turtles." (See pages 40, 260, and 300 for other recipes related to the much-missed McKenzie's bakeries.)

{MAKES 3 TO 4 DOZEN COOKIES}

COOKIES

1¼ cups (1½ sticks) unsalted butter,
    at room temperature

1 cup sugar

1 large egg

2 tablespoons milk

½ teaspoon vanilla extract

1¾ cups all-purpose flour

1½ teaspoons baking powder

¼ teaspoon salt

½ pound pecan halves or pieces

FROSTING

4 tablespoons unsalted butter

2 (1-ounce) squares unsweetened chocolate

⅓ cup milk

½ teaspoon vanilla extract

3 cups confectioners' sugar

Preheat the oven to 375 degrees F.

For the cookies: In a large mixing bowl, beat the butter and sugar with an electric mixer until light and fluffy. Beat in the egg, milk, and vanilla. In a medium bowl, mix the flour, baking powder, and salt. Add to the butter mixture and beat until well combined.

Place 3 pecan halves close together on an ungreased cookie sheet and drop a tablespoon of dough on top of the pecans. Continue in this way, placing the cookies about 1½ inches apart, until you've filled the cookie sheet. Bake for 10 to 12 minutes, until lightly browned on the edges. Let cool on racks before frosting.

For the frosting: In a small saucepan over low heat, melt the butter and chocolate with the milk. (This mixture will look a little curdled until it is completely melted.) Let the frosting cool and then beat in the vanilla and sugar with an electric mixer. Top each cooled cookie with a dollop of the thick frosting. 🐢

Chocolate Chewies

THIS SIMPLE RECIPE creates an all-around good cookie. Anne Easson sent it to us and said it came from a Domino confectioners' sugar advertisement.

{MAKES 2 DOZEN COOKIES}

3 cups confectioners' sugar

⅓ cup unsweetened cocoa powder

2 tablespoons all-purpose flour

3 large egg whites

1 cup chopped pecans or another nut, such as walnuts

Preheat the oven to 350 degrees F. Line a cookie sheet with parchment or wax paper.

In a large mixing bowl, blend the sugar, cocoa, and flour with an electric mixer on low speed. Beat in the egg whites, one at a time, and then beat at high speed for 1 minute. Use a spatula to fold in the nuts.

Drop the dough by the tablespoon, 2 inches apart, onto the prepared cookie sheet.

Bake for 15 minutes. Remove from the oven and let cool on the paper. Place the cookies, still on the paper, in the freezer for 1 hour. Remove and peel off the paper; then store the cookies in an airtight container. ❧

Fig Cakes

FIG CAKES, MORE commonly known as fig cookies, are often made to put on St. Joseph's Day altars for the March 19 celebration. Some historians believe the date and fig filling, rich with citrus and spices, reflects the Moorish influence in Sicily.

{MAKES ABOUT 100 COOKIES}

FILLING

2 (6-ounce) packages dried figs
1 (8-ounce) package diced dates
1 cup pecans
½ teaspoon grated orange zest
½ cup orange juice
1½ cups sugar
1 teaspoon ground cinnamon
½ teaspoon ground cloves
½ teaspoon ground nutmeg
2 teaspoons vanilla extract

DOUGH

6 cups all-purpose flour
½ cup sugar
1 teaspoon salt
4½ teaspoons baking powder
7 heaping tablespoons shortening
½ cup (1 stick) unsalted butter, at room temperature
3 large eggs
1½ cups cold milk
2 teaspoons vanilla extract

FROSTING

1 (1-pound) box confectioners' sugar
About ⅓ cup milk

For the filling: In a food processor, working in batches if necessary, process the figs, dates, and pecans until ground. Transfer to a large mixing bowl. Add the remaining ingredients and mix thoroughly. Cover and let stand while you make the dough.

For the dough: Combine the flour, sugar, salt, and baking powder in a large mixing bowl. With a pastry cutter or the tines of a fork, cut the shortening and butter into the dry ingredients until the pieces are the size of small peas. In a medium bowl, beat the eggs, milk, and vanilla. Add this liquid mixture to the bowl of dry ingredients and mix thoroughly. The dough should be very stiff.

Preheat the oven to 375 degrees F. Lightly grease at least two cookie sheets.

Working on a lightly floured surface, roll the dough into sheets about 12 inches square and ⅛ inch thick. Cut into strips 3 to 4 inches wide.

Place the fig filling evenly along the center of a strip. Lift one long side of the dough strip over the top of the filling, then roll the dough over to create a long tube with the filling inside. Use your hands to roll the dough with a backward-and-forward motion to even up the tube, keeping the overlapping edges on the bottom. With a sharp knife, cut the tube into 1½-inch pieces. Continue in this way until you've used up the dough and filling.

Place the cookies on the cookie sheets about 1½ inches apart and bake for 20 to 25 minutes, or until lightly browned. Remove from the oven and place the cookies on wax paper. Allow to cool.

For the frosting: Put the confectioners' sugar in a bowl and mix in the milk gradually, stirring well, until the frosting reaches the desired consistency (it should be thick) and there are no lumps. Spread the frosting on the cookies.

Ginger Cookies

CHILDREN'S ADVOCATE BABS Johnson made about 2,000 of these, her signature family cookies, to give away at a giant Thanksgiving 2005 meal for first responders.

They never fail, she said when she shared the recipe. And, like any cookies made with honey, molasses, or corn syrup, they keep well. The secret ingredients are blackstrap molasses and fresh ginger. This is not a gingersnap, so do not overbake them. This should be a soft cookie.

{MAKES 3 TO 4 DOZEN COOKIES, DEPENDING ON SIZE}

¾ cup (1½ sticks) unsalted butter, at room temperature

2 cups sugar, plus extra for rolling

2 large eggs

⅓ cup blackstrap molasses

2 teaspoons white or cider vinegar

3 tablespoons grated fresh ginger

3½ cups all-purpose flour

1½ teaspoons baking soda

1 teaspoon ground cinnamon

¼ teaspoon ground cloves

Preheat the oven to 350 degrees F. Lightly grease two cookie sheets.

In a large mixing bowl, beat the butter and sugar together with an electric mixer until creamy. Beat in the eggs and then the molasses, vinegar, and ginger.

Sift together the flour, baking soda, cinnamon, and cloves. Stir into the wet mixture with a wooden spoon, and mix well. If dough is too wet to handle, refrigerate briefly. (At this point you can freeze the dough for future use. Then simply thaw and continue with the recipe.)

Put some sugar on a pie plate. Shape the dough into walnut-size balls, and roll them in the sugar. Place on the prepared cookie sheets about 2 inches apart and bake for about 12 minutes, until golden brown. Immediately remove the cookies to racks to cool. When completely cooled, store in airtight containers or plastic storage bags. ✌

Gold Brick Fudge

ELMER'S GOLD BRICK EGGS are a local candy and have long been traditional Easter basket fillers. Lenny Lisotta of River Ridge uses the leftover chocolate eggs to create this super-simple and luscious fudge, which he serves in bite-size pieces. Writer Paulette Rittenberg featured the recipe in the Home Cooking column of *The Times-Picayune* in 2002.

{MAKES ABOUT 90 SMALL SQUARES OF FUDGE}

18 (1-ounce) Elmer's Gold Brick Eggs

1 (14-ounce) can sweetened condensed milk (regular or fat-free)

In the top of a double boiler (or a bowl set over a saucepan of simmering water) melt the chocolate eggs until creamy, stirring occasionally. Add the milk, and quickly stir to blend well. Promptly pour into a 9-inch square pan. Let the candy harden until firm, about 8 hours at cool room temperature, or roughly 2 hours if refrigerated. Cut into small squares for serving. Store at cool room temperature or in the refrigerator. ❧

Governor Blanco's Butter Brickle

In 2006, GOVERNOR Kathleen Blanco and six of her eight grandchildren made batches of a traditional family holiday recipe in the Governor's Mansion.

{MAKES 1¼ POUNDS}

¼ cup sliced almonds
1 cup sugar, preferably Louisiana cane sugar
1 cup (2 sticks) butter or stick margarine
1 (6-ounce) package semisweet chocolate chips

Preheat the oven or a small toaster oven to 300 degrees F. Spread out the almonds on a cookie sheet or pie pan and toast them for about 10 minutes, or until the almonds begin to turn golden brown. Let cool. Line a 10-by-15-inch shallow pan with wax paper.

In a heavy 2-quart saucepan, combine the sugar and butter. Cook over low heat for 25 to 30 minutes, stirring occasionally, until the syrup reaches 300 degrees F on a candy thermometer. Or test by dropping a very small amount into ice water, which should form brittle strands that are crunchy, but do not stick to your teeth.

Pour the syrup evenly into the prepared pan. Let sit for 1 or 2 minutes, then sprinkle the chocolate chips over the hot candy. Let sit for 2 or 3 minutes as the chocolate chips soften. With a spatula, spread the softened chocolate evenly over the candy. Sprinkle the toasted almonds over the melted chocolate. Let cool completely. (If you want to speed up the process, use the governor's preferred method, and put the candy in the freezer for about 30 minutes.)

Break into pieces, and store in tins or other airtight containers. 🏃

Halloween Cookies Like McKenzie's

IN LATE SUMMER of 2007, a reader named Emily wrote, "I was wondering if *The Times-Picayune* had the McKenzie's Bakery Halloween cookies recipe or something similar . . . I miss them!"

Readers frequently beg for recipes from the defunct local bakery chain. They did give out recipes to fill the patty shells they sold (see page 40), but the only recipes for their baked goods in circulation are copycats that readers or food professionals created.

Melanie G. of Metairie painstakingly re-created the Halloween cookies. "It's just a basic shortbread cookie, but the difference is the maple extract," Melanie wrote to us. "I've found a way to satisfy my craving for those big, striped cookies, and I'm happy to help others do the same!"

The glazelike chocolate frosting is the trickiest part of the process, Melanie explained. It has to be thin enough to drip over the sides of the cookie, but thick enough to cover. If you make it thin enough to pour, try two coatings. These cookies bake very quickly and must be watched. Melanie says that when they are firm to the touch, and just start to turn a bit golden (but not brown) on the bottom, take them out of the oven. They won't look done, but they are.

Pressing them out by hand gives the cookies an uneven, handmade look, just like the McKenzie's cookies. Melanie says that this same dough, with the addition of pecans, can be used to re-create McKenzie's turtle cookies. Top with a dollop of the same chocolate frosting, thinned slightly. (See page 294 for another interpretation of this cookie.) When we published Melanie's recipe, stores quickly sold out of the secret ingredient: maple extract.

{MAKES AT LEAST 12 BIG COOKIES}

COOKIES

2½ cups unbleached all-purpose flour

¼ cup cornstarch

½ teaspoon baking powder

¼ teaspoon salt

1 cup (2 sticks) cold unsalted butter (not margarine), cut into pieces

¾ cup confectioners' sugar

2 teaspoons vanilla extract (use clear vanilla for best cookie color)

1 teaspoon maple extract

CHOCOLATE FROSTING

2 (1-ounce) squares semisweet chocolate

1½ cups confectioners' sugar

½ teaspoon vanilla extract

5 to 6 tablespoons hot water

ORANGE STRIPES

About 1 cup confectioners' sugar

Orange paste food coloring

Hot water

Preheat the oven to 300 degrees F. Line one or two cookie sheets with parchment paper.

For the cookies: Stir together the flour, cornstarch, baking powder, and salt in a medium mixing bowl. In a large bowl, beat the butter, confectioners' sugar, and vanilla and maple extracts with an electric mixer until smooth and creamy. Add the flour mixture gradually, beating at low speed, until the dough holds together in big clumps.

Flour your hands to prevent sticking, and form the dough into about 12 balls with your hands. Press each ball down onto the parchment-covered cookie sheets. Make the cookies as thick as you like, but remember that thinner cookies cook faster. (If you are making more than one batch, refrigerate the remaining dough while waiting to bake.)

Bake the cookies until set but not brown, 10 to 15 minutes, depending on your oven and the thickness of the cookie. Lift one cookie slightly. The bottom should just be turning golden, and the cookie should be able to hold its shape.

Remove from the oven and put the cookie sheet(s) on a rack to cool. Let cool until the cookies are cool enough to pick up. Carefully use a large spatula to transfer the cookies to a rack covered with wax paper. The cookies will be very tender, and you may break a few before you get the hang of taking them off the cookie sheet(s).

For the chocolate frosting: Melt the chocolate squares in the top of a double boiler (or a bowl set over a saucepan of simmering water), or put in a microwave-safe bowl and microwave on high for 30-second intervals, stirring after each interval, until melted. Using an electric mixer, beat in some of the confectioners' sugar and the vanilla. Add more confectioners' sugar and hot water, a tablespoon at a time, until the frosting is thick but spreadable.

While the cookies are still on the rack, spoon the frosting over them and spread to cover the entire surface. When the frosting has set to the touch and looks glossy, make the Orange Stripes.

For the orange stripes: Combine the confectioners' sugar and a squeeze of the paste food coloring in a small bowl. Add just enough hot water to make a thin frosting.

Use a pastry bag fitted with a small round tip, or cut a tiny hole from the corner of a zip-top bag. Put the orange frosting in the bag and practice, over a piece of wax paper, applying even pressure to make stripes while moving your hand back and forth. When you are comfortable with the process, add stripes to the cookies. ❧

Italian Seed Cookies

SEVERAL KINDS OF cookies, including these seed cookies, are made by the thousands for the many annual St. Joseph's Day altars around the region. Ann Silva asked that we find one that included baking ammonia, which gives the cookies a light, crispy texture. Going through the piles of recipes sent in for the recipe restoration project, we came across this one, from Julie Pizzuto Crawford. The recipe was featured in *The Times-Picayune* "Home Cooking" column on March 11, 2004.

Seed cookies are always a popular treat from altars. "What most people like is that they're crispy, light, and not too sweet," said Crawford, a grandmother who has been making seed cookies since childhood. Usually, she bakes four times the number yielded by the recipe below. Recipes for these cookies are made in such quantities that the ingredients are typically given in pounds, not cups.

In the New Orleans area, brown sesame seeds are sold by the pound at Nor-Joe Importing Company in Metairie and Central Grocery in the French Quarter. Nor-Joe's also carries the leavening agent baking ammonia (ammonium bicarbonate), as do commercial bakery suppliers.

{MAKES ABOUT 10 DOZEN COOKIES}

About ¾ pound brown sesame seeds (sold loose at Italian grocery stores)

1 teaspoon powdered baking ammonia (ammonium bicarbonate)

1 cup water

1 pound sugar

1 pound butter-flavored solid vegetable shortening, such as Crisco

1 cup (2 sticks) margarine, cut into ½-inch cubes

2 teaspoons vanilla extract

3 pounds all-purpose flour

Preheat the oven to 350 degrees F. If you have insulated cookie sheets, you do not need to grease them; otherwise, line cookie sheets with parchment paper. Spread out several clean dish cloths to use for cooling the cookies.

Line a colander with a cloth dinner napkin, and pour in the sesame seeds. Soak the seeds thoroughly with running water. Drain, then wring out the napkin with the seeds inside until it no longer drips. Mound the wet seeds on a rimmed baking sheet or baking pan that you will not need for baking the cookies, and set aside.

Mix the baking ammonia with the 1 cup water and set aside. In a very large mixing bowl, blend the sugar, shortening, margarine, and vanilla with your hands, squeezing the mixture through your fingers until the mixture is smooth and the ingredients are well distributed. Add the flour and the baking ammonia mixture alternately, about a third at a time, beating with a wooden spoon until a stiff dough forms.

Pinch off a small amount of dough and roll it into a log roughly 8 inches long and ¾ inch in diameter, tapering at both ends. Place the log on the sesame seeds and roll the log in them, lightly pressing the seeds into the dough.

Transfer the log to a cutting surface, and with a knife, cut the log on a sharp diagonal into 2-inch-long cookies. If necessary, remoisten the sesame seeds.

Place the cookies about ¼ inch apart on the cookie sheets and bake until lightly browned on the bottom, about 25 minutes. Turn the cookies onto the dish cloths to cool. Store in cardboard boxes or tins (not plastic) to keep the cookies crispy. ❧

Justines

B.H. of Pass Christian, Mississippi, who lost nearly all of her cookbooks and clippings files, sent in a request for Justines.

"About two years ago, you published a recipe for cookies called Justines. These were great cookies and everyone who tasted them loved them. My recipe is gone and I would love to have a copy," she wrote.

This recipe was given to us by Barbara Wedemeyer. She got it years ago from a famous restaurant in Memphis, Tennessee, named Justine's, for which the cookies are named. For a moister taste, start with fresh whole dates and chop them yourself.

{MAKES 6 TO 7 DOZEN SMALL COOKIES}

1 cup (2 sticks) unsalted butter, at room temperature

⅔ cup granulated sugar, plus about 1 cup for rolling

1 cup light or dark brown sugar

1 large egg, lightly beaten

2½ cups all-purpose flour

2 teaspoons baking soda

⅛ teaspoon salt

1 teaspoon vanilla extract

1 cup chopped dates

1 cup rolled (old-fashioned) oats

1 cup chopped pecans

Preheat the oven to 350 degrees F. Grease cookie sheets for baking.

In a large mixing bowl, with an electric mixer, beat together the butter, ⅔ cup of the granulated sugar, and the brown sugar until fluffy. Add the egg, beating well. Sift together the flour, baking soda, and salt onto a piece of wax paper or aluminum foil. Beat into the butter and sugar mixture. Beat in the vanilla, dates, oats, and pecans. The mixture will be stiff.

Roll the dough into marble-size balls. Place the remaining 1 cup of granulated sugar in a shallow bowl. Roll the dough balls in the sugar, and place on the greased cookie sheets about 1 inch apart. Flatten the cookies a little with your fingertips or the side of a knife.

Bake for 10 to 12 minutes, or until the tops of the cookies are puffed and the bottoms are browned. Let cool for a few seconds on the cookie sheets before transferring to a wire rack to cool. Store in airtight containers. 🐘

McMain Brownies

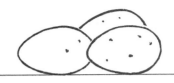

"GUESS I DON'T have to tell you: I lost all my cookbooks and recipes to Katrina," wrote a former New Orleans resident, who moved 200 miles north to Natchitoches, Louisiana. One recipe she wanted was for brownies, published by *The Times-Picayune*. These old-fashioned brownies had been served at McMain Girls High School in the 1940s, and were a favorite of many readers.

{MAKES ABOUT 2 DOZEN BROWNIES}

Butter for greasing
1 cup all-purpose flour
¾ cup unsweetened cocoa powder
¾ teaspoon salt
1 cup (2 sticks) margarine, at room temperature
2 cups sugar
4 large eggs, lightly beaten
1 teaspoon vanilla extract
1 cup pecans (optional)

Butter and flour a 9-by-13-inch baking pan. Preheat the oven to 275 degrees F.

Mix the flour, cocoa, and salt in a medium mixing bowl. Set aside.

In a large mixing bowl, beat the margarine with an electric mixer until fluffy and add the sugar and beaten eggs. Beat in the vanilla, then the dry ingredients. Stir in the pecans (if using) by hand. Pour the batter into the prepared pan. Bake for about 1 hour, or until the edges pull away slightly from the pan. Let cool in the pan on a rack. 🐀

Mrs. Trumm's Sand Tarts

THIS HEIRLOOM RECIPE was sent to the Food section by A.E. of New Orleans, who wrote, "I would like to pass on to you a terrific cookie recipe that's been in our family for 40 years."

{MAKES 12 SERVINGS}

1 cup vegetable shortening
1 cup (2 sticks) unsalted butter or margarine
2 cups sugar, plus extra for the tops of the cookies
½ teaspoon salt
2 large eggs, well beaten
½ teaspoon almond extract
3 cups all-purpose flour

In a large mixing bowl, beat together the shortening, butter, 2 cups sugar, and salt with an electric mixer until light and fluffy. Add the eggs and almond extract and beat well. Blend in the flour. Put the dough in the refrigerator until well chilled for easy handling.

Preheat the oven to 400 degrees F.

Roll the dough into balls the size of small walnuts and place them on a greased cookie sheet about 1½ inches apart. Use the bottom of a small glass dipped in sugar to lightly flatten each ball. Bake for about 7 minutes, or until the cookies are browned around the edges. Remove from the cookie sheet at once and let cool on wire racks. ❧

Mulhall Cookies

M.M., LIVING IN New Orleans post-Katrina, wrote to us about a recipe sent in years ago by a woman in Slidell. "Since I lost everything in the flood/oil, the only thing I can remember is that she called them Mulhall cookies," M.M. said. "I would love to have this recipe again if possible."

The recipe was shared in 1999 by Janet Calvet Fouert of Slidell, who named them after Flo Mulhall, who had introduced Fouert's aunt to the cookies thirty-five years before that. Fouert was on a mission to spread the recipe around so more people could enjoy this crisp, homey brown cookie.

{MAKES ABOUT 5 DOZEN COOKIES}

2½ cups all-purpose flour

1 teaspoon baking soda

1 teaspoon cream of tartar

1 cup (2 sticks) unsalted butter, or ½ cup butter and ½ cup margarine, at room temperature

1 (1-pound) box light brown sugar

2 large eggs

1 tablespoon vanilla extract

1 cup pecan pieces

Preheat the oven to 325 degrees F. In a large bowl, sift together the flour, baking soda, and cream of tartar three times; set aside.

In the large bowl of an electric stand mixer set on medium speed (use a dough hook if available), thoroughly mix together the butter and sugar, 2 to 3 minutes. Beat in one egg at a time, and continue beating until the mixture is very light in color and texture, about 5 minutes, scraping the sides down with a rubber spatula. Gradually add the flour mixture, a few tablespoons each time, then add the vanilla and pecans, mixing well. The batter will be quite stiff.

Drop the batter by slightly heaping teaspoons onto an ungreased cookie sheet, 2½ to 3 inches apart. Bake until golden brown, 12 to 15 minutes. Remove from the oven and let the cookies cool for about 1 minute on the cookie sheet. Then, working quickly, loosen them with a spatula and transfer to a wire rack to cool. (If you remove the cookies from the pan too soon, they break apart; if you wait more than about 2 minutes total, they tend to stick.) Store in airtight tins or freeze. 🍃

Basic Oatmeal Cookies

Several readers asked that we include a basic oatmeal cookie recipe. This one should make everyone happy.

{MAKES 6 TO 8 DOZEN COOKIES, DEPENDING ON WHETHER YOU ADD RAISINS}

¾ cup vegetable shortening (no substitutes)
1 cup firmly packed light brown sugar
½ cup granulated sugar
1 large egg
¼ cup water
1 teaspoon vanilla extract
1 cup all-purpose flour
1 teaspoon salt
½ teaspoon baking soda
3 cups rolled (old-fashioned) oats

Preheat the oven to 350 degrees F. Grease the cookie sheets.

In a large mixing bowl, with an electric mixer, beat together the shortening, brown and granulated sugars, egg, water, and vanilla until creamy. Sift together the flour, salt, and soda; then beat the dry ingredients into the creamed mixture. Stir in the oats by hand.

Drop by the teaspoon onto the prepared cookie sheets. Bake for 12 to 15 minutes, until lightly browned. Let cool on the cookie sheets for a few minutes before removing to racks to cool completely.

VARIATION:

Oatmeal-Raisin Cookies—Add 1½ cups of raisins to the dough after you stir in the oats.

Home-Style Peanut Butter Cups

PEANUT BUTTER CUPS are a favorite for trick-or-treaters. When someone requested a recipe for making them, former *Times-Picayune* food columnist Constance Snow found this one in Mable Hoffman's *The Peanut Butter Cookbook*. For smaller candies, use mini-cupcake liners instead of the regular size.

{MAKES 8 LARGE CUPS}

½ cup confectioners' sugar

⅓ cup sour cream

¼ teaspoon vanilla extract

¾ cup crunchy peanut butter

½ pound sweet baking chocolate or milk chocolate

In a small bowl, combine the sugar, sour cream, vanilla, and peanut butter. Refrigerate while preparing the chocolate.

Melt the chocolate in a pan or in the top of a double boiler (or a bowl set over a saucepan of simmering water). With a narrow ½-inch brush, brush the melted chocolate over the bottom and ¾ inch up the sides of eight 2¼-inch paper cupcake liners. Place the cups on a tray and refrigerate for about 15 minutes, until firm. Keep the remaining chocolate warm.

Shape about 2 tablespoons of the cooled peanut butter mixture into a flattened ball and use it to fill a chocolate-lined cup. Continue in this way to fill the remaining 7 chocolate cups. Spoon about 1½ teaspoons of the remaining melted chocolate over the top of each cup and refrigerate until firm. ❧

Praline Cookies

Anne Easson generously sent in this recipe, which came from a cookbook she found when she was working at Latter Library in New Orleans. "I had the opportunity to peruse all kinds of cookbooks during the eleven years I worked at Latter," Easson wrote. "This is my favorite cookie recipe of all the ones I looked at and it is truly a cookie New Orleanians would love." We agree.

{MAKES 3 TO 4 DOZEN COOKIES}

1½ cups coarsely chopped pecans

½ cup (stick) margarine or butter

1 cup packed dark brown sugar

1 large egg

1 teaspoon vanilla extract

1¼ cups all-purpose flour

¼ teaspoon baking soda

¼ teaspoon salt

Preheat the oven to 325 degrees F. Grease the cookie sheets.

Do not skip this step! Toast the pecans. Spread out the nuts in a single layer on an ungreased pan and bake until fragrant, about 10 minutes. Let cool.

In a large mixing bowl, beat the margarine and brown sugar with an electric mixer until fluffy. Beat in the egg and vanilla extract. In a separate bowl, whisk together the flour, baking soda, and salt. Mix this into the brown sugar mixture. Fold in the pecans by hand.

Drop the dough by the teaspoon onto the baking sheets. Bake for 15 to 20 minutes or until the cookies are lightly browned on the bottoms. Let cool on the cookie sheets for 5 minutes, then use a spatula to transfer the cookies to cooling racks.

Rosemary Cookies

THIS HAS BEEN one of the most requested cookie recipes since it was published in *The Times-Picayune* in September 2000. The recipe is from Mary Youngblood Cooper, and is one of her favorite cookies, too.

"I love people's reactions to these cookies and like the idea of putting a fresh herb in them," Cooper said. "Everyone always checks my cookie jar and is so disappointed if there's not a supply of rosemary cookies there."

Cooper was inspired to make the cookies after reading that the French like to include herbs in their cookies. To bake these Rosemary Cookies, she altered a standard butter cookie recipe, replacing the vanilla with fresh rosemary, an easy-to-grow herb, and an aromatic member of the mint family. The crisp cookies are perfect for serving with coffee whenever friends drop in. They're also elegant enough to offer with Champagne at fancy parties.

{MAKES 2½ TO 3 DOZEN COOKIES}

½ cup (1 stick) unsalted butter, at room temperature
1 cup all-purpose unbleached flour
½ cup confectioners' sugar
2 tablespoons minced fresh rosemary leaves
Squeeze of fresh lemon juice (optional)
About 2 teaspoons granulated sugar

Preheat the oven to 350 degrees F.

In a large mixing bowl with an electric mixer, beat together the butter, flour, confectioners' sugar, rosemary, and lemon juice (if using). Spoon the dough by teaspoons onto ungreased cookie sheets, about 1½ inches apart. Press the dough flat with a cookie stamp or the bottom of a small drinking glass dipped in granulated sugar.

Bake the cookies until light brown around the edges, about 10 minutes. Cool on a wire rack and store in an airtight container. ❧

Toasted Coconut Cookies

For Christmas 2005, a reader we know only as A.W. shared a gift with other readers. She wrote, "I'm happy to be able to read your column again, and I want to contribute something to those trying to rebuild their New Orleans recipe collections. I'm one of the lucky ones: I didn't lose my house and I didn't lose my treasured recipe collection. In fact, my recipe box was one of the items I took with me when I evacuated!

"I am fond of Christmas cookie baking, and I want to share my very best, longtime favorite cookie recipe, for Toasted Coconut Cookies. I've had it for forty years, and the recipe card is yellowed and stained from much use. I'm a faithful T-P Food section reader, and I've never seen this recipe or one like it published before."

A.W. started making these cookies when she was raising young children on a low budget, because coconut was cheaper than nuts. These crisp delicacies might become your favorite, too.

{MAKES ABOUT 3 DOZEN COOKIES}

1 cup sifted all-purpose flour

½ teaspoon baking soda

½ teaspoon salt

½ cup shortening

1 cup light brown sugar

1 large egg

1 teaspoon vanilla extract

1 cup quick-cooking oats

1 cup shredded coconut, toasted and crushed (see Note)

½ cup chopped pecans (optional)

Preheat the oven to 325 degrees F.

Mix the flour, baking soda, and salt in a medium mixing bowl. In a large mixing bowl, beat the shortening and brown sugar with an electric mixer until fluffy, then add the egg and vanilla. Beat again until fluffy. Stir in the flour mixture by hand, and then stir in the oats, toasted coconut, and pecans (if using).

Form the dough into balls 1 to 1½ inches in diameter, and place 2 inches apart on an ungreased cookie sheet. Flatten each cookie with the bottom of a glass dipped in flour. Bake for 12 to 15 minutes, until lightly browned. ❧

NOTE: *To toast the coconut, spread it out in a large shallow pan and bake in a slow oven (275 to 300 degrees F) for about 15 minutes, stirring once or twice, until toasted a delicate brown. Let cool and crush in a food processor, or put the cooled coconut in a plastic zip-top bag and crush with a rolling pin.*

Turtle Candies

CHOCOLATE CANDIES ARE always a good gift for your Valentine, so consider making these for that special someone. Sure, they take a little effort, but, hey, your sweetheart is worth it, right?

{MAKES 16 CANDIES}

1 (12-ounce) package semisweet chocolate morsels
1¼ cups pecan halves
28 caramels, unwrapped
2 tablespoons heavy cream

Microwave the chocolate morsels in a microwave-safe bowl on high power for 1 minute. Stir and microwave for another 30 seconds. Stir until smooth and let cool until slightly thickened.

Drop the chocolate by the tablespoon about 2 inches apart onto a baking sheet lined with wax paper or parchment paper, shaping the chocolate into small circles. Make a total of 16 circles. Reserve the remaining chocolate. Arrange 4 pecans over each circle, and refrigerate until firm.

Combine the caramels and heavy cream in a microwave-safe bowl. Microwave on high for 1 minute. Stir and microwave for 1 more minute, or until the caramels melt. Let stand for about 4 minutes, or until the mixture thickens slightly.

Spoon the caramel mixture evenly over the pecans. Microwave the remaining chocolate on high for 30 seconds. Stir and microwave for another 30 seconds. Quickly spread the chocolate over the caramel. Refrigerate until firm. Store in an airtight container. 🐢

Whiskey or Rum Balls

R.M. OF WESTWEGO asked us to reprint this recipe. If you make these treats and you want them sweeter, she suggests using amaretto or banana liqueur instead of whiskey or rum.

{MAKES ABOUT 5 DOZEN CANDIES}

1 pound vanilla wafers, finely crushed

2 cups finely chopped pecans

2 tablespoons unsweetened cocoa powder

3 tablespoons light corn syrup

¾ cup whiskey or rum

About ½ cup sifted confectioners' sugar, plus more for storage

Line a baking sheet with a large piece of wax paper. In a large bowl, combine the vanilla-wafer crumbs and pecans. Add the cocoa powder and mix to combine. Add the syrup and mix again. Add the whiskey or rum and mix until thoroughly incorporated.

Pinch off about 1 tablespoon of the mixture and roll it between your palms to form a ball. Transfer it to the baking sheet. Repeat with the remaining mixture. Set aside for 5 minutes.

Place the sugar in a large shallow bowl or in a zipper-top plastic bag. Working with a few at a time, roll or shake the balls in the sugar to coat them. Transfer the balls to a large container and sprinkle them with more confectioners' sugar. Cover and refrigerate. 🐜

PUDDINGS & OTHER DESSERTS

W e never realized there were so many recipes for bread pudding, a dessert that was created by thrifty cooks who didn't want to throw out stale bread. The Tennessee Bread Pudding (page 333) has a combination of coconut, pineapple, and raisins added to the custard. The Bon Ton Cafe's version (page 322) is a classic one, but if you want something different, try the Eggnog Bread Pudding with Rum Sauce (page 328). If you want something really elegant and over the top, you might want to make the Palace Café's White Chocolate Bread Pudding (page 332)—delicious! Another pudding that Marcelle likes is the old-time one made with rice (page 323), which is a tasty way to use leftover rice.

How can something so simple to make taste so good—Bananas Foster (page 320) is always a crowd-pleaser! Old favorites like Chocolate Pots de Crème (page 326) and Floating Islands (page 329) are also included here. And if you can't get to Brocato's here in New Orleans, then by all means try your hand at making your own Cannoli (page 324).

PUDDINGS & OTHER DESSERTS

Baked Rice Pudding

THIS RECIPE AND the Creole Bread Pudding on page 327 have been in Jamie Stevens's family for decades. "My mother cut [the] two recipes . . . out of *The Times-Picayune* sometime in the early to mid-1950s (I know this based on my sister's age, she is the oldest)," the Harvey resident wrote us. "My mother used to make both of these recipes for the family. My sister said Mother made them when she was a child, and later for me. We still use these recipes when we make bread pudding or rice pudding."

{MAKES ABOUT 12 SERVINGS}

1 quart milk

4 large eggs, lightly beaten

¾ cup sugar

2 teaspoons vanilla extract

1¼ cups cooked rice

1 cup raisins (optional)

1 teaspoon ground nutmeg

1 teaspoon ground cinnamon

Preheat the oven to 350 degrees F. Grease a 2-quart glass casserole dish.

Heat the milk in a large saucepan until just below the boiling point and gradually add the beaten eggs, stirring constantly. Stir in the sugar, vanilla, rice, and raisins (if using). Combine the nutmeg and cinnamon in a small dish and then blend into the rice mixture. Pour into the prepared dish.

Set the casserole dish in a large baking pan and add about 1 inch of hot water to the larger pan. Bake, uncovered. After 15 minutes, stir the pudding with a fork very gently, back and forth. Bake for 25 minutes longer, or until a metal knife inserted in the pudding comes out clean. Serve warm. ❧

Bally's Casino Bread Pudding

BREAD PUDDING IS a classic dessert in New Orleans. Just about every restaurant and cafe has its own version, with some being firm while others are more custardy. This recipe from Bally's Casino first appeared in *The Times-Picayune* in 1996. It has proven to be a favorite of readers, several of whom requested that we reprint it.

{MAKES 6 TO 8 SERVINGS}

PUDDING

1 pound stale French bread

½ cup raisins

5 large eggs

6 cups milk

1½ cups sugar

2 tablespoons vanilla extract

SAUCE

1½ cups (3 sticks) unsalted butter

1 cup granulated sugar

⅔ cup light brown sugar

¼ teaspoon salt

½ cup heavy cream

½ cup bourbon

Preheat the oven to 350 degrees F.

For the pudding: Tear the bread into 2-inch pieces and put in a greased 9-by-13-inch baking dish. Scatter the raisins on top and set aside.

In a large mixing bowl, beat the eggs with a wire whisk until they are well blended. Whisk in the milk, sugar, and vanilla. Pour over the torn bread and push the bread down with your fingers until saturated. Let the mixture soak for 3 minutes.

Place the pudding pan in a larger pan, then fill the larger pan with enough hot water to come half-way up the sides of the pudding pan. Bake for 65 minutes, until it sets and is lightly browned.

For the sauce: Meanwhile, in a medium sauce-pan, melt the butter over medium heat. (Do not boil.) Add the granulated and brown sugars and beat with a wire whisk until creamy. Remove from the heat and beat in the salt and heavy cream. Add the bourbon and whisk until well blended.

Remove the pudding from the oven. Let cool slightly. To serve, pour the sauce over the entire bread pudding, or over individual servings. 🥢

Bananas Foster

BANANAS FOSTER, A favorite New Orleans dessert, was created by the Brennan family in the 1950s when they opened Brennan's restaurant in the French Quarter. It was named for a regular customer, Dick Foster. It never fails to please and is easy to prepare.

If you're a New Orleanian old enough to remember NOPSI, (New Orleans Public Service, Inc.), you've probably sampled some of the hundreds of recipes the utility company published over the years, which were created by the company's home economists. This is one of their recipes.

{MAKES 4 SERVINGS}

2 bananas, peeled
1 tablespoon fresh lemon juice
2 tablespoons unsalted butter
¼ cup dark brown sugar
⅛ teaspoon ground cinnamon
2 tablespoons banana liqueur
¼ cup white rum
1 pint vanilla ice cream

Slice the bananas in half lengthwise and brush with the lemon juice. Melt the butter with the sugar in a flat chafing dish or 10-inch skillet. Add the bananas and sauté until just tender. Sprinkle with the cinnamon.

Remove from the heat and add the liqueur and rum. Carefully ignite with a long match. Use a large long-handled spoon to baste the bananas with the warm liquid until the flame burns out.

Divide the ice cream among four dishes. Top each one with a banana half and some of the sauce. Serve immediately. ❧

Blueberry Buckle

A BUCKLE IS much like a coffee cake. The batter is dense and has a streusel topping. While the dessert bakes, the topping "buckles" and the batter sinks to the bottom of the pan.

Blueberry recipes are quite popular in the greater New Orleans area because of the large number of blueberry farms north of Lake Pontchartrain and in western Mississippi. This recipe has been requested often.

{MAKES ABOUT 8 SERVINGS}

STREUSEL TOPPING

¼ cup granulated sugar

¼ cup packed light brown sugar

¼ cup all-purpose flour

4 tablespoons unsalted butter

½ teaspoon ground cinnamon

CAKE

¾ cup sugar

4 tablespoons unsalted butter

2 large eggs, beaten

1 teaspoon vanilla extract

2 cups all-purpose flour

2 teaspoons baking powder

½ teaspoon salt

½ cup buttermilk

2½ cups blueberries

For the streusel topping: With a fork or your fingers, combine all the streusel ingredients in a small bowl until the mixture has a crumbly consistency. Set aside.

Preheat the oven to 375 degrees F. Lightly grease a 9-inch square pan and set aside.

For the cake: Beat the sugar and butter with an electric mixer in a large mixing bowl until fluffy. Beat in the eggs, then the vanilla.

Mix together the flour, baking powder, and salt in another mixing bowl. Add this to the sugar and butter mixture alternately with the buttermilk, beating well after each addition. Fold in the blueberries until just mixed in. Spread out the mixture in the pan and top with the streusel.

Bake until a cake tester inserted in the cake comes out clean, 25 to 30 minutes. Serve warm or at room temperature. ❧

Bon Ton's Bread Pudding

WHEN THE BON TON Cafe opened in 1953 in New Orleans, it was deemed the first Cajun restaurant of note to appear in the city. The owner, the late Al Pierce, served authentic Cajun dishes like crawfish étouffée, crawfish bisque, gumbos, and a delicious bread pudding.

The restaurant, still on Magazine Street but across the street from the original site, continues to serve many of its signature dishes. If you ask for the bread pudding recipe, voilà, the waitress will kindly hand you a sheet of paper with the original recipe of Alzina Pierce, Mr. Al's wife.

{MAKES 8 TO 12 SERVINGS}

1 quart milk
5 thick slices French bread, torn into pieces (about 5 cups)
3 large eggs, beaten
2 cups sugar
2 tablespoons vanilla extract
1 cup raisins
3 tablespoons margarine or butter, melted
Whiskey Sauce (recipe follows) for serving

Preheat the oven to 350 degrees F.

Pour the milk into a large mixing bowl. Soak the bread in the milk for about 30 minutes, pressing the bread down into the milk occasionally. Then add the eggs, sugar, vanilla, and raisins and stir well.

Coat a 6- or 8-cup baking dish with the margarine, and transfer the bread mixture to the dish. Bake until very firm, about 1 hour.

Cut the pudding into serving sizes and serve warm or cold on dessert dishes, accompanied by the warm Whiskey Sauce.

Whiskey Sauce

½ cup (1 stick) unsalted butter or margarine, at room temperature
1 cup sugar
1 large egg, well beaten
3 tablespoons bourbon

Combine the butter and sugar in the top of a double boiler (or a bowl set over a saucepan of simmering water) and whisk until the sugar dissolves. Remove from the heat and whisk in the well-beaten egg, whipping vigorously so the egg doesn't curdle. Whisk in the bourbon. 🍧

Butterscotch Rice Pudding

G.M. SENT ONE of the lighter notes that have come in since we started on our mission to rebuild New Orleanians' recipe collections. "My daughter rescued a lot of my clipped recipes from my house and I had them hanging on her clothesline drying out. And this was over two months after Katrina hit!" she wrote. They dried well and that made her very happy, G.M. said.

"Whenever I see a request I always go to my stash and look for it," G.M. told us. But there was one old-fashioned recipe that she wanted, which she didn't manage to rescue. It was originally published in *The Times-Picayune* and here it is. She said it is quick and easy and tastes divine.

{MAKES 4 SERVINGS}

1 cup water
Pinch of salt
⅓ cup short-grain rice
1½ cups milk
1 teaspoon vanilla extract
2 tablespoons unsalted butter
½ cup heavy cream
⅓ cup firmly packed dark brown sugar

Preheat the oven to 350 degrees F. Grease a 1-quart ovenproof casserole dish.

Bring the cup of water to a boil in a large saucepan. As soon as the water boils, add the salt and the rice. Cover and cook over low heat for 15 minutes, or until all the water is absorbed. Stir in the milk and heat for 5 to 10 minutes, or just until the milk comes to a boil. Remove from the heat and stir in the vanilla extract.

In a small, heavy-bottomed skillet, melt the butter over medium heat. Add the cream and brown sugar. Bring to a boil, reduce the heat to low, and simmer for 2 minutes, stirring constantly. Pour the cream mixture into the rice. Stir well and spoon into the casserole dish.

Bake for 20 minutes, or until the pudding is thick and has a golden crust. Let cool for 15 minutes before serving.

Cannoli

THERE IS A LARGE Sicilian community in and around New Orleans, which may be why we had several requests for cannoli, that delicious confection of pastry shells filled with sweetened ricotta, chocolate, and pistachios. However, most New Orleanians opt to purchase them, ready-made, at Angelo Brocato's Original Italian Ice Cream Parlor.

That century-old tradition stopped for a while when Brocato's suffered damage from Hurricane Katrina. Brocato's reopened in September 2006, much to the delight of their many loyal patrons. Food editor Judy Walker wrote the following when Brocato's reopened their doors:

For a Mid-City neighborhood on the long road back from Katrina, Saturday's reopening was a moment as sweet as the legendary cannoli that Angelo Brocato first started selling in the French Quarter in 1905.

"I hope we can bring you as much joy in the next 100 years as we have in the past 100 years," Arthur Brocato said as he cut the crepe ribbon to open the Carrollton Avenue store.

It was just last July when the family celebrated 100 years since Angelo Brocato started selling ice cream. A month before Katrina, the company had completed a major renovation of the store and the consolidation of their wholesale cookie and ice cream operation in a building behind the shop.

Then Katrina pushed five feet of water into the area.

In the year that it took to rebuild, the level of support the Brocatos received from their devoted fans never wavered.

"It's unbelievable, the very sincere e-mails we've gotten," Arthur Brocato said. "People were so heartsick when they saw the business so severely damaged. They kept us in their prayers and well wishes. It has really been wonderful."

Brocato said they made 7,000 cannoli shells for the grand reopening, and it seemed as if every single person who went in was soon cradling a box.

This is not Brocato's recipe (it's a family secret), but it's darn good.

{MAKES 6 SERVINGS}

¾ cup ricotta cheese

¾ cup mascarpone cheese

1½ cups confectioners' sugar, plus extra for sprinkling the shells

1 teaspoon vanilla extract, or 1 tablespoon Grand Marnier

3 tablespoons chopped candied orange peel

½ cup finely chopped semisweet or bittersweet chocolate

2 to 3 tablespoons finely chopped pistachios (optional)

6 cannoli shells (see Note)

In a food processor, combine the ricotta, mascarpone, confectioners' sugar, and vanilla. Process until the mixture is very smooth. Remove the blade and by hand, stir in the orange peel, chocolate, and pistachios (if using). Continue stirring until well blended. (The ricotta mixture can be prepared in advance, covered, and refrigerated.)

To prevent the shells from getting soggy, stuff them just before serving. With a pastry bag fitted with an open star tip, pipe some of the cheese mixture into each side of the cannoli shells. Or use a small spoon to stuff it in. Sprinkle the tops of the shells with additional sifted confectioners' sugar. Serve immediately. ❧

NOTE: *Cannoli shells are available at some supermarkets and at Italian markets.*

Chocolate Pots de Crème

POTS DE CRÈME, a creamy custard dessert, was a popular dessert at many New Orleans restaurants for years, but for some reason, it is hard to find these days. It's a delightful ending to any meal, and just enough to satisfy anyone's sweet tooth.

The classic flavoring of these creamy-rich custards is vanilla, but there are many variations. And the great thing is they can be easily made in advance and kept chilled in the refrigerator until it's time to serve. Garnish them just before bringing them to the table.

There are tiny (about three-ounce) pot-shaped cups made just for these custards, but you can certainly serve the desserts in small ramekins, wine glasses, or even in saucer-shaped champagne glasses.

{MAKES ABOUT 6 SERVINGS}

2 cups half-and-half

2 large eggs, lightly beaten

2 tablespoons sugar

3⅓ cups semisweet chocolate morsels

3 tablespoons amaretto or another almond-flavored liqueur

2 teaspoons vanilla extract

Pinch of salt

Whipped cream for garnish

Chocolate shavings for garnish

Combine the half-and-half, eggs, and sugar in a heavy saucepan. Cook over medium heat, stirring often, for about 12 minutes, or until the mixture registers 160 degrees F on a candy or deep-fat thermometer. Add the chocolate morsels, amaretto, vanilla, and salt. Stir until smooth.

Spoon the custard into individual ramekins or glasses, cover, and chill. Just before serving, garnish with the whipped cream and chocolate shavings. ❧

Creole Bread Pudding

THE ACADIANS AND Creoles were always thrifty and economical, but you could hardly tell by the elegant and delicious dishes that emerged from their kitchens. Think creamy smooth bread pudding made with day-old bread, or *calas* (rice fritters) made from leftover rice. This bread pudding recipe was sent in by Jamie Stevens of Harvey, who also contributed the recipe for Baked Rice Pudding on page 318.

{MAKES 8 TO 10 SERVINGS}

Butter for greasing
3 large eggs
1 cup sugar
1 quart milk
1 teaspoon vanilla extract
½ teaspoon grated nutmeg
10 cups stale French bread cubes (1-inch cubes)
1 cup raisins
Bourbon Whiskey Sauce (recipe follows) for serving

Preheat the oven to 350 degrees F. Generously butter a 9-by-13-inch baking dish.

In a large mixing bowl, beat the eggs with an electric mixer or a whisk until frothy. Beat in the sugar, milk, vanilla, and nutmeg. Mix thoroughly. Add the bread and raisins and stir well by hand. Set aside and let the bread soak for 15 minutes.

Pour the bread mixture into the prepared dish and smooth the top. Bake just until set, about 45 minutes. Serve warm or at room temperature with the sauce.

Bourbon Whiskey Sauce

1¼ cups water
½ cup packed light brown sugar
¼ teaspoon ground nutmeg
¼ cup bourbon
1½ teaspoons cornstarch
2 teaspoons unsalted butter or margarine

Combine the water, brown sugar, and nutmeg in a medium saucepan and bring to a boil over high heat. In a small bowl, stir together the bourbon and cornstarch, then stir into the sugar mixture and cook until the mixture thickens and is smooth, about 8 to 10 minutes. Stir in the butter and serve warm. ❧

Eggnog Bread Pudding with Rum Sauce

THIS APPEARS TO have been a very popular recipe, since many readers have requested it. For extra fiber, use whole-grain bread.

{MAKES 8 SERVINGS}

BREAD PUDDING

5 slices white bread, halved
⅓ cup sugar
1 cup fat-free evaporated milk
1 teaspoon vanilla extract
1 large egg
2 tablespoons raisins
½ teaspoon ground nutmeg

RUM SAUCE

⅓ cup loosely packed light brown sugar
¼ cup light corn syrup
⅓ cup orange juice
2 tablespoons dark rum

For the bread pudding: Preheat the oven to 350 degrees F. Coat an 8-inch square baking dish with cooking spray. Lay the bread slices in the dish, overlapping them.

In a medium bowl, beat together the sugar, milk, vanilla, and egg with a whisk or an electric mixer. Pour the custard over the bread slices and press the bread into it to help soak it up. Sprinkle with the raisins and nutmeg. Bake until firm, about 30 minutes.

For the rum sauce: Stir together all the sauce ingredients in a small saucepan and simmer for 2 minutes.

To serve, cut the pudding into 8 rectangles and top each serving with warm Rum Sauce. ᕽ

Floating Islands

SOMETIMES SIMPLE IS GOOD. Take floating islands, for instance, a dessert that often appeared on many restaurant menus years ago in New Orleans. Pastry chefs continue to reinterpret this dish, which is nothing more than creamy custards on which puffs of meringue float. But oh, how this cooling dessert pleases the palate, especially after a heavy, rich meal.

This is a great dessert to make for small dinner parties, or when children are visiting, as they are enchanted by the islands of meringue floating happily on the custard. And the best part is, they can be made ahead of time. The custard is also delicious over angel food or pound cake.

{MAKES 6 TO 8 SERVINGS}

6 cups milk
1⅔ cups sugar
6 large eggs, separated
2 tablespoons cornstarch
2 teaspoons vanilla extract
¼ teaspoon cream of tartar

Preheat the oven to 350 degrees F. Pour 1 inch of warm water into a baking pan and set aside.

Heat the milk in a heavy saucepan until warm.

With a whisk or electric mixer, beat together ⅔ cup of the sugar, the egg yolks, and the cornstarch in a medium mixing bowl, and then add the mixture to the milk. Cook over medium heat, stirring constantly, until thick enough to coat a spoon. Remove from the heat and pour into a large mixing bowl. Stir in the vanilla.

With an electric mixer, beat the egg whites with the cream of tartar in a mixing bowl until stiff. Slowly add the remaining 1 cup of sugar, beating well until glossy. Drop the egg white mixture by spoonfuls into the pan of warm water and bake the islands for 20 minutes to set.

With a slotted spoon, transfer the islands to the surface of the custard, mixture and refrigerate for at least 2 hours before serving.

To serve, scoop up each island and some of the custard, and put in dessert bowls. ༃

Frosty Cherry Parfaits

Bernice S. Preis from Covington nominated this recipe to be included in this post-Katrina cookbook. "I found this recipe in *The Times-Picayune* in the 1960s," she wrote. "I use it every year when cherries are in season."

{MAKES 6 TO 8 SERVINGS}

2 cups sweet cherries

1½ tablespoons cornstarch

½ cup sugar

1 cup orange juice

2 tablespoons fresh lemon juice

¼ teaspoon almond extract

3 or 4 drops red food coloring (optional)

1 quart vanilla ice cream

Sweetened whipped cream for serving

Chill six to eight parfait glasses. Halve and pit the cherries and set aside.

In a medium saucepan, mix the cornstarch and sugar until well blended. Stir in the orange juice. Cook, stirring, over medium heat until thickened and clear, about 2 minutes. Stir in the cherries, lemon juice, almond extract, and food coloring (if using) and remove from the heat. Let cool.

Alternate the cherry mixture with scoops of ice cream in the chilled parfait glasses. (The parfaits may be assembled in the glasses and stored, well wrapped, in the freezer.) To serve, top each parfait with whipped cream. 🐚

Masson's Almond Torte

MASSON'S RESTAURANT FRANÇAIS operated for forty-two years before it closed in January 1993. Located on Pontchartrain Boulevard near the lakefront in New Orleans, it was a delightful and much-loved dining spot, where the menu was hand-written and included French dishes with a bit of a Creole accent, such as Escargots de la Maison, Fillet of Red Snapper Meunière, Filet Mignon au Champignon, and this Almond Torte, which became a local favorite. Because it must be made ahead and kept in the freezer until serving, the torte is an ideal dessert to keep on hand.

{MAKES 8 SERVINGS}

½ cup (1 stick) unsalted butter, at room temperature

1 cup light brown sugar, sifted

1 large egg

1 cup sliced almonds, toasted and ground (see Note), plus ¾ cup sliced almonds, toasted and ground, for garnish (optional)

¼ teaspoon almond extract

1 cup sweetened whipped cream

In a large mixing bowl, beat the butter with an electric mixer until light and fluffy. Gradually add the brown sugar, beating well after each addition. Add the egg and beat for 1 minute. Fold in the 1 cup of ground almonds and the almond extract by hand. Mix well. You should have a stiff dough. Place the dough on aluminum foil (do not wrap it) and refrigerate for 1 hour.

Shape the dough into a log about 8 inches long and 2 inches in diameter. If desired, sprinkle the log with the additional ¾ cup of ground almonds. Carefully wrap in aluminum foil and place in the freezer for at least 3 or 4 hours. (The log will keep in the freezer for up to 3 months.)

When ready to serve, let stand at room temperature for 10 minutes. Cut into 1-inch slices, frost with whipped cream. ❧

NOTE: *To toast the almonds, spread out on a cookie sheet and toast them in a 300-degree-F oven for about 5 minutes, or until the almonds begin to turn golden brown. Grind in a blender for 5 seconds.*

Palace Café's White Chocolate Bread Pudding

LEAVE IT TO the renowned Brennan clan of New Orleans restaurateurs to bring the lowly bread pudding to new heights. This over-the-top confection was on the menu when the Palace Café opened in March 1991, and it's been on the menu ever since. The yield is generous, so it's a great dessert to serve when entertaining a crowd.

{MAKES ABOUT 16 SERVINGS}

BREAD PUDDING
6 cups heavy cream

2 cups whole milk

1 cup sugar

1¼ pounds white chocolate (morsels or small pieces)

4 large eggs plus 15 egg yolks

One 24-inch loaf stale French bread (see Note)

WHITE CHOCOLATE GANACHE
½ cup heavy cream

½ pound white chocolate (morsels or small pieces)

2 ounces dark chocolate, grated, for garnish

For the bread pudding: Stir together the cream, milk, and sugar in a large heavy saucepan. Bring the mixture to a boil, then remove from the heat and carefully add the white chocolate pieces. Allow the chocolate to melt for several minutes, then stir until smooth.

Whisk together the whole eggs and egg yolks in a large mixing bowl. Slowly pour the hot cream and chocolate mixture into the eggs in a steady stream, whisking constantly as you pour. Use a rubber spatula to scrape out all of the chocolate from the warm pot. Set the pudding mixture aside.

Preheat the oven to 350 degrees F. Thinly slice the stale French bread and place in a 9-by-13-inch metal baking pan. Pour half of the pudding mixture over the bread and allow it to cool for about 5 minutes. Use your fingers or a rubber spatula to press the bread into the pudding so that the liquid is absorbed and the bread becomes very soggy. Pour the remaining pudding over the bread and stir.

Cover the pan with aluminum foil and bake for 1 hour. Remove the foil and bake, uncovered, for an additional 30 minutes, or until the bread pudding is golden brown. While the bread pudding is baking, make the ganache.

For the white chocolate ganache: Bring the cream to a boil in a small saucepan. Remove from the heat and carefully add the white chocolate. Allow the chocolate to melt for several minutes, then stir until smooth.

Spoon the warm bread pudding right out of the pan, or for a more elegant presentation, cut it into slices. To serve in slices, chill for 6 to 8 hours to allow it to set completely. When almost ready to serve, preheat the oven to 275 degrees F. Run a knife around the inside of the pan, and invert the pudding onto a wooden board. Cut into squares, then halve the squares to make triangular slices. Place on a cooking sheet and heat in the oven for 15 minutes, or until warm. Serve the pudding topped with warm White Chocolate Ganache and garnished with the grated dark chocolate. 🐝

NOTE: *If you don't have stale French bread on hand, thinly slice a fresh loaf and dry in a 275-degree-F oven.*

Tennessee Bread Pudding

M.D. OF MARRERO wrote to us, "Would you please print the recipe for Tennessee Bread Pudding? I lost my copy during Katrina."

Marcelle Bienvenu was given this recipe by a friend who lived in Tennessee. It has become a favorite, and we had to include it in this book. The coconut, crushed pineapple, and raisins make it a festive dessert.

{MAKES 6 TO 8 SERVINGS}

BREAD PUDDING

2 cups hot water

1½ cups sugar

1 (12-ounce) can evaporated milk

4 large eggs

1 cup coconut flakes

½ cup crushed pineapple, drained

½ cup raisins

⅓ cup unsalted butter, melted

1 teaspoon vanilla extract

½ teaspoon ground nutmeg

¼ teaspoon ground cinnamon

9 slices white bread with crust, cut into ½-inch cubes

BOURBON SAUCE

1 cup light corn syrup

4 tablespoons unsalted butter

¼ cup bourbon

½ teaspoon vanilla extract

For the bread pudding: Preheat the oven to 350 degrees F. Combine the water and sugar in a large bowl and stir until the sugar dissolves. Use a wire whisk to whisk in the milk and eggs, and continue whisking until blended. Stir in the coconut, pineapple, raisins, butter, vanilla, nutmeg, and cinnamon. Add the bread and let stand for 30 minutes, stirring occasionally.

Pour into a lightly greased 9-by-13-inch pan and bake until a cake tester inserted in the center comes out clean, about 45 minutes. Let cool slightly before serving with the Bourbon Sauce.

For the bourbon sauce: Bring the corn syrup to a boil in a small saucepan. Remove from the heat and let cool slightly. Whisk in the butter, bourbon, and vanilla. Serve warm. ❧

LAGNIAPPE— A LITTLE SOMETHING EXTRA

hese recipes are what we call lagniappe (pronounced LAN-yap—a little something extra). The Cranberry Relish (page 338) goes with not only turkey but also other meats like chicken and pork.

Make a batch or two of the Creole Mustard (page 341) to give as gifts to foodies! Ditto for Warren Leruth's Fig Preserves (page 347) and the Tomato Marmalade (page 346).

LAGNIAPPE—A LITTLE SOMETHING EXTRA

Cranberry Relish

B.B. of Baton Rouge sent this recipe to share with *The Times-Picayune* readers in November 2005. Adapted from a recipe in *Southern Living* magazine, it is easily made if you need a touch of cranberry for a holiday meal.

{MAKES ABOUT 4 CUPS}

2 cups sugar
¾ cup orange juice
2 (12-ounce) bags fresh cranberries
Grated zest of 1 orange

Combine the sugar and orange juice in a large saucepan and stir well. Add the cranberries and orange zest. Bring to a boil over medium heat, stirring often. Reduce the heat and simmer for 5 minutes, or until the cranberry skins pop and the mixture thickens. Serve warm or chilled. ❧

Creole Cream Cheese

CREOLE CREAM CHEESE is a unique New Orleans dish, which has been around for quite a while. Originally made from raw milk, it was clabbered by the addition of rennet, then strained through cheesecloth. The curds were then drained and fresh cream was added to make the final product, which was often eaten for breakfast with sugar, salt and pepper, or fruit.

When Gold Seal Dairy, which made it for years, went out of business, there was fear that the much-loved product would be extinct. But now it is available once again from several local purveyors.

However, the cream cheese can be made easily enough at home. If you don't have Creole cream cheese molds, just punch holes in the bottom and sides of seven or eight 8-ounce plastic margarine tubs (or similar containers) for the liquid to drain.

{MAKES 7 OR 8 SERVINGS}

1 gallon skim milk between 70 and 80 degrees F
½ cup cultured buttermilk
½ teaspoon liquid rennet
Half-and-half or heavy cream for serving

Pour the milk into a large plastic or glass container. Add the buttermilk and stir the mixture well. Then pour in the rennet and stir the mixture vigorously for 1 minute. Do not stir again or you will disturb the formation of cheese. Cover the container and let it stand at room temperature for 12 to 15 hours. All the while the rennet will be converting the milk solids to a "caked" cheese. Remember, the longer it stands, the firmer the cheese will be.

After the cheese has set, ladle it into Creole cream cheese molds or other perforated containers so that the water can drain off the cheese. Place the molds in a large roasting pan on an elevated rack. (You can place the rack on upside-down coffee cups.) Leave the pan in the refrigerator until no more water drips from the cheese. It will take at least 4 to 6 hours to form. The cream cheese will keep in your refrigerator for at least 1 month in clean containers.

When you are ready to serve, spoon the cream cheese into bowls, and cover with either half-and-half or heavy cream. ❧

Frozen Creole Cream Cheese

FOR YEARS, Frozen Creole Cream Cheese has been a delightful summer treat favored by New Orleanians. It has a somewhat tart taste, a welcome departure from heavily sugared desserts.

{MAKES 6 SERVINGS}

2 cups Creole cream cheese, store-bought or homemade (page 339)

¼ cup heavy cream

1 cup evaporated milk

1 cup sugar

½ teaspoon vanilla extract

1 large egg white, beaten until stiff peaks form

In a large bowl, mash the cream cheese with the cream and milk. Stir in the sugar and vanilla by hand and fold in the stiffly beaten egg white. Pour into a freezer tray and freeze. Alternatively, pour the mixture into the container of an ice-cream machine and follow the manufacturer's directions.

Creole Mustard

SPICY CREOLE MUSTARD is a must in New Orleans pantries. It's used to add zing to a remoulade sauce; to slather on po-boys, the quintessential New Orleans sandwiches (see page 345); and to tweak mayonnaise and salad dressings. Creole Mustard is similar to coarse-grained European mustards, and probably was first developed by German immigrants.

While Creole Mustard is readily available at local grocery stores and supermarkets, there are those who just might want to make their own, especially if they live many miles from south Louisiana. In response to a request for a recipe from B.M. of New Orleans, D.H. of Mandeville sent in this one, which she describes as "very zingy!" She credits *Bill Neal's Southern Cooking.*

{MAKES ½ CUP}

¼ cup white wine vinegar

2 tablespoons water

2 tablespoons vegetable oil

⅛ teaspoon celery seed

Pinch of white pepper

2 whole cloves

1 clove garlic, sliced

½ teaspoon salt

½ teaspoon sugar

¼ cup whole mustard seed

2 tablespoons dry mustard

Combine the vinegar, water, oil, celery seed, white pepper, cloves, garlic, salt, and sugar in a small saucepan. Cover tightly and bring to a rapid boil over high heat. When the boiling point is reached, remove the pan from the heat and let sit, covered, for 30 minutes to steep.

Strain the liquid and discard the solids. Put the whole mustard seed and dry mustard into a blender or food processor and blend or process for 1 minute. Slowly pour in the strained liquid and process until the mixture thickens. Alternatively, use a mortar and pestle to crack the mustard seeds well, and then whisk them and the dry mustard into the strained liquid. ❧

White Barbecue Sauce

IN THE MIDDLE of August 2005, *The Times-Picayune*'s food editor, Judy Walker, visited the Gulf Coast. She got this recipe from Matt Mayfield, who owns Tay's Barbecue, which has three locations in large gas stations around Biloxi, Mississippi. Yes, some of the best food in the South is served in gas stations.

White Barbecue Sauce is a northern Alabama thing, Mayfield explained. In 1925, Big Bob Gibson Bar-B-Q started in Decatur, Alabama, and the owner created a White Barbecue Sauce to use on turkey and chicken. The original Big Bob gave the recipe away and others in the area copied it.

Mayfield serves White Barbecue Sauce with smoked chicken and chicken wings, and many of his customers use it on their orders of ribs. Mayfield uses a secret ingredient in his spicy version: Huy Fong Sriracha Hot Sauce, the Thai hot sauce popularly known as rooster sauce, because of the illustration on the bottle.

The recipe was published August 25, four days before Katrina wiped out much of the Gulf Coast. Tay's survived.

To make the sauce spicier, add sriracha sauce to taste. To apply to chicken or turkey or wings, brush on only at the very end of cooking; otherwise it will break down and separate. Or serve on the side with grilled or smoked chicken, turkey, or other poultry.

{MAKES 1½ CUPS}

1 cup mayonnaise
1 cup apple cider vinegar
1 tablespoon lemon juice
1½ tablespoons cracked black pepper
½ teaspoon kosher salt, finely ground
¼ teaspoon cayenne pepper
Sriracha sauce, such as Huy Fong's, to taste (optional)

Combine all the ingredients in a large bowl and mix thoroughly. Transfer to an airtight container or bottle and refrigerate until you're ready to use. It keeps for up to 4 days. 🐜

Marinated Onions

C.O. OF METAIRIE offered this family favorite from her collection, which fortunately was not lost to Katrina. She says these onions are fantastic to serve over sliced beets or cucumbers, and on green beans.

{MAKES ABOUT 4 PINTS}

4 to 6 cups sliced Vidalia or other sweet onions
¾ cup white vinegar
⅔ cup sugar
½ cup water
1 tablespoon salt
1 teaspoon dried dill weed

Put the sliced onions in a glass bowl.

Combine the vinegar, sugar, water, salt, and dill in a saucepan and bring to a boil. Cook, stirring, until the sugar dissolves, about 1 minute. Pour the mixture over the onions and stir to coat evenly. Transfer to sterilized glass jars and store in the refrigerator for up to 3 months. ✺

Tailgate Muffuletta Sandwich

THE MUFFULETTA HAS been a favorite New Orleans sandwich since the early 1900s. It was created by Sicilians and named after the round loaf on which it is made. One muffuletta makes four generous servings, and is ideal for tailgating.

{MAKES 4 TO 6 SERVINGS}

OLIVE SALAD

1½ cups chopped pimiento-stuffed olives
1 cup chopped ripe olives
2 tablespoons capers, drained
3 anchovies, drained and chopped
⅔ cup olive oil
1½ tablespoons fresh lemon juice
½ cup chopped parsley
2 garlic cloves, minced
1 teaspoon dried oregano leaves

SANDWICH

1 round loaf Italian bread (8 to 10 inches in diameter)
⅔ pound mortadella, thinly sliced
⅔ pound provolone cheese, thinly sliced
⅔ pound Italian salami, thinly sliced

For the Olive Salad: Combine the ingredients in a bowl. Cover and chill for 2 to 4 hours.

For the sandwich: Cut the loaf of bread in half horizontally. Remove some of the soft inside from both the top and the bottom, leaving a ¾-inch-thick shell.

Brush the inside of the top and bottom shells with the marinade collecting at the bottom of the bowl with the Olive Salad. Stir the Olive Salad to blend and then spoon half onto the bottom round of bread. Arrange the mortadella slices over the Olive Salad, and then in layers add the provolone and salami. Mound the remaining Olive Salad on top and cover with the top shell.

Wrap the sandwich tightly with plastic wrap and chill for at least 1 hour. Cut the sandwich into wedges to serve. ❧

Shrimp or Oyster Po-boy

THIS ICONIC NEW ORLEANS sandwich showed up in the first few minutes of the premiere episode of *K-Ville*, the Fox TV cop drama set in post-Katrina New Orleans, starring Anthony Anderson, Cole Hauser, and John Lynch. The series was ended by the writers strike of 2007–2008, but a cookbook (what else?) was assembled for cast and crew as a party favor, and TV columnist Dave Walker wrote about it for the Food pages. This excellent recipe was in the book.

Fried shrimp and fried oyster po-boys are arguably the two most popular types of po-boys. The oyster loaf, as the sandwich is also called, is sometimes known as a peacemaker, or *la media-trice* in local lore. If a husband was detained in town, he would carry home an oyster loaf to make peace with his wife. (Nowadays, the half-oyster and half-shrimp po-boy is sometimes called a peacemaker, too.)

{MAKES 6 SERVINGS}

3 cups vegetable oil for frying

1 large egg, beaten

1 cup milk

1 cup water

2 tablespoons Creole mustard, homemade (page 341) or store-bought, or any coarse, grainy brown mustard

1 tablespoon yellow mustard

3 cups yellow corn flour

2 tablespoons granulated garlic

Salt

Cracked black pepper

6 (10-inch) po-boy loaves, or 3 loaves French bread, halved

3 dozen small shrimp, peeled and deveined; or 3 dozen freshly shucked oysters, drained; or a combination of the two

6 tablespoons tartar sauce (see Note)

6 tablespoons ketchup

18 thin slices tomato

2 cups shredded lettuce

Preheat the oven to 375 degrees F. Heat the oil to 350 degrees F in a deep fryer or large heavy pot.

In a shallow bowl, whisk together the beaten egg, milk, water, and mustards. In a mixing bowl, combine the corn flour, garlic, and the salt and pepper to taste. Set aside.

Slice the po-boy bread lengthwise and place on a large cookie sheet, crust-down. Put the bread in the oven and turn off the heat to allow it to become crispy and warm while you fry the seafood.

Dip the shrimp or oysters, 6 at a time, in the egg batter and then the corn flour mixture. Fry in 2 or 3 batches, 3 minutes per batch, or until the shrimp or oysters float on the surface of the oil. Drain and keep warm until all the seafood has been fried.

Remove the bread from the oven and top one side of each loaf with tartar sauce and the second side with ketchup. Place 3 slices of tomato on the bottom half and sprinkle with shredded lettuce. Place 6 shrimp, oysters, or a combination of both over lettuce, and top with the other po-boy half. Secure with toothpicks and slice in half. Serve hot. ❧

NOTE: *To make your own tartar sauce, mix together ½ cup of mayonnaise, 1 tablespoon of sweet pickle relish, ½ teaspoon of finely chopped onion, 1 teaspoon of fresh lemon juice, Creole seasoning to taste, and 2 dashes of hot sauce.*

Tomato Marmalade

A MONTH BEFORE Katrina, a reader from Chalmette asked for a recipe for tomato pepper jelly "like the one that is sold in the French market." We never found that recipe, but we ran this Tomato Marmalade recipe instead, since it was Creole tomato season.

{MAKES ENOUGH TO FILL ABOUT
9 HALF-PINT JARS}

3 quarts (about 5½ pounds) ripe tomatoes

3 oranges

2 lemons

4 sticks cinnamon (3-inch pieces)

6 whole allspice berries

1 tablespoon whole cloves

6 cups sugar

1 teaspoon salt

Sterilize nine half-pint canning jars and process nine new two-piece canning lids according to the manufacturer's instructions.

Peel the tomatoes, cut them into small pieces, and drain. Cut the oranges and lemons into very thin slices; quarter the slices. Tie the cinnamon, allspice, and cloves in a cheesecloth bag.

Put the tomatoes in a large pot. Add the sugar and salt and stir until dissolved. Add the oranges, lemons, and spice bag. Bring to a boil, stirring constantly. Continue to boil rapidly, stirring constantly, until thick and clear, about 50 minutes.

Remove from the heat and skim off the foam. Pour the hot marmalade into the hot, sterilized jars, leaving ¼ inch of headspace. Wipe the rims of the jars with a dampened clean paper towel. Adjust the two-piece metal canning lids. Process in a boiling water canner for 5 minutes. 🦐

Warren Leruth's Fig Preserves

When famed chef Warren Leruth died in November 2001, Brett Anderson, the restaurant writer for *The Times-Picayune*, wrote an appreciation of Leruth's career:

> *Warren Leruth, the chef, restaurateur, and food scientist who helped forge a renaissance in local cuisine, died Wednesday at a hospice in Diamondhead, Miss. He was 72. A failed physics student who went on to become a specialist in tastes and flavors, building a business as a sought-after consultant of national food manufacturers and restaurant chains, Mr. Leruth was first and foremost a chef.*
>
> *In 1965, he opened LeRuth's (the R is capitalized in the restaurant's name, not the founder's) in a renovated shotgun on Franklin Street in Gretna.*
>
> *"Before LeRuth's, the typical New Orleans restaurant menu was a fairly limited catalog of traditional dishes. Leruth sort of rewrote the script," said Gene Bourg, former restaurant critic for* The Times-Picayune.
>
> *Oyster-artichoke soup and sautéed soft-shells with lump crab meat are both Mr. Leruth inventions.*

This recipe for his fig preserves appeared in *The Times-Picayune* Food section in July 1991. We have updated the preserving process.

{MAKES ENOUGH TO FILL 10 TO
12 HALF-PINT JARS}

4 quarts local figs, small, ripe, on the firm side
7 pounds sugar
2½ quarts water
4 teaspoons vanilla extract

In a large pot, cover the figs with boiling water and soak for 15 minutes. Drain the figs and add 5 pounds of the sugar and 2 quarts of the water. Boil, carefully stirring occasionally, until the syrup registers 214 degrees F on a candy or deep-fat thermometer. Remove from the heat. Allow the figs and syrup to cool overnight.

The next day, sterilize twelve half-pint jars and process twelve new two-piece canning lids according to the manufacturer's instructions. Fill a boiling-water-bath canner with water and bring to a boil. (Don't overfill—the jars will take up some room.)

Meanwhile, add the remaining 2 cups of water and 2 pounds of sugar to the preserves. Boil until the syrup registers 218 degrees F. Add the vanilla extract.

Immediately fill the jars within ½ inch of the top and wipe the edge clean. Apply the lids and process in the boiling water for 10 minutes. ❧

WORDS TO EAT BY

Tourists to New Orleans have always needed glossaries to interpret the unique dishes on menus here. But the food culture of south Louisiana has dozens more terms that beg for clarification.

In general, the culinary terms reflect the rich complexity of the region's food culture. Most of the roots of these terms have French, Spanish, and African origins. The customs around some iconic foods, such as king cake, date back centuries.

A note about pronunciation: Is mirliton pronounced MUR-luh-tawn, MILLY-tawn or MEL-ee-tawn? Because New Orleans has many different accents, it often depends on how ya mama said it. The pronunciations offered here are only suggestions, and we welcome input from readers, as well as ideas for other culinary words not on this list, which will be archived at www.nola.com/entertainment on the Food/Dining page. E-mail your suggestions to our Food editor, Judy Walker, at jwalker@timespicayune.com.

AGUA FRESCAS (ag-WAH fres-CAHS): Literally, "fresh waters." Mexican fruit beverages made of water, sugar, and seasonal fruit.

AMANDINE (AH-mun-deen): Butter sauce with almonds for fish.

AMBERJACK: Lean, mild member of the Jack family of fishes.

ANDOUILLE (ahn-DOO-ee): Popular spicy Cajun smoked pork sausage. Kielbasa can be substituted for it.

BAHN MI (bahn ME): Vietnamese sandwich on French bread, usually made with various fillings, including pâté or headcheese and jalapeños. It is locally known as the Vietnamese po-boy.

BANANAS FOSTER: Dessert of bananas cooked in rum and brown sugar, flambéed, and served over vanilla ice cream. Named after Dick Foster, friend of restaurateur Owen Brennan, in the 1950s.

BARBACOA (bar-buh-COE-uh): On Mexican menus, beef slow-cooked over an open fire.

BARBECUE SHRIMP: Head-on shrimp baked in butter, Worcestershire, garlic, and copious amounts of black pepper. Created at Pascal's Manale restaurant.

BEIGNETS (BEN-yays): Square doughnuts liberally covered with confectioners' sugar.

BLACK DRUM: A cousin of red drum, also known as redfish.

BLACKENED: Paul Prudhomme's much-imitated technique of searing seasoned fish or meat in a smoking-hot cast-iron skillet. The food takes its color from the burnt butter and paprika.

BORDELAISE (BORE-duh-laze): New Orleans–style garlic and olive oil sauce, which has nothing in common with the French wine sauce of the same name.

BOUCHERIE (BOO-sher-ee): Communal Cajun gathering in autumn to slaughter a hog and make sausages and other products such as hogshead cheese, cracklin (see below), ponce, (see below) and backbone stew. The stew is traditionally served during the boucherie.

BOUDIN (BOO-dan): Cajun white sausage with cooked rice, green onions, bits of pork, and other seasonings.

BOULETTES (boo-LETS): French for "meatballs." Cajun interpretations can include balls of any minced or ground meat, chicken, fish, or seafood, such as crawfish or catfish boulettes.

BRANDY MILK PUNCH: Brunch favorite with brandy, cream and/or milk, simple syrup, and vanilla. It is garnished with nutmeg and always served chilled, never with ice.

BREAD PUDDING: Most common of all local desserts, made with stale French bread and often served with hard sauce.

BRUCCIOLONI (BRUSH- or BROOSH-a-loney): Also spelled braciola/brocioloni. A Sicilian beef or veal dish, rolled up around a stuffing and baked or braised in red gravy. Spelled differently on every menu, and in every cookbook where it appears.

BUCHE (BOO-chay): On Latin menus, stomach of the beef.

CAFÉ AU LAIT (CAH-fay o LAY): Hot coffee (traditionally flavored with chicory) mixed with an equal quantity of hot milk.

CAFÉ BRÛLOT (CAH-fay brew-LOW): Elaborate old-school Creole dessert coffee presentation made in a flameproof bowl with coffee, spices, sugar, orange and lemon zest, and brandy, ladled into cups. *Brulot* is French for "burnt brandy."

CALAS (cuh-LAHZ): Hot fritters of cooked rice, eggs, and leavening; an old Creole dish revived by the Slow Food movement in the 1990s.

CANE SYRUP: A thick sweetener made from sugarcane, and a south Louisiana staple on pancakes and biscuits, as well as in many old and new dishes and recipes.

CARNE CON PAPAS (car-NAY con PAH-pahs): Spanish for "meat with potatoes."

CHAURICE (shoh-REECE): Full-flavored, spicy sausage eaten as a main dish, or on the side with red or white beans, and used as an ingredient in gumbo, jambalaya, and other dishes.

CHICHARRON (CHEECH-a-rone): Seasoned Mexican-style pork rinds, fried and moist, not dry.

CHICORY (CHICK-a-ree or CHICK-ree): Traditional in New Orleans coffee blends. Chicory root is dried, roasted, ground and added for body and flavor.

CHORIZO (chor-EE-zoh): Mexican fresh spicy pork sausage with garlic, onion, and seasoning. (Spanish chorizo is a thin, dry sausage.)

COCHON DE LAIT (co-CHON de LAY): Cajun dish of roasted suckling pig, lovingly adapted by some New Orleans chefs in the mid-2000s. Literally, "pig of milk" in French, a reference to the piglet still suckling milk; milk is not involved in the dish at all.

COCKTEL DE CAMARON (cocktail de cam-ah-ROAN): Mexican shrimp cocktail—cooked shrimp in lime-tomato juice with chopped vegetables.

COURTBOUILLON (COO-bee-yawn): In Creole cookery, a spicy roux-based tomato sauce or broth for cooking or saucing fish. In Cajun country, a hearty, thick soup of fish, tomatoes, other vegetables, and seasonings. (Neither is like the French court-bouillon, which is a type of broth.)

COWAN (cow-WAHN): Old term for snapping turtle.

CRAB BOIL: Two meanings. A crab boil, like a crawfish boil, is a party at which seafood is boiled in traditional seasonings. Dry crab boil, a mix of spicy seasonings, is used to season seafood of all kinds. In liquid form, crab boil is also widely used by local cooks as a flavoring ingredient in many dishes, from red beans to hot dogs to seafood gumbo.

CRACKLINS or **CRACKLINGS**: Crunchy pieces of pork or poultry fat after it has been rendered, or the crisp brown skin of fried or roasted pork.

CRAWFISH: Freshwater crustacean resembling a tiny lobster, widely cultured and used in south Louisiana cooking. (Never called "crayfish" or "crawdad.")

CRAWFISH BISQUE: Labor-intensive, seldom-found soup or stew of stuffed crawfish heads in a bisque containing the crawfish tails. Served with rice.

CREOLE CREAM CHEESE: Tangy local soft cheese, similar to a combination of cottage cheese and sour cream, often eaten for breakfast. The Slow Food movement and local dairies revived it in the 1990s.

CREOLE MUSTARD: Grainy coarse brown local mustard first created in Bayou country by German settlers.

CREOLE SEASONING: In recipes the term usually refers to a dry seasoning mix (such as the popular Tony Cachere's brand). It can also mean the fresh "trinity" of iconic seasoning vegetables: onion, green bell pepper, and celery, which are available locally chopped, often with garlic, green onions, and parsley.

CREOLE TOMATOES: Locally grown tomatoes, often from Plaquemines Parish.

CUCUZZA (cuh-COOT-zuh): Oversized Sicilian heirloom squash. Eaten like summer squash, especially in red gravy, when young and under two feet long. Older, longer squash are treated like winter squash.

CUP CUSTARD: Classic New Orleans dessert, close relative of flan and crème caramel, baked in a cup with its own caramel sauce.

CUSHAW (COO-shaw): Elongated, multistriped heirloom member of the winter squash and pumpkin family, often used to make pies. Still found in the Mississippi Delta and the Southwest.

DAUBE (DOBE): The Creole classic daube is a braised roast. Now most often found on menus and homes in red gravy (red sauce), undoubtedly a Creole-Sicilian adaptation.

DAUBE GLACE (dobe glah-SAY): Seldom found now, Creole classic luncheon or Christmas dish of cooked, spiced, shredded roast in gelatin, usually eaten on crackers.

DEBRIS: Bits and pieces of roast beef after it has been sliced. Popularized in po-boys at Mother's Restaurant.

DIRTY RICE: Rice cooked with ground chicken giblets and seasonings.

DOBERGE CAKE (DOE-berge in New Orleans, DOE-bash in Lafayette): Multilayered bakery specialty credited to Beulah Ledner, who opened a New Orleans bakery in 1933 and adapted it from the Austrian Dobos cake.

DRESSED: As in "Do you want that sandwich dressed?" Refers to lettuce, tomato, mayonnaise, and sometimes other condiments.

ESCOLAR: Deep-water Gulf fish with rich, tender flesh, sometimes called white tuna. Known as white fish in sushi bars.

ÉTOUFFÉE (ay-too-FAY): Literally, "smothered." Very popular Cajun dish of crawfish and vegetables, served over white rice.

FILÉ (FEE-lay): Powdered sassafras leaves used to thicken gumbo; introduced by the Choctaw people.

FRENCH BREAD: Local version has a shatteringly crisp crust and soft center. The most popular bakeries carrying French bread actually have German or Italian heritages.

GINGER CAKES/STAGE PLANKS: Hard-to-find traditional gingerbread cookie. Around 1900, Stage Planks got the name from wooden planks that connected riverboats to the shore.

GORDITA (gore-DEE-tah): Mexican sandwich of thick corn tortillas, cheese, and meat, pressed together. Literally, Spanish for "little fat one."

GRILLADES (GREE-yahds) **AND GRITS**: Favorite brunch dish of scallops of beef or veal cooked in a rich tomato gravy and served with grits.

GROUPER (GROO-per): Lean, firm fish in the sea bass family found in the Gulf and Atlantic, usually sold whole and cooked many different ways.

GUMBO: Iconic roux-based soup usually made with seafood, okra, tomatoes, and filé. Another popular version, gumbo ya ya, is made with chicken and sausage. Gumbo z'herbes (green gumbo) is made with a variety of greens and is served during Lent. All are served with rice. The word "gumbo" comes from *gombo*, the word for okra in many west African languages.

HEADCHEESE: Rustic pate of jellied pork, usually eaten with crackers. Called souse elsewhere in the South.

HERBSAINT: Anise-flavored liqueur developed and made in New Orleans to fill the void when absinthe was outlawed.

HORCHATA (or-CHA-tah): Latin American beverage of rice, sugar, and cinnamon.

HOT SAUSAGE: Fresh sausage generally made with ground beef or pork, highly seasoned with cayenne, garlic, and other spices. Used in po-boys, gumbo, and other dishes.

HUCKLEBUCK: Brightly colored child's treat made with Kool-Aid or other punches, frozen in cups. Most often homemade and also known as frozen cups.

HURRICANE: Potent fruit punch and rum drink developed at Pat O'Brien's Bar.

JAMBALAYA (jam-bah-LIE-uh): Extremely popular Cajun-Creole rice dish usually made with seafood and often with sausage. Its roots are often traced to Spanish paella. The red Creole version generally includes tomatoes; the brown Cajun jambalaya does not.

JAPANESE PLUM: Small mild fruit of a common backyard tree, also called loquat (LOW-quat).

KING CAKE: Iconic Carnival season coffee cake/ dessert, usually an oval ring of brioche dough decorated with purple, green, and gold frosting. The person who is served the piece with a small plastic baby doll inside brings the cake to the celebration the following year. Rooted in European Twelfth Night or Feast of the Epiphany customs, which some historians trace back to the Roman festival of Saturnalia.

LENGUA (len-GWAH): Spanish for beef tongue, an authentic taco filling.

MAQUE CHOUX (mock SHOE): Cajun creamed corn dish with onions, bell peppers, and tomatoes.

MARCHAND DE VIN (mar-SHAWN de van): Literally means "the wine merchant" in French. Arguably the most famous of New Orleans sauces, usually made with beef stock, red wine, minced ham, onions, garlic, butter, and sometimes mushrooms, served over meats or breakfast dishes.

MENUDO (muh-NOO-doh): Spicy soup of tripe, hominy, chiles, and other seasonings. A traditional Mexican hangover cure.

MEUNIÈRE (men-YER): A classic French method, widely used in New Orleans, to cook fish, which is lightly floured and fried in butter.

MIRLITON (MEL-a-tawn, MILLY-tawn, or MUR-la-tawn): Pear-shaped, mild-flavored squash known elsewhere as chayote. Often stuffed with seafood or meat dressing.

MOJEJA (moe-HAY-ha): A Spanish dish of fried chicken livers.

MUFFULETTA (muff-a-LOT-uh or muff-a-LET-uh): Sandwich invented by New Orleanians of Sicilian descent in the early 1900s. It is made on thick, round Italian bread with layers of cheese and deli meats, plus a layer of olive salad.

(MY-NEZ): Believe it or not, this is one local pronounciation for "mayonnaise."

NATCHITOCHES MEAT PIES: Turnovers stuffed with seasoned ground meat, first sold by peddlers on the streets of Natchitoches, and possibly created by the Natchitoches Indians.

NECTAR FLAVOR, NECTAR SODA: Vanilla-almond flavor in a vivid pink syrup, invented by apothecary owner I.L. Lyons in the late 1800s, and popularized at soda fountains. Still available in snowball syrup and as a locally produced soda, it is also made at home from local recipes.

NOPALITOS (no-pall-EE-toes): Pickled or canned strips of prickly pear cactus.

OLIVE SALAD: Mixture of black and green olives, olive oil, garlic, capers, seasonings, and often other pickled vegetables. Mandatory on muffulettas and also used in south Louisiana homes on green salads and in pasta salads.

OYSTERS BIENVILLE: Both Arnaud's and Antoine's, two famous old-line Creole restaurants, claim to have created oysters Bienville. The dish is named after Jean-Baptiste Le Moyne, Sieur de Bienville, one of the founders of New Orleans. The oysters are served on the half shell and topped with a sauce of shrimp, cream, and cheese.

OYSTERS EN BROCHETTE (on bro-SHET): Skewered oysters wrapped in bacon, battered, and deep-fried.

OYSTERS ROCKEFELLER: Invented by Jules Alciatore, the son of the founder of the legendary Antoine's, on the occasion of John D. Rockefeller's visit in the late 1800s. Absinthe-flavored, greens-topped oysters on the half shell.

OYSTER STUFFING: Thanksgiving staple of oysters, French bread crumbs, seasoning, and, sometimes, ground meat.

PAIN PERDU (pah per-DOO): French toast, translated literally from French, "lost bread."

PAN BREAD: Thick-sliced white bread often used for fried seafood sandwiches. Seldom seen these days, except at Casamento's Restaurant, an old-school shrine to oysters.

PANEE (PAH-nay): Breaded and pan-fried (as opposed to deep-fried).

PEACEMAKER: Po-boy with oysters, or sometimes with half shrimp, half oysters. Said to be the favored gift for irate wives, given by husbands coming home late at night. Also called *la mediatrice*.

PECAN RICE: Aromatic rice grown in Cajun country.

PEYCHAUD'S BITTERS: A tonic, or bitters, for stomach disorders, developed by the French apothecary Antoine Amédée Peychaud, who fled to New Orleans after the Haitian uprising in 1793. Peychaud opened a shop and served his bitters with Cognac in an egg cup (*coquetier*), and is known to history as the father of the cocktail.

PICKLE MEAT: Picked pork shoulder, a primary seasoning meat in Creole dishes, such as red beans and rice.

PIMM'S CUP: The signature cocktail at Napoleon House, made with Pimm's No. 1 (a low-alcohol liqueur of aromatics steeped in gin). The cocktail also contains a citrus blend, usually lemon-lime soda, and a distinctive garnish of cucumber.

PISTOLETTE (pis-toe-LET): An elongated French bread roll made by local bakeries.

PLATILLOS (plah-TEE-ose): A Spanish word that refers to a plate of food, usually including meat, rice, beans, salad, and at least one tortilla.

PO-BOY/POOR BOY: Sandwich invented in the 1920s to feed "poor boys" during a streetcar strike. Fried seafood or roast beef and gravy is stuffed into long loaves of French bread (known as po-boy or poor boy loaves).

POMPANO EN PAPILLOTE (on pah-pee-YOHT): An old French recipe in which seasoned fish is steamed and served in folded parchment paper.

PONCE: Hard-to-find, legendary Cajun charcuterie item of ground pork, rice, vegetables, and seasoning sewn in a pig's stomach and baked or steamed, then sometimes smoked. Also called chaudin (sho-DAHN).

PRALINE (prah-LEEN): Candy made of pecans, carmelized sugar, and cream.

RAMOS GIN FIZZ: Cocktail of gin, egg white, fresh lemon and lime juice, simple syrup, orange flower water, and cream or milk. It was developed in the late 1800s by bar owner Henry Ramos.

RAVIGOTE (rahv-ee-GOAT) **SAUCE**: Creole staple sauce, most often served cold with seafood and salads; crabmeat ravigote is a standard. Modern recipes differ widely, but most include mayonnaise (unlike the French ravigote) and Creole mustard, as well as minced vegetables and various seasonings.

RED BEANS AND RICE: Iconic dish of red kidney beans, widely made in homes and restaurants and served on Monday, the traditional wash day, because the cook could put beans on the stove to cook all day with little tending.

RED GRAVY: Red (tomato) sauce, such as spaghetti sauce.

REMOULADE (REM-o-lahd): Spicy sauce usually served as an appetizer with boiled shrimp; usually made with mustards, horseradish, oil, ketchup, chopped vegetables, and seasonings.

ROMAN TAFFY CANDY: Sicilian confection produced and sold in New Orleans in 1890 in a goat-drawn cart by Sam Cortese, who later had a horse-drawn candy cart on wheels made. Cortese's grandson, Ron Kottenmann, still sells candy from the cart outside schools and other venues, one of New Orleans' most picturesque and beloved culinary sights.

ROUX (ROO): Flour browned in fat and used to thicken and/or flavor many Creole and Cajun dishes, such as gumbo, and stews.

SATSUMA (sat-SUE-muh): Cold-hardy mandarin orange, widely planted in the lower Gulf South from 1908 to 1911. Does not ship well, so almost all are consumed instate. Grown in Plaquemines Parish and backyards.

SAUCE PIQUANTE (pee-KAWNT): Spicy, tomato-based sauce similar to spicy gumbo or étouffée, often used with wild game, turtle, alligator, or rabbit. Probably from the Spanish *picante*, which means "spicy heat."

SAZERAC: A (if not *the*) signature local cocktail; contains rye whiskey, a sugar cube, Peychaud's bitters, herbsaint, and lemon peel. Developed in 1850 at an Exchange Alley bar. Associated with the Sazerac Bar at the Fairmont Hotel.

SEED CAKES: Sesame seed cookies, one of the most popular offerings on the St. Joseph's Day altars tended by families of Sicilian descent on St. Joseph's Day, March 19.

SHEEPSHEAD: Popular, firm, mild, shallow-water Gulf fish that feeds on crustaceans, nibbling them with little teeth.

SHRIMP CREOLE: Stew of tomatoes and shrimp served over rice.

SNOWBALLS: Similiar to a snow cone in the rest of the country, perhaps descended from hand-shaved Italian ice served at Sicilian corner groceries. The ice is mechanically shaved into fine "snow" and flavored with an infinite variety of syrups, juices, sweetened condensed milk, or chocolate syrup.

SOUFFLÉ POTATOES: Thinly sliced potatoes are deep-fried, cooled, and deep-fried again so they inflate into crisp golden puffs.

SQUAB: A young domesticated pigeon; and the signature dish at Peristyle Restaurant in New Orleans.

TASSO (TAHS-oh): Cajun dried pork seasoned with cayenne, garlic, and salt, then heavily smoked. Possibly derived from the Spanish *tasajo*, dried, cured beef.

TORTA (TORT-uh): Mexican po-boy. Includes meat dressed with the diner's choice among avocado, cheese, lettuce, tomato, and mayonnaise.

TURDUCKEN (tur-DUCK-ehn): Cajun invention of stuffed deboned chicken inside a deboned duck, which is stuffed inside a partially deboned turkey. Popularized by Paul Prudhomme and, later, football announcer John Madden, who orders custom six-legged versions at Thanksgiving from the Gourmet Butcher Block in Gretna.

WAHOO (WAH-hoo): Fish with moderate- to high-fat white, almost sweet flesh, and known as ono in Hawaii.

YA-KA-MEIN (ya-keh-MEAN): One-bowl dish of cooked spaghetti or ramen noodles in a beef and soy broth, topped with chopped meat, green onions, and hard-cooked egg. Popular in corner groceries, perhaps brought home to New Orleans by African American veterans returning from the Korean War.

ZATARAIN (ZAT-a-ran): Local manufacturer of a big line of Louisiana products, including mixes and seasonings.

Index

Table of Equivalents

The exact equivalents in the following tables have been rounded for convenience.

LIQUID/DRY MEASUREMENTS

U.S.	Metric
¼ teaspoon	1.25 milliliters
½ teaspoon	2.5 milliliters
1 teaspoon	5 milliliters
1 tablespoon (3 teaspoons)	15 milliliters
1 fluid ounce (2 tablespoons)	30 milliliters
¼ cup	60 milliliters
⅓ cup	80 milliliters
½ cup	120 milliliters
1 cup	240 milliliters
1 pint (2 cups)	480 milliliters
1 quart (4 cups, 32 ounces)	960 milliliters
1 gallon (4 quarts)	3.84 liters
1 ounce (by weight)	28 grams
1 pound	448 grams
2.2 pounds	1 kilogram

LENGTHS

U.S.	Metric
⅛ inch	3 millimeters
¼ inch	6 millimeters
½ inch	12 millimeters
1 inch	2.5 centimeters

OVEN TEMPERATURE

Fahrenheit	Celsius	Gas
250	120	½
275	140	1
300	150	2
325	160	3
350	180	4
375	190	5
400	200	6
425	220	7
450	230	8
475	240	9
500	260	10